South France Pilot
V. The Riviera

EX LIBRIS

George & Barbara Ormerod

Published by
Imray, Laurie, Norie & Wilson Ltd
Wych House, St Ives, Huntingdon,
Cambridgeshire, PE17 4BT, England.

All rights reserved. No part of this publication may be reproduced, transmitted or used in any form by any means – graphic, electronic or mechanical, including photocopying, recording, taping or information storage and retrieval systems or otherwise – without the prior permission of the Publishers.

©Robin Brandon 1990

1st Edition 1975
2nd Edition 1982
3rd Edition 1990

British Library Cataloguing in Publication Data
Brandon, Robin
   South France Pilot. – 3rd ed.
   Chapter 5: The Riviera
   1. Southern France. Coastal waters – Pilots' guides
   I. Title
   623.89'29448

ISBN 0 85288 130 4

IMPORTANT

This work has been corrected to October 1989.

While every effort has been made to check and crosscheck the data and information given in this book, the Author and Publishers cannot accept responsibility for any accidents, injury or damage occasioned by the use of this information or data.

Readers should use this book with prudence and in a seamanlike manner. Their attention is directed to the many changes both man-made and natural that are certain to occur subsequent to publication. Furthermore reference should always be made to any amendments issued by the Publishers as well as the latest Admiralty *Notices to Mariners*, *List of Lights Volume E* and *Lists of Radio Signals*.

Furthermore, users of this guide themselves are asked to report any changes, omissions or corrections to the Publishers or Author. A correction reported immediately when noted, briefly on a postcard or by rough sketch, may subsequently avoid another yachtsman getting into difficulties. Your cooperation in this matter, therefore, is gratefully requested.

Set in Plantin by Cromwell Graphics Ltd, St Ives, Huntingdon, Cambridgeshire direct from the Publishers' disks.

Printed in Great Britain by The Bath Press, Avon.

South France Pilot

V. The Riviera

CAP ROUX TO THE ITALIAN FRONTIER

Robin Brandon

Imray Laurie Norie & Wilson Ltd
St Ives Cambridgeshire England

Preface

TO THE THIRD EDITION

The changes that have taken place on the Riviera coast since the last edition of this pilot was published have not been numerous and the only major changes have been at Port Vauban (Antibes) and Golfe Juan (Vallauris).

The facilities at most harbours have been improved and in many places extra berths have been provided, but these have not been sufficient for the numbers of yachts in the area during the high season of June, July, and August. Early arrival at a port is essential to be certain of a berth for the night.

Some additional anchorages have been included in this edition in view of the crowding of the harbours and extra aerial photographs have been added. Details of harbours, anchorages and headlands together with their photographs and plans have been listed in geographical order to make the pilot easy to use.

During the last seven years there has been a continuing rise in the coastal population and therefore a great increase in the number of houses, apartment blocks, shops and local industrial areas. This increase is very noticeable on the roads and the number of cars on the move during the winter months must have trebled, however it is still a wonderful and attractive sailing area even in the high season and much more so during the rest of the year.

Robin Brandon
Grimaud
France

October 1989

Key to symbols

Where practical symbols are used in the plans and French terms are applied where the meaning is obvious. Users are referred to the comprehensive glossary in Volume I of this pilot.

⚓	Port office	*Bureau de Port/ Capitainerie*
	Harbourmaster	*Capitaine de Port*
	Water	*Eau*
	Fuel	*Gasoil*
	Yacht chandler	*Ship chandler*
	Crane	*Grue*
✉	Post office	*PTT*
	Telephone	
	Travel-lift	
V	Visitors' berths	*Passagères*
	Yacht club (with initials)	
	Showers	*Douches*
i	Information	*Syndicat d'initiative*
	Mechanics	*Mécaniciens*
	Ship/yacht yard	*Chantier navale*
	Customs	*Douane*
	Ice	*Glace*
	Swimming pool	*Piscine*
	Slip	*Cale*
	Hard	*Terre-plein*
⚓	Anchorage	*Mouillage*
	Anchoring prohibited	*Mouillage interdit*

Contents

Preface, iv

INTRODUCTION, 1
  General description, 1
  Warnings, 1
    Winds and seas, 1
    Dangers, 2
    Submarines, 2
    Restricted areas, 2
  Data, 2
    Charts, 2
    Tides, 2
    Currents, 2
    Sea levels, 2
    Marine radiobeacons, 2
    Air radiobeacons, 2
    Weather forecasts, 2
    Major lights, 2
  Visits, 2
  Sports, 3
  Festivals, 3
  History, 3

PLANNING GUIDE, 4

PILOTAGE, 6

110   Port de la Figueirette (Port Miramar-le-Trayas), 12
111   Port de la Galère, 16
112   Port de Théoule-sur-Mer, 19
113   Port de la Rague, 22
114   Port de la Mandelieu-la Napoule, 25
115   Port du Riou de l'Argentière, 28
116   Port de Cannes-Marina, 30
117   Port de Marco-Polo Marina, 33
118   Port de la Siagne (Port Sec), 35
119   Port du Béal, 35
120   Vieux Port de Cannes (Port St Pierre), 37
121   Port Pierre-Canto, 41
122   Ports de la Croisette (Port de Palm Beach and Port Bijou), 44
123   Les Iles de Lérins, 47
124   Port de St Honorat (Port aux Moines), 49
125   Port de Ste Marguerite, 51
126   Port du Mouré-Rouge, 53
127   Port de Golfe-Juan (Vallauris), 55
128   Port Gallice, Juan-les-Pins, 58
129   Port du Crouton, 61
130   Port de la Salis (Rous-Chaffey), 66
131   Port Vauban-Antibes, 68
132   Port de Marina, Baie des Anges, 73
133   Port de Cros-de-Cagnes, 75
134   Port de St Laurent-du-Var, 78
135   Port de Nice, 82
136   Port de Villefranche-sur-Mer, 88
137   Port de St Jean-Cap Ferrat, 95
138   Port des Fourmis, 98
139   Port de Beaulieu-sur-Mer, 99
140   Port de Silva-Maris (Port d'Eze-sur-Mer), 103
141   Port de Cap d'Ail, 107
142   Port de Fontvieille, 111
143   Port de Monaco (Monte Carlo), 114
144   Port de Menton-Ville (Vieux Port), 121
145   Port de Menton-Garavan, 124

Index, 129

South France Pilot

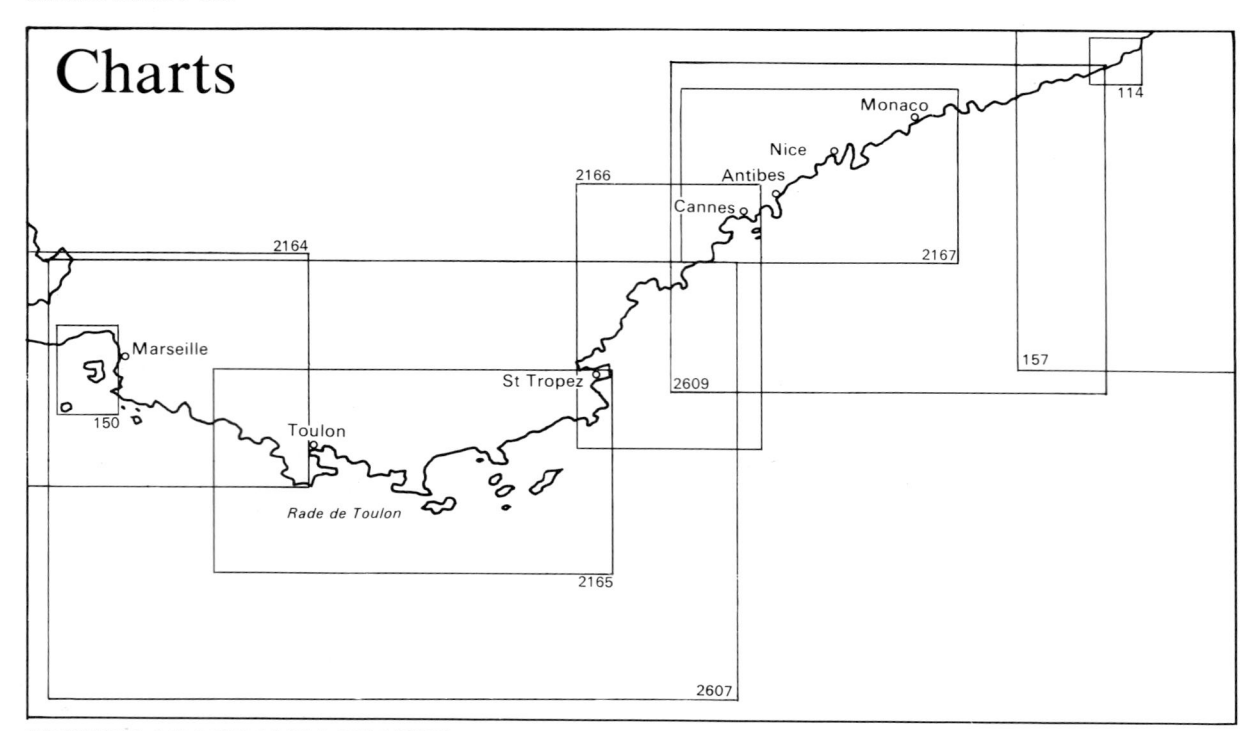

Charts

BRITISH ADMIRALTY CHARTS

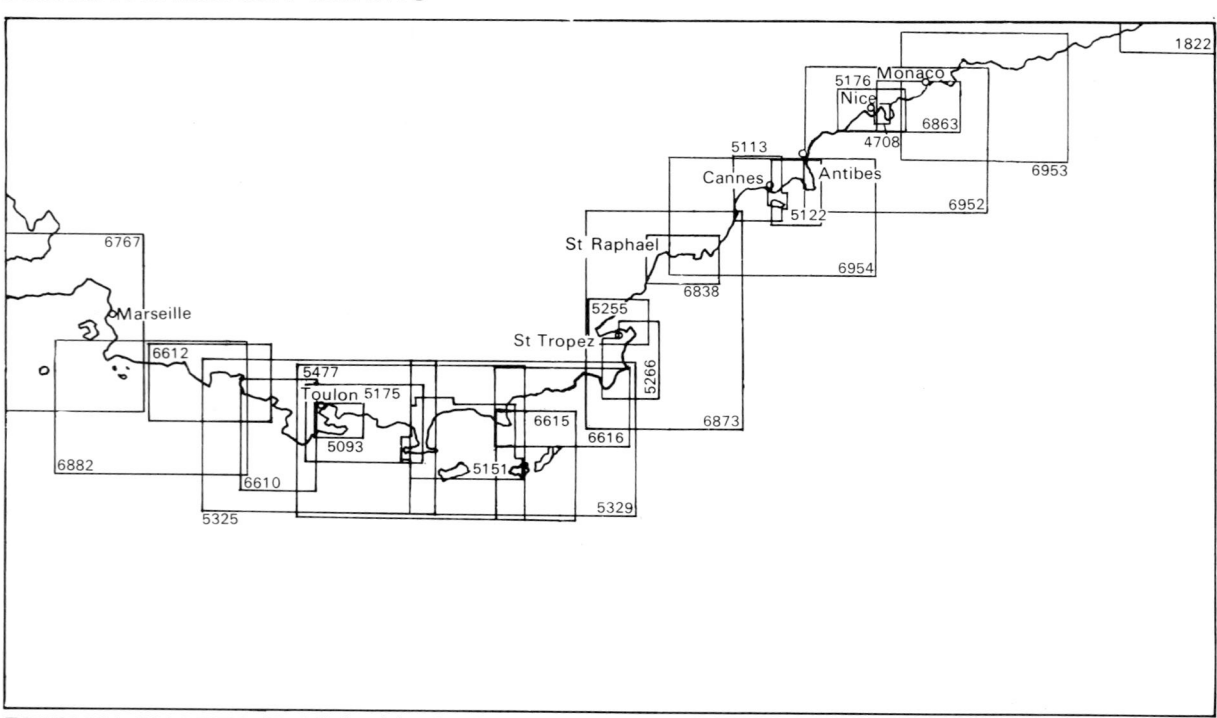

FRENCH CHARTS (Published by La Service Hydrographique de la Marine)

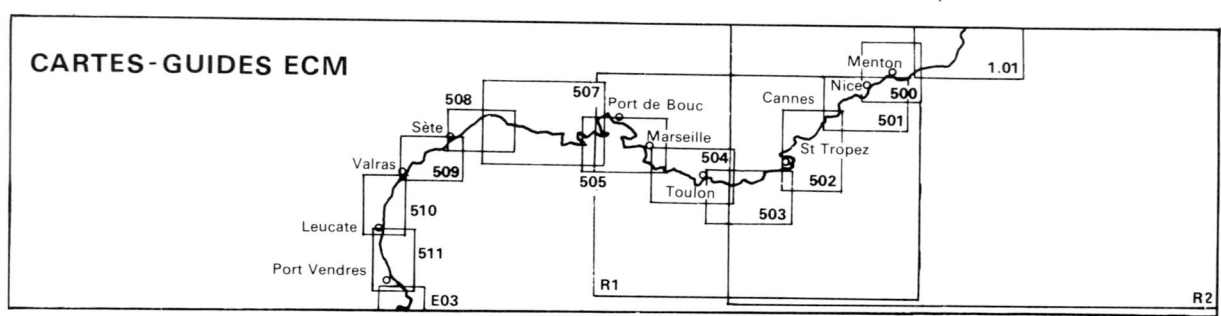

CARTES-GUIDES ECM

Introduction

General description

This 35M section of coast which stretches from the E side of the Massif de l'Esterel as far as the Italian frontier is spectacular with numerous harbours and a number of pleasant towns. The greater part of the coast follows the foothills of the Alpes Maritimes which have high buttress ridges running down to the sea in places. Between these features lie wide sandy bays such as the Golfe de la Napoule, Golfe Juan and Baie des Anges. Further E beyond Nice where the mountain ridges are higher and steeper, a number of smaller bays with broken rocky shores are to be found of which Rade de Villefranche, Baie de Beaulieu and Baie de Roquebrune are examples. From far out to sea the high snow-covered mass of the Alps will be seen and the coastal features will be difficult to identify, but on closing the coast these features will become apparent as they progressively obscure the high land in the background.

The only offshore dangers are the Iles de Lérins, two large tree-covered islands which are of low elevation located 2 to 3M S of Cannes. These islands and their offlying dangers have no lights except one on the S side. Most of the coast is rocky with high cliffs which are steep-to. The parts that have sandy coasts slope steeply out to sea except at the mouth of the river Var where there are offlying shoals.

This area is well provided with harbours, for instance there are eleven around the Golfe de Napoule, and most of them have been constructed recently as yacht harbours. There are a fair number of original fishing and commercial harbours still in existence though some have been so 'improved' that it is difficult to recognise them from the attractive places they once were.

This area saw the first invasion by foreign tourists in the late 19th century and many resorts remind one of similar Victorian and Edwardian watering places in England. Because this area has been receiving foreign visitors for so long the facilities are very much better than those which are normal on the coast further W where tourism is of quite recent origin.

The old areas of the main ports are most attractive and in general have not been swamped by modern developments which have usually taken place outside the older parts of the town. The mountainous hinterland is very beautiful and is very useful in that it shelters major sections of the coast from the effects of the *mistral*, producing a very pleasant climate even in the winter months.

Warnings

Winds and seas The winds on this section are not nearly so savage as those on the sections of coast to the W. The strength of the NW *mistral* near the coast is much reduced by the high mass of the Alps. Far out to sea this wind is considerably stronger but still below that experienced in the Golfe du Lion and near Marseille.

On the other hand the winds from NE–E–SE are stronger, especially in winter, and send heavy seas onto this coast and into those harbours facing their direction. (See wind diagrams below). When at sea a listening watch should be kept on the radio for warnings of these conditions and shelter taken in the nearest suitable harbour without delay. Due to the considerable number of modern all-weather yacht harbours on this coast little difficulty will be experienced in finding one quickly where shelter may be found.

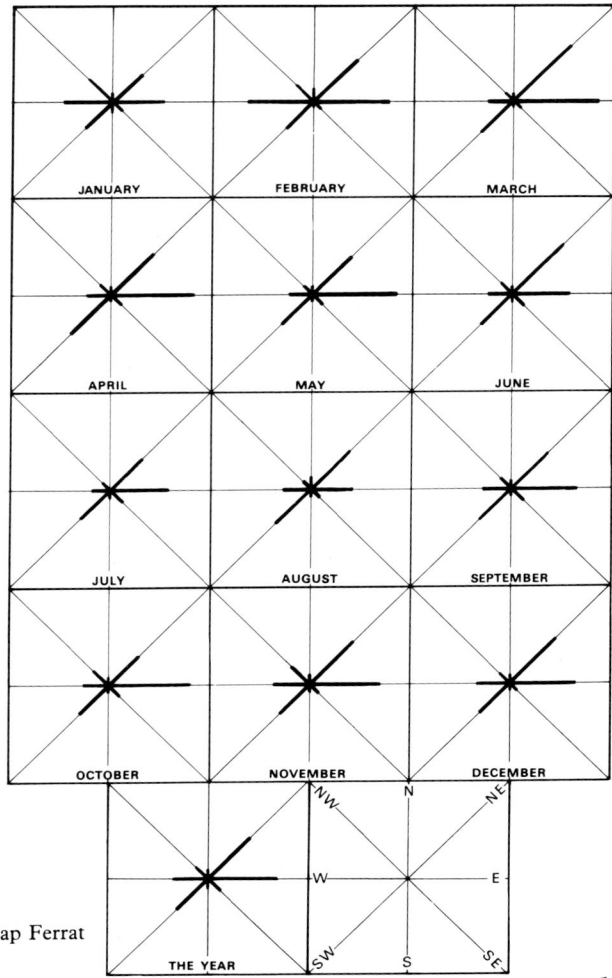

Relative wind directions. Cap Ferrat

South France Pilot

Dangers There are two dangerous shallow areas which should be avoided, the delta and the mouth of the Var which has shoals extending over ½M, and the area of rocks at Pointe Bacon to the NE of La Garoupe lighthouse.

Submarines may use the area covered by this book surfaced or submerged.

Restricted areas Anchoring, mooring and fishing are not permitted in the following areas:
- Cable area between the Iles de Lérins and Pointe de la Croisette.
- Marine reserve E side of Golfe Juan and off the beach.
- Cables to the N of Port de la Mouré-Rouge.
- Explosives dump E of La Salis.
- Cables to N of Port Vauban-Antibes.
- A small area for military and naval exercises to SW of Cap Ferrat (see chart). When in use International code flags NE2 are flown from the signal station on Cap Ferrat.
- Restricted areas off Nice and Cap Ferrat.

Buoys and lights

Buoyage on this section of the coast conforms to IALA System A.

Data

Charts The following small-scale charts cover this area:
Admiralty 2166, 2167
French 6954, 6952, 6953
Spanish 121
ECM 500, 501, 502

Tides The tidal range in this part of the Mediterranean reaches a maximum of 0·15m (0·5ft) at springs and is hardly detectable at neaps. For all practicable purposes tidal heights and streams can be ignored.

Currents Currents are weak on this section of coast and rarely exceed 1 knot. They are usually W-going but the indentations of the coast often cause a reverse swirl which can also be found behind headlands. A counter-current can sometimes be experienced close inshore. Heavy winds from the E sector tend to augment these currents while those from the W sector tend to decrease their strength and may sometimes reverse their direction.

Sea levels In very strong winds from the SE the level of the sea has been known to rise 1m (3·3ft) while those from the NW cause a drop of up to 0·5m (1·6ft). In the winter and early spring the sea levels are often as much as 1m (3·3ft) below the normal levels.

Marine radiobeacons
La Garoupe lighthouse GO (— —/— — —) 294·2 kHz 100M every 6 minutes. Sequence 5, 6, grouped with Punta Revellata (RV).

Air radiobeacons
Nice. Mont Leuza LEZ (·— ··/·/— — ··) 398·5 kHz 75M Continuous 43°43'·7N 7°20'·2E.
Sénétose SNE (···/— ·/·) 394·5 kHz 15M Continuous 41°33'·5N 8°47'·9E.

Coast radio stations
Grasse (TKM) (1648) RT MF: Transmits 1834, 2182, 2649 3722 kHz. Receives 2182 kHz, plus at Ile Sainte Marguerite 1988, 2049, 2056, 2153, 2167, 2286, 2321, 2449, 3168 plus 2009, 2023, 2477 kHz. Traffic lists on 2649 kHz every even H+33 (0633–2033 UT). Remotely controlled from Marseille (FFM) 2200–0630 UT, one hour earlier during DST.
VHF: Transmits Ch 02, **04, 05,** 16. Receives Ch 02, 04, 05. 0630–2100 UT, one hour earlier during DST.
Monaco (3AF) (2500) VHF: Transmits Ch 16, 20, 22, 86. Receives Ch 16, 20, 22, 86. Continuous service. Traffic lists on Ch 16 every H+03 (0700–2300, one hour earlier during DST).

Radio weather forecasts

This section of coast falls inside Area No.531 Golfe du Gênes and the most effective weather forecast is from Grasse (TKM) which also broadcasts storm warnings on receipt on 2649 kHz at even H+33 from 0633 to 2233. Weather bulletins and forecasts are transmitted regularly as follows; (add 1 hour to UT for local time, *l'heure légale*, add 2 hours during DST unless the broadcast is 1 hour earlier):

Grasse (TKM) 2649, 3722 kHz, 0·35 kW at 0733, 1233 and 1645 UT (in French at dictation speed) and VHF Ch 02 at 0633, 1133 UT[1]. Storm warnings on 2649 kHz on receipt at end of next two silence periods and at every even H+33. Storm warnings on VHF Ch 02 at end of next two silence periods.
La Garde (Toulon) (CROSS) VHF Ch 09 at 0810 UT[1] and at 1730 UT[1].
France Inter Toulon 1584 kHz and Nice 1350 kHz at 0555, 1905 UT[1]. (Rapid French. Covers a large area.)
Monte Carlo 1466 and 218 kHz 0800 and 1900 UT[1]
Navimet VHF Ch 23, 0700 to 2100 hours.
Monaco VHF Ch 23 at 0600 to 2200 UT[1]. Continuous in French and English.

1. Broadcasts given 1 hour earlier during DST.

Automatic prerecorded coastal forecasts At almost every *Bureau de Port* on this coast will be found a small loudspeaker with a button nearby labelled *Météo*. Upon pressing this button the latest tape-recorded coastal forecast originating from Monaco will be heard.

Meteorological offices Weather forecasts can be obtained from the following by phone:
Nice. Station Météo, aerodrome ☎ 93 83 17 24, automatic prerecorded forecast ☎ 93 83 00 25
Cannes. Station Météo, aerodrome ☎ 93 47 20 48

Navigational warnings
Grasse (TKM) 2649 kHz at 0633 and 1833 UT (French and English).
Monaco (3AF) VHF Ch 22 at 0703 (French, English on request).

Major lights
Cannes. Jetée Ouest Head VQ(3)R.2s22m8M. White tower, red top.
La Garoupe Fl(2)W.10s104m31M. White square tower.
Antibes Digue du Large Fl(4)WR.15s13m15/11M. Yellow tower, red top.
Nice Jetée du Large Fl.R.5s21m20M White square tower, red lantern, white cupola.
Cap Ferrat Fl.W.3s69m25M. White 8-sided tower, green band at base, green lantern.
Menton-Ville Jetée Head VQ(4)R.3s16m10M. White tower, red top. Obscured by Cap Martin when bearing more than 036°.

Visits

Details of local places of interest will be found in the sections dealing with the harbour concerned. There are however a number of other places a little way inland that are worth visiting and which can be reached by taxi or in some cases by bus and rail. Full details are available gratis from the nearest office of the Syndicat d'Initiative.

These interesting places include:
- Grasse, the perfume capital of the world where there are also several museums.
- Tende, where there are prehistoric cave drawings.
- Eze, a hilltop village with a medieval château.
- La Turbie, which has Roman remains.
- Roquebrune, with its 10th-century castle.
- Grand Canyon du Verdon. This river gorge is the deepest in Europe.

Sports

There are excellent alpine ski slopes not far inland on this section of coast in winter, and in summer, climbing, mountaineering, shooting and river fishing are available in the same area. Water sports such as water-skiing, fishing and sub-aqua swimming are popular in the summer months and riding, golf, tennis and canoeing and many other sports are also readily available.

Festivals

There are many festivals during the year at most of the major resorts and a number of the smaller places have similar affairs. Details of these and the dates concerned, which vary from year to year, can be obtained from the office of the nearest Syndicat d'Initiative.

History

There are many traces of prehistoric man in this area, but recorded history, as with the other sections of the southern French coast, commences with the Ligurians in occupation around 1000 BC. In 600 BC the Greeks from Marseille and later the Romans established outstations at the natural harbours of Cannes, Antibes, Nice and Monaco which lasted until between the 4th and 6th centuries AD when the Vandal invasion caused the withdrawal of the Roman forces. It should be noted here that the Roman road leading to the huge area that they had conquered in Gaul ran along this coast between the Alps and the sea.

The monks of the Iles de Lérins established control of a large coastal area in the 7th century as did the Grimaldis of Monaco in the 14th century. In the 8th century and later, the Saracens frequently raided the area from the sea and the number of hilltop fortified villages to be found just inland from the coast is the natural result of these incursions. During the ensuing centuries the area was in frequent turmoil as various royal and noble families acquired and lost sections of it. The border between what was to be France and Italy moved repeatedly. At different times several harbours and areas, notably Villefranche (Free town), Menton and Monaco declared themselves as independent. The establishment of the rule of the French crown in the 15th and 16th centuries did much to establish peace and order in the area but no real progress or prosperity was possible before the arrival of the first foreign tourists in the 19th century who brought new ideas, new requirements and wealth to a very poor and backward area.

South France Pilot

Planning guide

Note Anchorages closest to harbours are described under the heading *Anchorage in the approach* of the harbour concerned.

Ports, harbours, anchorages and landing places

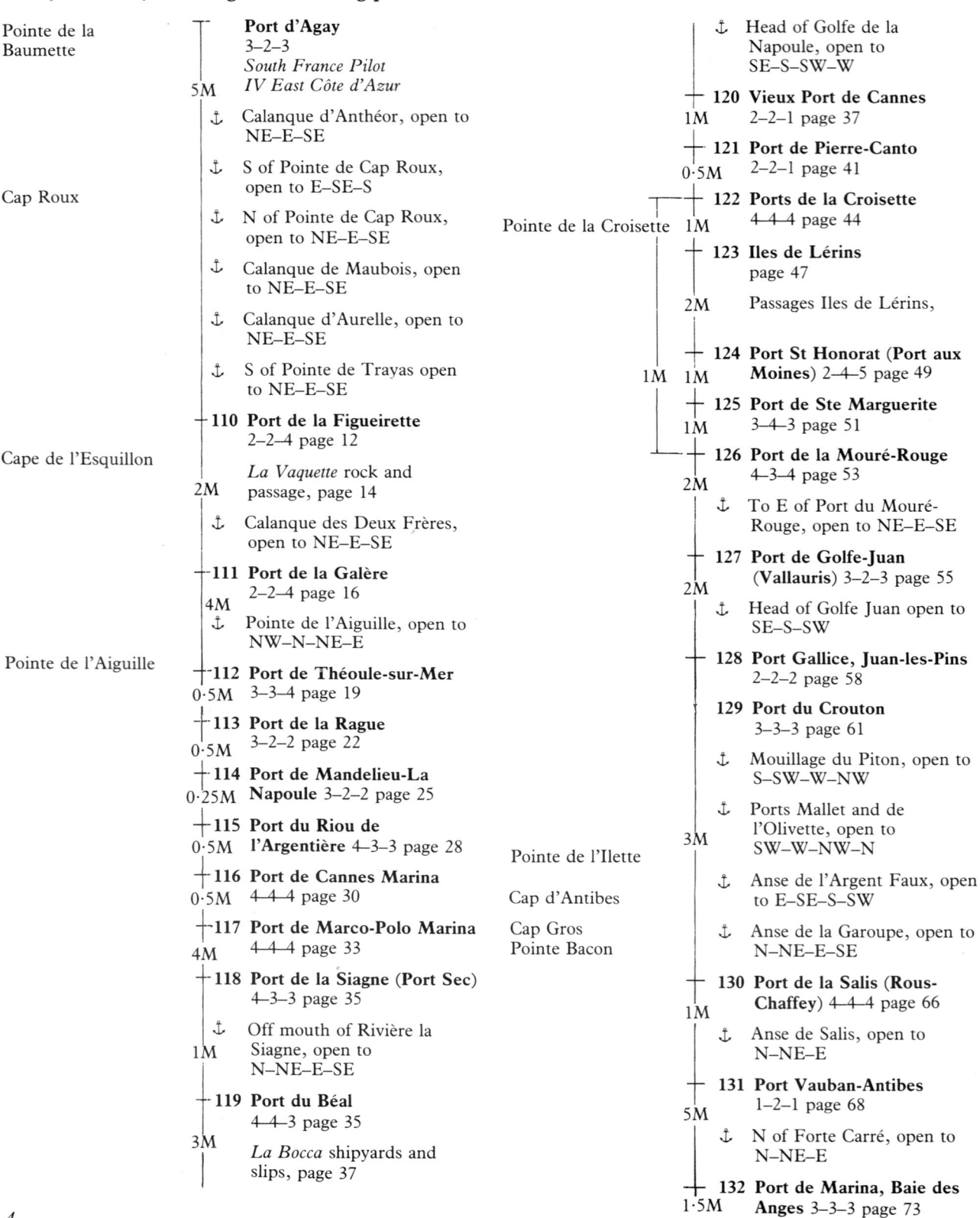

Pointe de la Baumette		**Port d'Agay** 3–2–3 *South France Pilot* IV East Côte d'Azur
	5M	
	⚓	Calanque d'Anthéor, open to NE–E–SE
Cap Roux	⚓	S of Pointe de Cap Roux, open to E–SE–S
	⚓	N of Pointe de Cap Roux, open to NE–E–SE
	⚓	Calanque de Maubois, open to NE–E–SE
	⚓	Calanque d'Aurelle, open to NE–E–SE
	⚓	S of Pointe de Trayas open to NE–E–SE
	110	**Port de la Figueirette** 2–2–4 page 12
Cape de l'Esquillon		*La Vaquette* rock and passage, page 14
	2M ⚓	Calanque des Deux Frères, open to NE–E–SE
	111	**Port de la Galère** 2–2–4 page 16
	4M ⚓	Pointe de l'Aiguille, open to NW–N–NE–E
Pointe de l'Aiguille	**112** 0·5M	**Port de Théoule-sur-Mer** 3–3–4 page 19
	113 0·5M	**Port de la Rague** 3–2–2 page 22
	114 0·25M	**Port de Mandelieu-La Napoule** 3–2–2 page 25
	115 0·5M	**Port du Riou de l'Argentière** 4–3–3 page 28
	116 0·5M	**Port de Cannes Marina** 4–4–4 page 30
	117 4M	**Port de Marco-Polo Marina** 4–4–4 page 33
	118	**Port de la Siagne (Port Sec)** 4–3–3 page 35
	1M ⚓	Off mouth of Rivière la Siagne, open to N–NE–E–SE
	119	**Port du Béal** 4–4–3 page 35
	3M	*La Bocca* shipyards and slips, page 37

	⚓	Head of Golfe de la Napoule, open to SE–S–SW–W
	120 1M	**Vieux Port de Cannes** 2–2–1 page 37
	121 0·5M	**Port de Pierre-Canto** 2–2–1 page 41
	122 1M	**Ports de la Croisette** 4–4–4 page 44
Pointe de la Croisette	**123**	**Iles de Lérins** page 47
	2M	Passages Iles de Lérins,
	124 1M 1M	**Port St Honorat (Port aux Moines)** 2–4–5 page 49
	125 1M	**Port de Ste Marguerite** 3–4–3 page 51
	126 2M	**Port de la Mouré-Rouge** 4–3–4 page 53
	⚓	To E of Port du Mouré-Rouge, open to NE–E–SE
	127 2M	**Port de Golfe-Juan (Vallauris)** 3–2–3 page 55
	⚓	Head of Golfe Juan open to SE–S–SW
	128	**Port Gallice, Juan-les-Pins** 2–2–2 page 58
	129	**Port du Crouton** 3–3–3 page 61
	⚓	Mouillage du Piton, open to S–SW–W–NW
	⚓ 3M	Ports Mallet and de l'Olivette, open to SW–W–NW–N
Pointe de l'Ilette	⚓	Anse de l'Argent Faux, open to E–SE–S–SW
Cap d'Antibes Cap Gros Pointe Bacon	⚓	Anse de la Garoupe, open to N–NE–E–SE
	130 1M	**Port de la Salis (Rous-Chaffey)** 4–4–4 page 66
	⚓	Anse de Salis, open to N–NE–E
	131 5M	**Port Vauban-Antibes** 1–2–1 page 68
	⚓	N of Forte Carré, open to N–NE–E
	132 1·5M	**Port de Marina, Baie des Anges** 3–3–3 page 73

4

Planning guide

Delta du Var	⊢ **133 Port de Cros-de-Cagnes** 4–3–4 page 75	Cap Roux	⊢ **140 Port de Silva Maris** 3–3–4 page 103
	1M ⚓ SE of Port de Cros-de-Cagnes, open to SE–S–SW		⚓ N of Cap Roux, open to NE–E–SE
	⊢ **134 Port de St Laurent-du-Var** 3–3–3 page 78		3M ⚓ Baie de St Laurent, open to S–SW
	6M Aéroport Nice-Côte d'Azur,		⚓ W of Cap d'Ail, open to SE–S–SW
Cap de Nice	⊢ **135 Port de Nice** 1–2–2 page 82	Cap d'Ail	⊢ **141 Port de Cap d'Ail** 3–2–3 page 107
	2M ⚓ W side of Rade de Villefranche, open to SE–S	Pointe St Martin	0·5M
Pointe des Sans Culottes	⊢ **136 Port de Villefranche-sur-Mer** 1–1–2 page 88	Pointe de St Antoine	⊢ **142 Port de Fontvieille** 3–2–3 page 111
	⚓ Head of Rade de Villefranche, open to S		0·5M ⊢ **143 Port de Monaco** 3–2–3 page 114
	⚓ E side of Rade de Villefranche, open to S–SW (Anse de Grasseut, de l'Espalmador and de Passable)		⚓ W of Pointe de la Veille open to E–SE–S–SW
	4M		5M ⚓ Baie de Roquebrune, open to SE–S–SW
Cap Ferrat	⚓ Des Fosses and des Fossettes, open to SE–S–SW	Cap Martin	⚓ E of Cap Martin, open to NE–E–SE
Pointe St Hospice	⚓ Anse de la Scalletta, open to NW–N–NE		⊢ **144 Port de Menton-Ville (Vieux-Port)** 1–3–3 page 121
	⊢ **137 Port de St Jean-Cap Ferrat** 2–3–3 page 95		1M ⚓ N of Port de Menton-Ville, open to E–SE–S
	1M ⚓ N of Pointe Rompa-Talon, open to N–NE–E		⊢ **145 Port de Menton-Garavan** 3–3–2 page 124
Pointe de Beaulieu	⊢ **138 Port des Fourmis** 3–4–4 page 98	Capo della Martola	0·5M Franco-Italian frontier
	1M ⊢ **139 Port de Beaulieu-sur-Mer** 3–2–2 page 99		
	1M		

Rade d'Agay looking NW

5

South France Pilot

Pilotage

Pointe de la Baumette
A low wooded point with houses and an hotel on it. The lighthouse partly hidden by trees has a white tower (15m) and is set back from the coast. The point is foul with many rocky heads awash extending 200m offshore. 1M to E of the point is Les Vieilles, a rocky reef with an island which is marked by *La Chrétienne* S Card beacon tower YB with ▼ topmark (9m) ½M offshore. The red section of La Baumette light covers these dangers.

Pointe de la Baumette lighthouse

La Chrétienne S cardinal beacon tower looking WNW

Anchorages between Pointe de la Baumette and Pointe de l'Aiguille
The coast between these two points is of steep rocky cliffs backed by high reddish rocky hills broken by small bays which offer very many anchorages for use in good conditions. There are numerous small isolated rocks close inshore and a few further out. These anchorages should be approached with care at slow speed with a forward lookout stationed as high as possible; rocky dangers are easily seen in the clear water, especially with *Polaroid* glasses. A number of the larger anchorages are described below.

⚓ Calanque d'Anthéor
This bay has a conspicuous railway viaduct with nine arches at its head. There is a sandy beach ashore then the coast road, a beach restaurant, an hotel and several houses which lie beyond the viaduct. Enter on a NNW heading and anchor in 6m sand in the middle of the bay. The N side is rocky. Open to NE–E–SE and to NW wind down the valley.

Pointe de Cap Roux
A red rocky-cliffed headland which is not easily recognised unless coasting close in, the point is low with a lone house on it. Behind the Cap starts the steep-sided Mont de Cap Roux (451m) of reddish rock and some pine woods.

⚓ S of Pointe de Cap Roux
An anchorage in very attractive surroundings between the Pointe de l'Observatoire which has disused gun emplacements and pill boxes on its top and the Pointe de Cap Roux. The road and railway run along the top of the cliffs and there is a track to a rocky and sandy beach. Approach on a NNW heading, there are rocks on each side, anchor in 6m sand and rock, open to E–SE–S

Pointe de Anthéor

Calanque d'Anthéor looking S–SW

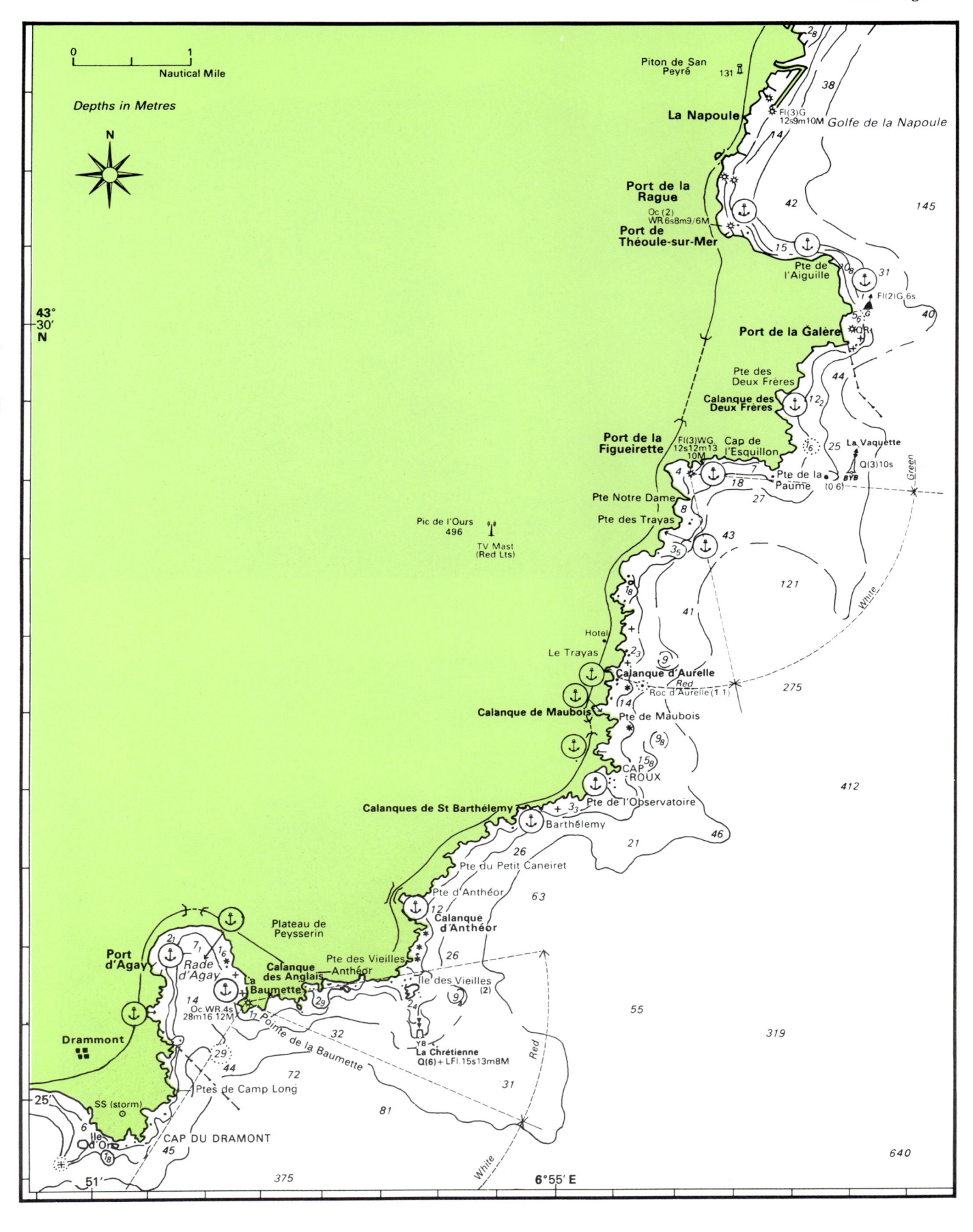

Anchorages

South France Pilot

Calanque d'Anthéor looking SW. Note Multi-arch viaduct

Pointe de la Baumette and Rade d'Agay looking NW

Anchorages

Pointe de Cap Roux, S anchorage looking W

Pointe de Cap Roux and N anchorages

South France Pilot

Pointe de Cap Roux

S of Pointe de Cap Roux

⚓ N of Pointe de Cap Roux

Another attractive anchorage but only use the N half of the bay, several beaches otherwise similar to that to the S of the point. A lone awash rock 200m offshore to N of this bay. Approach on a W heading and anchor in 5m rock and sand. Rocky beaches. Open to NE–E–SE.

Calanque de Maubois looking W

North of Pointe de Cap Roux

⚓ Calanque de Maubois

Yet another beautiful anchorage 800m to N of Pointe de Cap Roux. The Pointe de Maubois to the S has a lone ruined house. Road and rail at head, beaches and stairway to cliff top. Awash rocks lie 200m and 300m offshore to the N of this anchorage. Rocky beach. Enter on a W heading a third nearer the S side of the bay. Anchor in 5m sand and rock. Open to NE–E–SE.

⚓ Calanque d'Aurelle

A large lone house on point to S of this bay with a ruined house and walled garden on the point to N. Three awash rocks 300m off point to S. High embankment for railway behind bay, shingle beach. Enter on a W course towards the ruined house and divert towards head of bay. Anchor in 5m rock and sand. Open to NE–E–SE.

Pic de l'Ours

A tall (58m) TV/radio tower (F.R Lts) on a hill (496m) is very conspicuous. It lies 1¼M to W of Pointe de Trayas.

⚓ S of Pointe de Trayas

A larger bay with no outlying dangers, attractive but has some houses around it. Sand and shingle beach at head with stairs to road, railway has a large arch. Café up steps. Enter on a W course and anchor in 8m sand and rock. Open to NE–E–SE.

10

Anchorages

Pic de l'Ours ↓

Pic de l'Ours looking NW

Calanque d'Aurelle looking W

S of Pointe de Trayas looking NW–N

11

South France Pilot

110 PORT DE LA FIGUEIRETTE (PORT DE MIRAMAR-LE-TRAYAS)
06590 Alpes Maritimes

Position 43°29'·0N 6°56'·0E
Minimum depth in the entrance 6m (20ft)
               in the harbour 6 to 2m (20 to 6·6ft)
Width of the entrance 30m
Number of berths 235
Maximum length overall 15m (49ft)
Population 1000 (approx)
Rating 2–2–4

General
A small artificial yacht harbour situated in a sheltered bay in very attractive mountainous surroundings now covered with houses. The approach and entrance are easy but would be difficult and dangerous in heavy weather from E–SE–S, good protection is however offered once inside. The harbour is also sheltered to a large extent from the NW *mistral* wind. Local facilities are limited but improvements are planned. Experimental fish farms are located outside the harbour.

Data
Charts   Admiralty 2166
         French 5113
         Spanish 121
         ECM 501

Magnetic variation 1°19'W (1990) decreasing by about 8' each year.

Current There is a permanent SW-going current of 1 knot along this coast.

Port radio VHF Ch 9, call sign *Miramar* (French).

Weather forecasts Posted at the *Bureau de Port* once a day.

Speed limit 3 knots

Lights
Môle Sud Head Fl(3)WG.12s12m13/10M. White column, green top. 275°-W-348°-G-275°
Spur head F.R

Buoys **La Vaquette** Q(3)10s E Card BYB ♦ topmark.

Port de la Figueirette looking SW. Note fish farm and line of buoys.

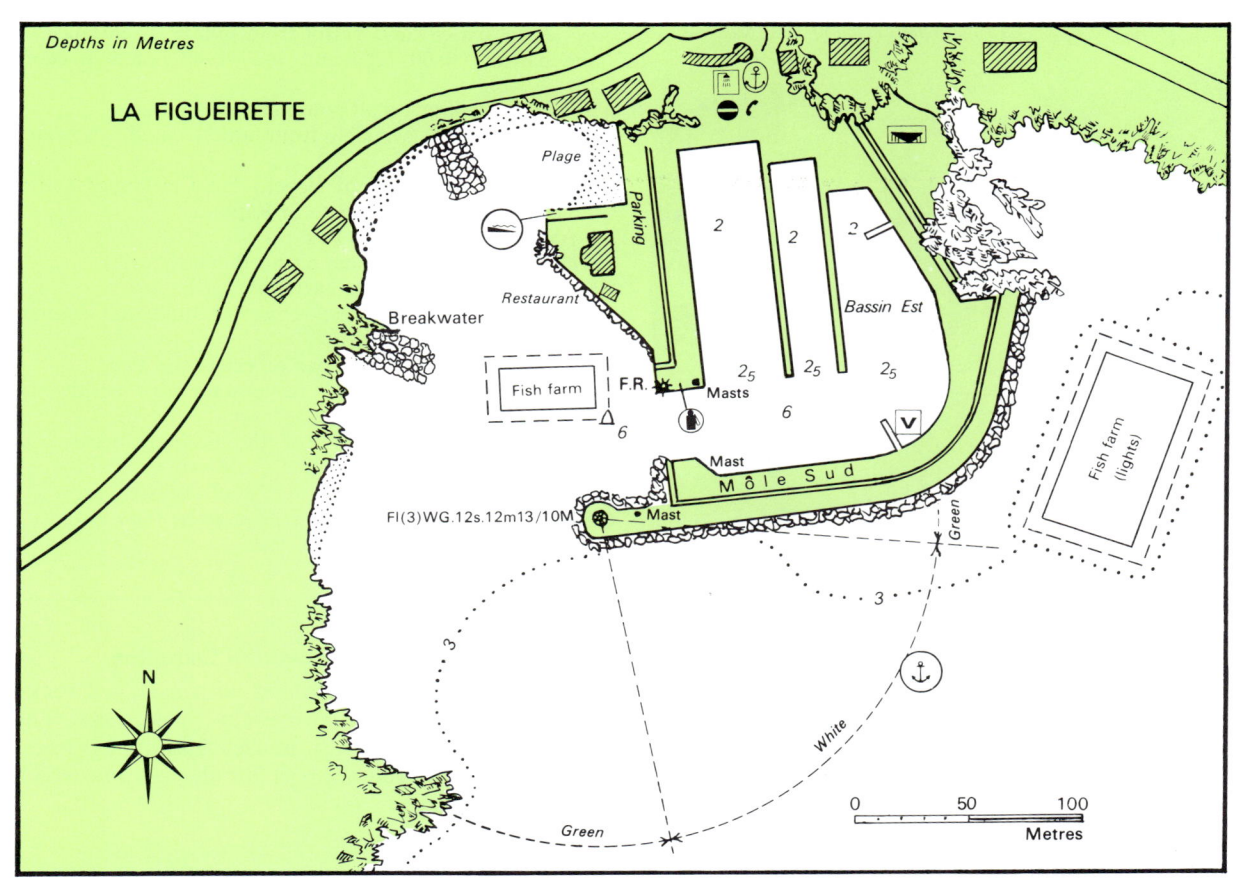

Port de la Figueirette (Port Miramar-le-Trayas)

Port de la Figueirette

Warning
La Vaquette, a low rock, lies 500m off Cap de l'Esquillon and has an E Card lightbuoy BYB ♦ topmark, Q(3)10s, marking it. The rock can usually be seen by the sea breaking over it, but it is dangerous in calm weather because it is difficult to locate. It is in the green sector of the Fl(3)WG.12s on the Môle Sud head. There is a tendency for this harbour to silt up and it is dredged from time to time, depths shown may not be accurate. Fish farms are located near the harbour surrounded by Y buoys. White lights illuminate the areas at night.

Approach by day
From SW Very high rocky cliffs of a red colour stretch to this harbour from Cap Dramont which has a white signal station on its summit. There is a deep bay, the Rade d'Agay, which with *La Chrétienne* S Card beacon YB ♦ topmark, Q(6)+LFl.15s, at its E end, is identifiable if close to the coast; if further out, the lighthouse at Pointe de la Baumette and viaduct at Anthéor will help. The TV tower on the Pic de l'Ours (F.R) (496m) leads to this harbour, it lies 1M to SSW of the harbour.
From NE Cross the wide Golfe de la Napoule and follow the high reddish rocky-cliffed coast of the Massif de l'Esterel at ½M: Cap de l'Esquillon is prominent and has La Vaquette, a dangerous isolated rock, 500m off its point, marked by an E Card BYB ♦ topmark lightbuoy, Q(3)10s, outside it. Round this point preferably outside *La Vaquette* lightbuoy, when the harbour will be seen at the head of the Baie de la Figueirette. There is a passage 300m wide inside the danger.

By night
Using the lights listed below navigate to a position where the harbour lies 400m to NW:
Pointe de la Baumette Oc.WR.4s15/12M
La Chrétienne lightbeacon Q(6)+LFl.W.15s8M
La Garoupe Fl(2)W.10s31M
Pic de l'Ours (TV tower)2 F.R
La Vaquette lightbuoy Q(3)W.10s

Anchorage in the approach
Anchor 200m to SE of the entrance in 10m (33ft) sand. Open to E–SE–S.

Entrance
By day Approach the head of Môle Sud which has a unique 4-pillared lighthouse on a NW course and round it at 20m leaving it to starboard and some small R and Y buoys to port. Enter on an E course leaving the fuel station to port.
By night Approach Fl(3)WG.12s in W sector on a NW course. Leave it 20m to starboard and round it onto an E course. Enter on this course leaving F.R to port.

13

South France Pilot

La Figueirette   Head of Môle Sud

Port de la Figueirette, approach looking N

Berths
Secure stern to vacant berth in SE corner with bow to chain and report to *Bureau de Port* for allocation of a berth which is sometimes allocated verbally from the fuel station.

Formalities
Report to the *Bureau de Port* (☎ 93 75 41 00) on arrival; open summer 0730–1230 and 1300–2030, winter 0830–1200 and 1430–1730. The customs office is alongside.

Charges
There are harbour charges. There is no charge for a visit between 1100 and 1500.

Facilities
Hard A small sandy beach which can be used as a hard to the W of the harbour.
Crane An 8-tonne mobile crane.
Fuel Diesel (*gasoil*) and petrol from pumps at entrance to the harbour 0800–1200 and 1400–1900 hours in summer.
Water Water points on all pontoons and quays.
Electricity 220v AC available from outlets on all quays and pontoons.
Provisions A small shop at Espero Pax-Le Trayas half a mile away along the road to St Raphael.
Ice At the shop in Espero Pax.
Garbage Rubbish containers round the harbour.
Chandlery Shop beside the harbour.
Repairs A small yard where repairs to hulls and engines can be carried out.
Hotels Three ** hotels and two others in the area.
Restaurants There are three restaurants, one beside the harbour.
Showers Showers to the N of the harbour beside the Bureau de Port.
Beaches A small sandy beach to NW of the harbour.
Communications Frequent bus service along the coast.

Pointe de la Paume and Cap de l'Esquillon
A rounded prominent headland with dark red rocky cliffs (102m) which has two rocky projections. The headland is covered with houses and many trees. There is a multi-arch support for the railway which is conspicuous.

La Vaquette rock and passage
An awash rock 500m to E of Pointe de la Paume is marked by a W Card buoy. A passage 300m wide and 10m deep lies in a NE/SW direction halfway between this rock and the coast.

Fish farm   Head of Môle Sud

Port de la Figueirette, entrance looking E

14

Anchorages

Pic de l'Ours   W cardinal buoy   La Vaquette rock   Iles de Lérins   Cap l'Esquillon   La Vaquette
                      Port de la Figueirette

La Vaquette rock and buoy looking W

Port de la Figueirette looking E

Calanque des Deux Frères looking W

15

South France Pilot

⚓ Calanque des Deux Frères

A beautiful bay with several houses with a road to main coast road above this and high on the hill are some 'flying saucer' type buildings. The N side of the entrance is foul with rocks as is the SW corner of the bay. Approach on a NW course and anchor in 4m sand and rocks open NE–E–SE and swell from S.

---

111 PORT DE LA GALERE
06590 Alpes-Maritimes

Position 43°30'·0N 6°57'·3E
Minimum depth   in the entrance 4m (13ft)
                  in the harbour 3 to 1·5m (9·8 to 4·9ft)
Width of the entrance 45m
Maximum length overall 12m (39ft)
Number of berths 220
Population 1000 (approx)
Rating 2–2–4

General

A most attractive small artificial yacht harbour that is a part of a housing development of unique design. The approach and entrance are easy and good shelter obtained from the NW *mistral*, but winds and swell from the E–SE can make the entrance dangerous and it is narrow and uncomfortable inside the harbour. Facilities are limited.

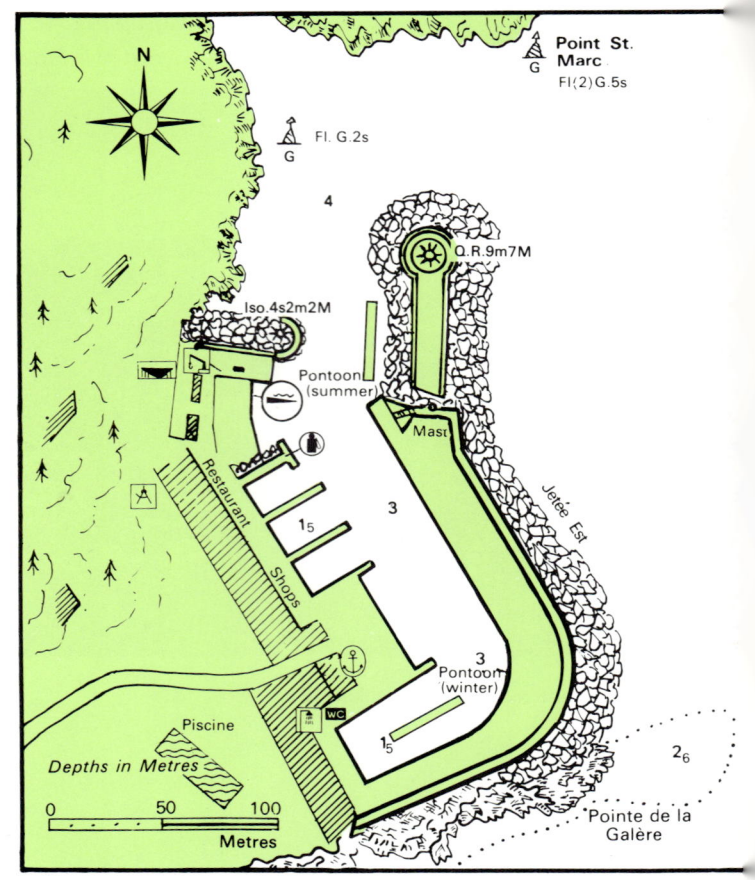

Port de la Galère

Port de la Galère looking SW

16

Port de la Galère

Entrance

Data

Charts Admiralty 2166
French 5113
Spanish 121
ECM 501

Magnetic variation 1°19′W (1990) decreasing by about 8′ each year.

Current There is a permanent SW-going current of about 1 knot off this harbour.

Weather forecasts Forecasts are posted daily outside the *Bureau de Port* and also a tape-recorded service (*Navimet*).

Speed limit 3 knots.

Lights
Jetée Est Head Q.R.9m7M. White tower, red top.
Spur Iso.W.4s. Line of light along top of spur.

Buoys Small G lightbuoy (Fl(2)G.5s) off Pointe St Marc. Small G lightbuoy (Fl.G.2s) on W side of entrance. Both have ▲ topmarks.

Warning

La Vaquette, a low rock, lies 500m off Cap de l'Esquillon; just awash, it is sometimes very difficult to see in calm weather. An E Card BYB lightbuoy topmark, Q(3)W.10s, is moored outside it.

Approach by day

From SW The reddish rocky Massif de l'Esterel, with high broken cliffs along the coast, commences at Cap Dramont which has a conspicuous signal station. Also conspicuous are the lighthouse at Pointe de la Baumette, the 9-arched rail viaduct at Anthéor, the TV tower at Pic de l'Ours and the group of houses of Moorish-type futuristic design on the cliff-face around and to the SW of this harbour. Follow the coast along at ½M, outside *La Chrétienne* S Card YB beacon tower topmark, Q(6)+LFl.15s, and outside *La Vaquette* lightbuoy until the entrance is W when approach on this course.

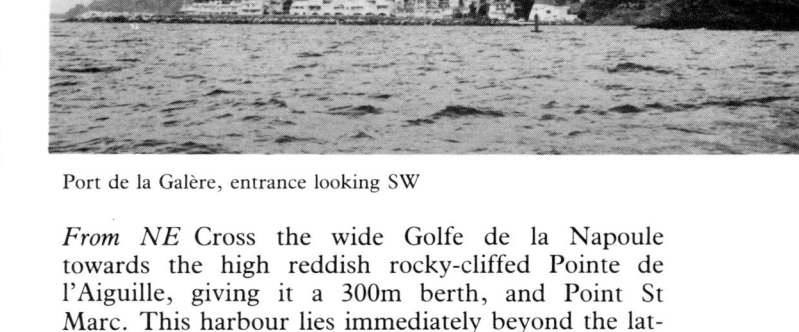

Port de la Galère, entrance looking SW

From NE Cross the wide Golfe de la Napoule towards the high reddish rocky-cliffed Pointe de l'Aiguille, giving it a 300m berth, and Point St Marc. This harbour lies immediately beyond the latter point and can be recognised by the group of houses of futuristic N African design. Approach the entrance on a W course.

By night

Using the lights below navigate to a position where the entrance lies W at 300m:
La Napoule Fl(3)G.12s10M
La Chrétienne lightbeacon Q(6)+LFl.W.15s8M
Pointe de la Baumette Oc.WR.4s15/12M
La Garoupe Fl(2)W.10s31M
La Vaquette lightbuoy Q(3)W.10s

Anchorage in the approach

Anchor 200m to E of the entrance in 20m (66ft) sand and shingle. Open to N–NE–E–SE–S.

Entrance

By day Enter on a W course towards the head of Jetée Est, leave it 15m to port and round it leaving two small lightbuoys with G ▲ topmarks to starboard onto a S course.

By night Approach Q.R on a W course leave it 15m to port and round it onto a S course leaving Fl(2)G.5s, Fl.G.2s and Iso.W.4s to starboard.

Fuel *Chantier*

Port de la Galère looking S–SW–W–NW

South France Pilot

Berths
Secure alongside or stern to quay, bow to mooring chain in a vacant space or to fuel station and report to *Bureau de Port* for an allocation of a berth. In summer a pontoon for visitors is established just inside the entrance to port, in winter it is moved to the S end of the harbour.

Formalities
Report to *Bureau de Port* (☎ 93 57 41 74) on arrival, open day and night. Customs have an office at Cannes and officers visit occasionally (☎ 93 39 22 77).

Charges
There are harbour charges.

Facilities
Slip A slip to NW of the harbour.
Crane A mobile 19-tonne crane to the NW of the harbour.
Fuel Diesel (*gasoil*) and petrol are available from pumps at head of a pontoon. 0800–2200 hours in summer, 0800–1800 in winter (☎ 93 75 42 11).
Water Water points on all quays and pontoons.
Electricity 220v AC supply points on all quays and pontoons.
Provisions Some shops around the harbour including a supermarket and more to be found in Théoule about 1M away over the hill.
Ice Available in season at the supermarket.
Duty-free goods Arrangements can be made for the supply of duty-free goods on application to the *Bureau de Port*.
Garbage Rubbish containers are on the quays.
Chandlery A limited amount available at the shipyard.
Repairs Minor repairs to hull and engine are carried out by the small shipyard to NW of the harbour.
Post office The nearest is at Théoule.
Hotels Being built.
Restaurants One restaurant and a café.

Yacht club There is a club but it is not really a yacht club but a social club. It has bars, restaurant, swimming pool and showers.
Showers Showers are available near the *Bureau de Port*.
Lifeboat A small lifeboat is stationed here in the season.
Communications A frequent coastal bus service.

History
The harbour has been named after the wreck of a Roman galley which was discovered here.

⌘ E of Pointe de l'Aiguille
An open anchorage lies between this point and the port of Théoule-sur-Mer. The coast is of high cliffs covered with houses. Anchor close inshore in 5m mud. Open to NW–N–NE–E.

Piton St Pierre

Pointe de l'Aiguille looking NW into Golfe de la Napoule

112 PORT DE THÉOULE-SUR-MER
06590 Alpes-Maritimes

Position 43°30′·5N 6°56′·4E
Minimum depth in the entrance 3·4m (11ft)
in the harbour 3·4 to 1·6m (11 to 5·2ft)
Width of the entrance 30m
Number of berths 180
Maximum length overall 13m (43ft)
Population 3000 (approx)
Rating 3–3–4

General

A very small old fishing harbour that has been improved by the provision of two jetties and pontoons. Not difficult to approach and enter but some care is needed owing to off-lying rocks. The entrance is dangerous in strong E–SE winds and swell. Shelter from the NW *mistral* wind is fair. Facilities are limited.

Data

Charts Admiralty 2166
French 5113
Spanish 121
ECM 501

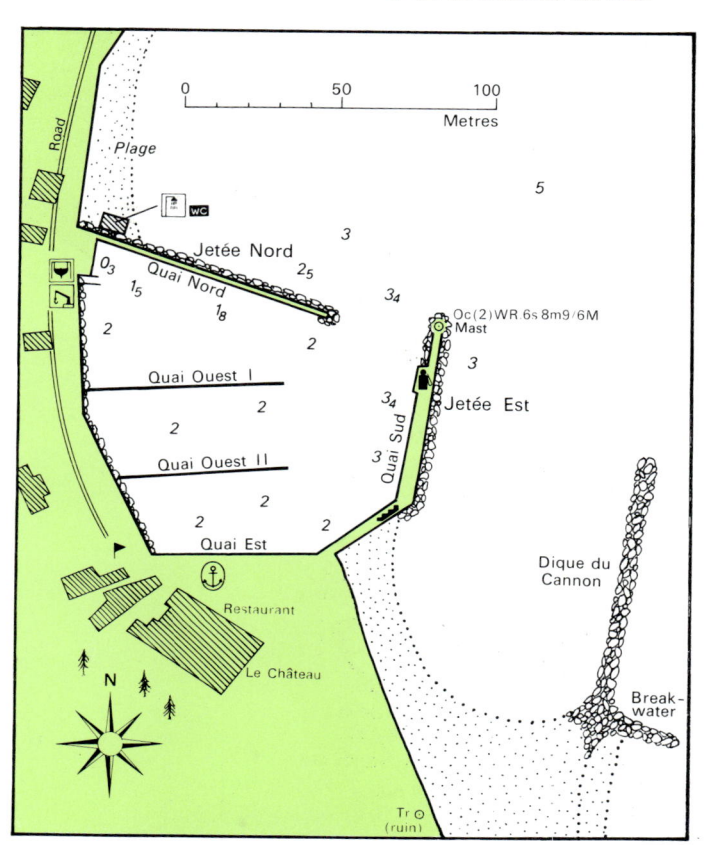

Port de Théoule-sur-Mer

Port de Théole-sur-Mer looking W

South France Pilot

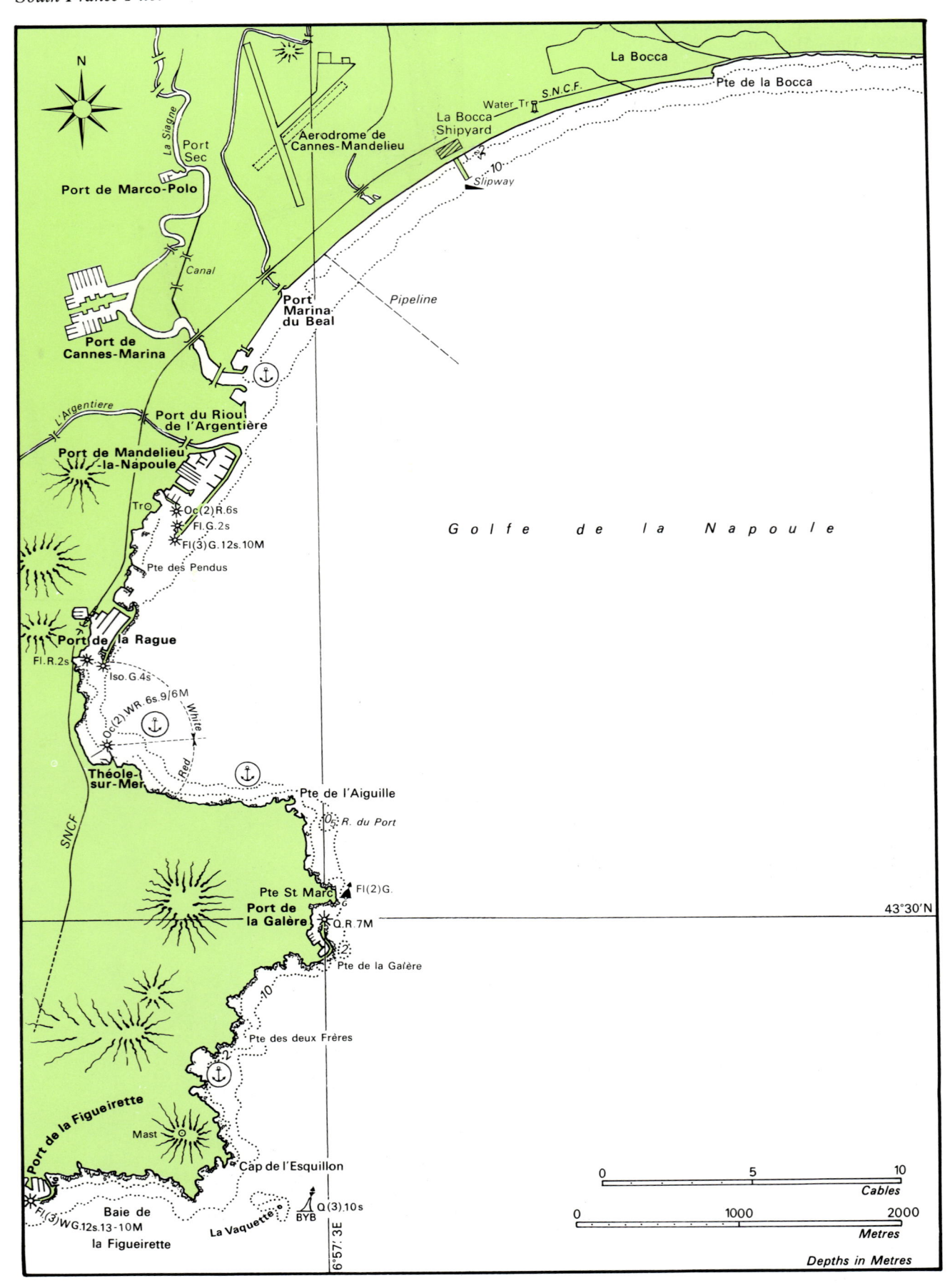

Magnetic variation 1°19'W (1990) decreasing by about 8' each year.

Weather forecasts Posted twice a day at the *Bureau de Port* and automatic tape-recorded service (*Navimet*).

Speed limit 3 knots.

Port radio VHF Ch 16 and 9 (French)

Lights
Jetée Est Head Oc(2)WR.6s8m9/6M.

Warning

As there is little space for manoeuvre in this harbour, enter with care and at slow speed. In the approach pay attention to the Digue du Cannon.

Approach by day

From SW Round the high reddish rocky-cliffed Pointe de la Galère, Pointe St Marc and Pointe de l'Aiguille at 400m. The small town and château of Théoule will be seen at the foot of two steep-sided valleys with the conical hill Piton de San Peyré (131m) lying 1M to N of the harbour. Do not cut the corner towards the harbour but remain 400m from the coast until the entrance bears SW when approach on this course.

From NE Cross the wide Golfe de Napoule towards the high reddish coloured rocky Massif de l'Esterel. Set course for this harbour that lies at the foot of two steep-sided valleys which are located to the N of Pointe de l'Aiguille and to the S of a conspicuous viaduct at La Rague. Approach the harbour on a SW course. The Piton de San Peyré (131m) which is 1M to the N of the harbour may also be identified.

By night

Using the following lights navigate to a position where the entrance lies 300m to SW:

La Napoule Fl(3)G.12s10M
Cannes VQ(3)R.2s8M
Pointe de la Baumette Oc.WR.4s16/12M
La Garoupe Fl(2)W.10s31M

Anchorage in the approach

Anchor 200m to NE of the entrance in 10m (33ft) mud and weed. Open to N–NE–E.

Entrance

By day Approach the head of Jetée Est on a SW course, round it at 15m leaving it to port.
By night Approach Oc(2)WR.6s on a SW course in the W sector, round it at 15m leaving it to port.

Berths

Secure to fuel station just inside the harbour on the port hand or in a vacant berth stern-to, bow to chain, and report to *Bureau de Port* for allocation of a berth.

Formalities

Report to the *Bureau de Port* (☎ 93 49 97 38) on arrival. Open 0800–1230 and 1330–1830.

Charges

There are harbour charges.

Facilities

Hard In the SW corner of the harbour to N of Quai Nord there is a sand hard.
Crane A mobile 6-tonne crane.
Fuel Diesel (*gasoil*) and petrol are available from pumps at the head of Jetée Est (☎ 93 47 12 62)
Travel-lift 3 tonnes in NW corner of the harbour.
Water There are water points on the quays.
Electricity A few outlets for 240v AC on the quays.
Provisions A number of shops in the town nearby and a market on Friday mornings.
Ice Delivered to the harbour once a day in the season.
Garbage A very few rubbish containers around the harbour.
Repairs Minor repairs by two local shipyards and mechanic for hulls and engines.
Chandlery A small shop with limited stock in the town.
Post office A PTT in the town to SW of the harbour.
Hotels One ****, three ***, four ** and some unclassified.
Restaurants Thirteen restaurants and some café/bars.

Digue du Canon   *Head Jetée Este   Entrance*

Port de Théoule-sur-Mer, approach looking SE

South France Pilot

Yacht clubs The Yacht Club de Théoule (YCT) (☎ 93 49 98 80) and the Cercle de Voile Théoule (CVT) (☎ 93 49 13 14) have offices here in season (mid-June to mid-September and weekends).
Showers 3 showers and WCs.
Information office The Syndicat d'Initiative has an office near the PTT and town hall (*mairie*).
Lifeboat A small lifeboat is stationed here.
Beaches A small sandy beach each side of the harbour.
Communications A coastal bus service and rail service.

Future development
A new yacht club is to be built to the SW of the harbour.

History
Used as a natural harbour for centuries it was first developed in the 17th century by the construction of the jetty. It remained a small fishing village of some 50 persons until with the advent of the railways in the 19th century it became a popular tourist resort.

---

113 PORT DE LA RAGUE
06590 Alpes-Maritimes

Position 43°30′·9N 6°56′·3E
Minimum depth in the entrance 5m (16ft)
in the harbour 4·5 to 1m (15 to 3·3ft)
Width of the entrance 50m
Number of berths 540
Maximum length overall 30m (98ft)
Population 1000 (approx)
Rating 3-2-2

General
A medium-sized new yacht harbour created by the construction of a large jetty. Easy to approach and enter with good protection even from the NW *mistral* once inside. There are good facilities available for yachtsmen.

Data
Charts Admiralty 2166
French 5113
Spanish 121
ECM 501

Magnetic variation 1°19′W (1990) decreasing by about 8′ each year.

Port radio VHF Ch 9. Listening watch on 2649 kHz (French and a little English).

Weather forecasts Forecasts are posted once a day at the Bureau de Port. *Météo* telex, French and Italian. Also an automatic tape-recorded forecast (*Navimet*).

Speed limit 3 knots.

Storm signals Storm signals are flown from a mast at the Bureau de Port and announced over a public address system.

Lights
Jetée Est Head Iso.G.4s9m10M. White tower, green top.
Epi Ouest Fl.R.2s4m2M. Red post.

Buoys A series of small R buoys with square red flags marks the shallows on the W side of the harbour.

Approach by day
From SW Round the high reddish rocky-cliffed Pointe de la Galère, Point St Marc and Pointe de l'Aiguille at 400m onto a NW course towards a conspicuous railway viaduct, leaving the town and harbour of Théoule to port. The entrance will be seen just to the S of the viaduct which has 6 arches. Approach on a W course.

From NE Cross the wide Golfe de Napoule towards its W extremity. A conspicuous railway viaduct with 6 arches will be seen which is located behind this harbour. The harbour of Mandelieu-La Napoule which is situated ½M to NE of La Rague should not be confused with this harbour. The entrance lies at the S end of the Jetée Est and it should be approached on a W course.

Port de la Rague, entrance looking NE

Entrance *Piton de San Peyr*

Port de la Rague, approach looking NW–N

Port de la Rague

Quai d'Accueil

Port de la Rague

Port de la Rague looking SW

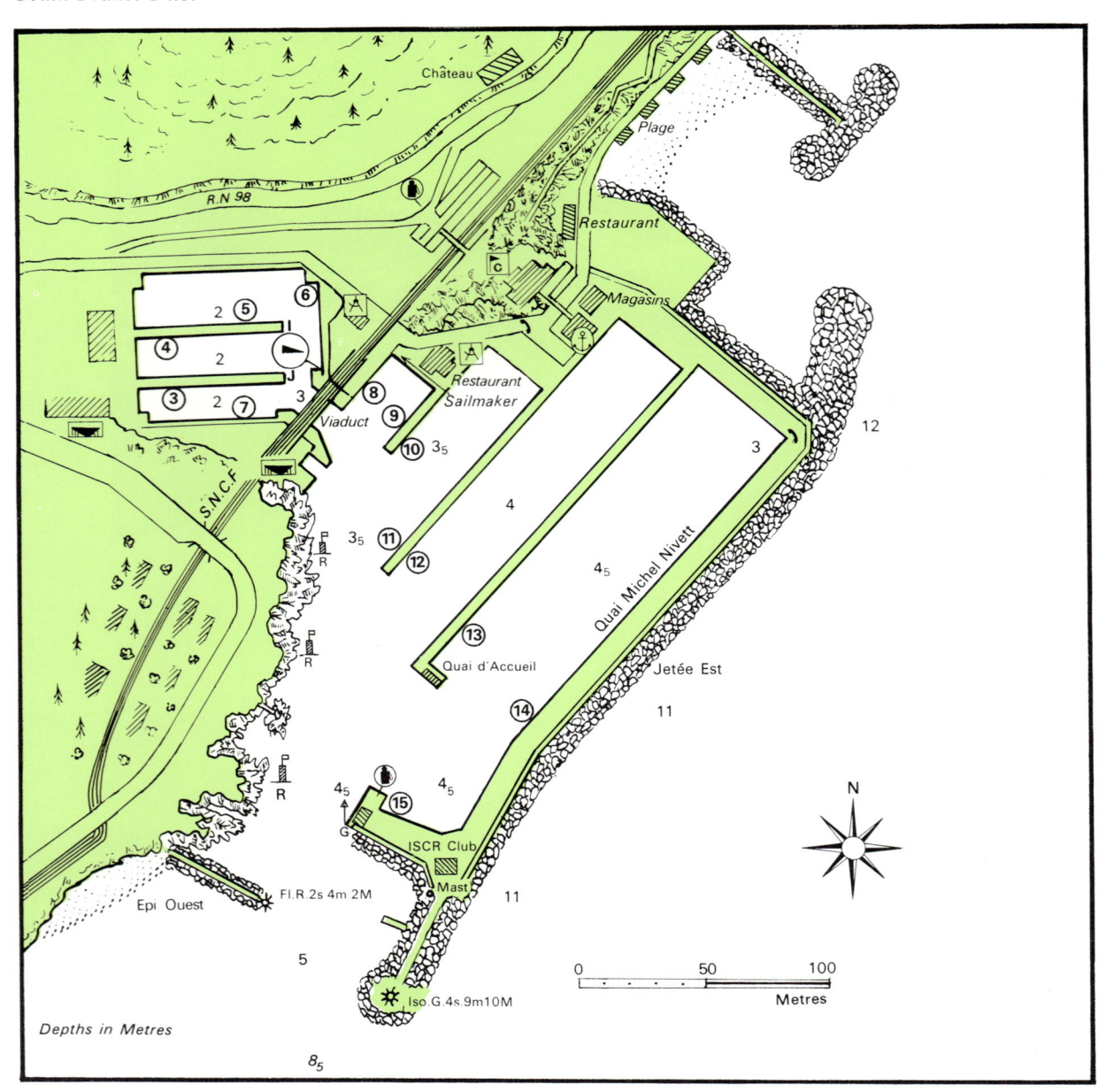

South France Pilot

Port de la Rague

By night
Using the following lights navigate to a position where the entrance to the harbour lies 300m to W:

Port de la Galère Q.R.7M
Théoule Oc(2)WR.6s9/6M
Cannes VQ(3)R.2s8M
La Garoupe Fl(2)W.10s31M

Anchorage in the approach
Anchor 200m to E of the entrance in 10m (33ft) sand, mud and weed. Open to NE–E–SE.

Entrance
By day Approach the head of the Jetée Est on a W course, round it at 20m leaving it to starboard. Then leave the Epi Ouest head 10m to port and a spur with a small G beacon ▲ topmark 10m to starboard. There is a line of small R buoys that have now to be left to port.

By night Approach Iso.G.4s on a W course, leave it 20m to starboard and round it onto a N course leaving Fl.R.2s 10m to port, enter harbour passing close to a spur on the starboard hand.

Berths
Secure to the head of 'B', the first pontoon No.13 (Quai d'Accueil) and report to the *Bureau de Port* for the allocation of a berth. Secure stern-to, bow to mooring chain. In season berths are allocated direct from Quai d'Accueil or call when 1M off on VHF Ch 9 for a berth.

Formalities
Report to the *Bureau de Port* on arrival, open 0600–2200, (☎ 93 49 81 55/56). Telex 470673/263 FLASH.

Facilities

Slip A small slip underneath the viaduct.
Travel-lift A 30-tonne travel lift.
Crane A 20-tonne mobile crane and a 3-tonne crane.
Fuel Diesel (*gasoil*) and petrol are available from pumps at the head of the spur just inside the entrance. 0830–1130 and 1430–1730 hours in summer.
Water Water points on all quays and pontoons.
Electricity Electricity points 230v AC on all quays and pontoons. Also 380v AC on certain deep-water quays.
Provisions Some small shops alongside the harbour and many others in La Napoule.
Ice From shop near the *Bureau de Port*.
Duty-free goods Available by arrangement with the *Bureau de Port*.
Garbage Many rubbish containers around the harbour.
Repairs One shipyard and engine repair workshop; can carry out most repairs to engine and hull. Sails and electronics can also be repaired.
Laundrette Théoule and La Napoule.
Post office At La Napoule and Théoule.
Restaurants Restaurants and café/bars in the harbour area.
Yacht club The International Sporting Club de la Rague (ISCR) (☎ 93 49 56 72) has a clubhouse at the head of Jetée Est.
Showers Four showers and WCs are at the *Bureau de Port*.
Information office At La Napoule.
Beach A small sandy beach to N of the harbour.
Communications Bus and rail services, also air service 2M away.

Future development

Shopping area is to be constructed.

---

114 PORT DE MANDELIEU-LA NAPOULE
06210 Alpes-Maritimes

Position 43°31'·3N 6°56'·7E
Minimum depth in the entrance 7m (23ft)
in the harbour 7 to 2m (23 to 6·6ft)
Width of the entrance 100m
Maximum length overall 50m (164ft), (35m (115ft) visitors)
Number of berths 1129
Population 6792
Rating 3–2–2

General

A large new artificial yacht harbour which is easy to approach and enter and offers good protection once inside from winds including the NW *mistral* but open to some swell from SE. Facilities for yachtsmen are good but expensive.

Data

Charts Admiralty 2166, 2167
French 5113
Spanish 121
ECM 501

Magnetic variation 1°19'W (1990) decreasing by about 8' each year.

Port radio VHF Ch 9. 0800–2000 hours only (French and a little English).

Weather forecasts Weather forecasts are published every morning at the *Bureau de Port* and 3 other places. Automatic tape-recorded forecasts (*Navimet*).

Speed limit 3 knots.

Traffic signals Shown from mast at entrance.

Day	Meaning
Red flag	Entrance forbidden
Green flag	Exit forbidden
Red and green flags	Entrance and exit forbidden

Storm signals Storm signals are hoisted on the mast at the entrance and announced over the public address system.

Lights
Jetée Est Head Fl(3)G.12s9m10M. White tower, green top.
Jetée Est Spur Fl.G.2s2m2M. Dark green post.
Jetée SW Head Oc(2)R.6s2m2M. Red post.

Buoys Y buoys established in summer only on the port side of the entrance mark the bathing areas.

Approach by day

From SW Round the high reddish-cliffed Pointe de la Galère, Point St Marc and Pointe de l'Aiguille at 400m onto a NW course and approach a large low dark stone château with a small conical hill Piton de San Peyré (131m) behind it. ½M to SW will be seen a conspicuous railway viaduct with Port de la Rague in front. When closer in the Jetée Est will be seen with a light tower, white with green top at the entrance.

From NE Cross the wide Golfe de Napoule towards where the first coastal hills rise on the SW side of the flood plain and mouth of the Rivière la Siagne. In the closer approach a large group of white apartment blocks and a long low dark stone château will be seen which is near the entrance to this harbour. The long Jetée Est will also be seen, round the SW end for the entrance.

By night

Using the lights listed below navigate to a position where the harbour entrance lies 300m NW:
Port de la Galère Q.R.7M
Théoule Oc(2)WR.6s9/6M
Cannes VQ(3)R.2s8M
La Garoupe Fl(2)W.10s31M

Anchorage in the approach

Anchor 200m to E of harbour entrance in 10m (33ft) mud and weed. Open to NE–E–SE.

Entrance

By day Approach the head of Jetée Est on a NW course, round it at 20m leaving it to starboard onto a N course. Leave a short spur to starboard and the head of Jetée SW to port.
By night Approach Fl(3)G.12s on a NW course and round it at 20m leaving it to starboard, then leave Fl.G.2s to starboard in a similar manner and finally leave Oc(2)R.6s 20m to port.

South France Pilot

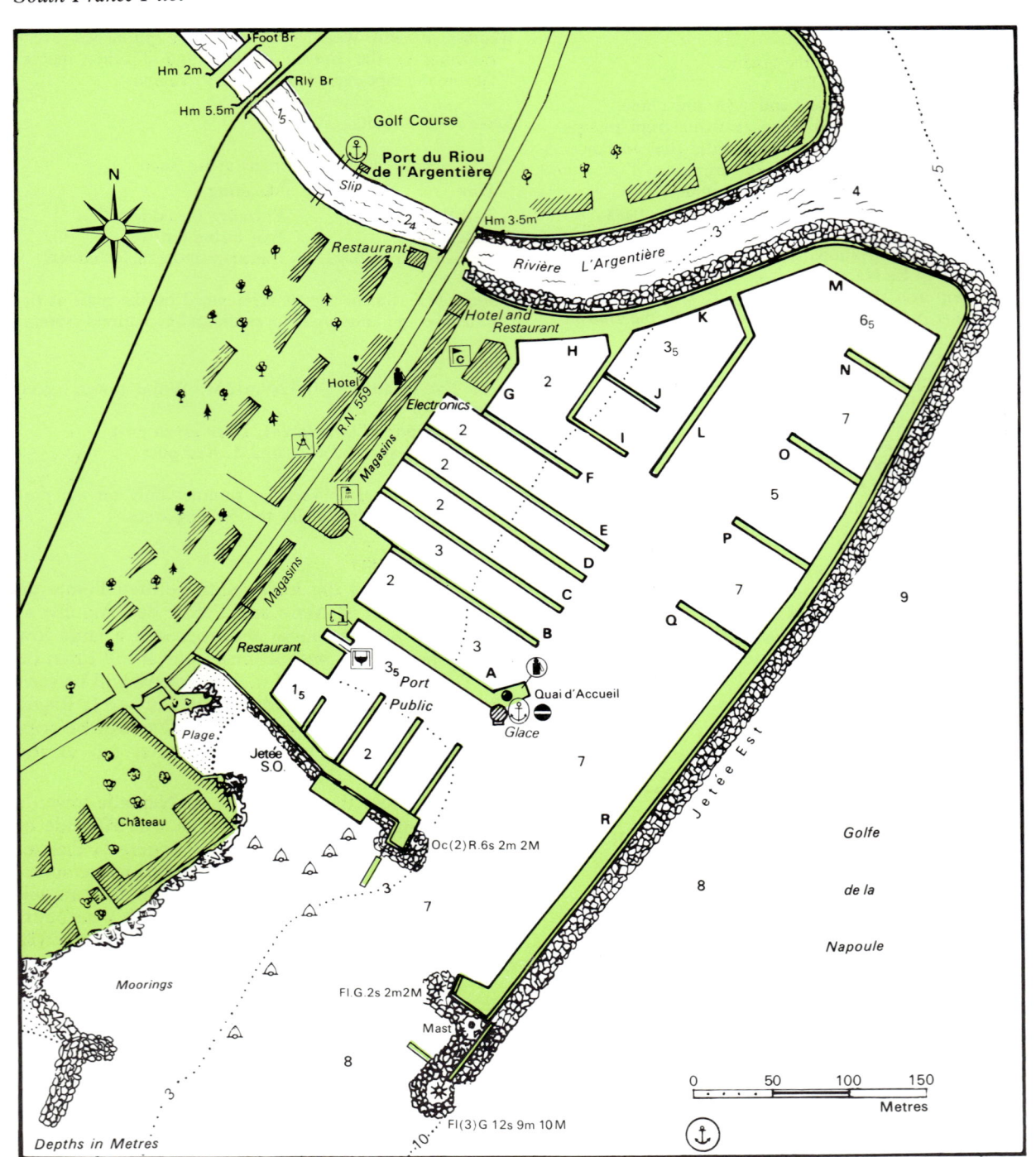

Port de Mandelieu-la-Napoule

Château → ← *Bureau de Port*

Port de Mandelieu-La Napoule

26

Port de la Mandelieu-la Napoule

Cannes Marina

Le Château

Marco Polo   Port Sec

Mouth of R. L'Argentière

Block of white flats   Mouth of R. La Siagne

Port de Mandelieu-la-Napoule looking NNW

Berths
Secure alongside the Quai d'Accueil close to the *Bureau de Port* and the fuel pumps. Report to the Bureau for allocation of a berth and secure stern-to, bow to mooring chain. Berths may be reserved by calling on VHF Ch 9 when 1M out.

Formalities
Report at once on arrival to the *Bureau de Port* (☎ 93 93 36 36) open day and night. Customs at Cannes (☎ 93 93 36 13) have an office in the *Bureau de Port* if required. Reservation of berths is on ☎ 93 93 36 14 and 93 49 80 64.

Charges
There are harbour charges.

Facilities
Travel-lift There is a 70-tonne travel-lift elevator in the SW corner of the harbour. Maximum dimensions: LOA 22m (72ft), width 7m (23ft), draught 3·2m (10ft)
Cranes An 8-tonne mobile crane.
Fuel Diesel (*gasoil*) and petrol from pumps near the *Bureau de Port* 0800–1900 hours in summer and 0900–1200, 1400–1800 in winter. Not open on Tuesdays.
Water Water points are established on all quays and pontoons.
Electricity Supply points are on all quays and pontoons for 220v AC and others for 380v AC on deep-water quays.

Provisions A supermarket and a number of shops around the harbour and more are to be found in the town nearby.
Ice Supplies are obtainable from the fuel station in summer.
Duty-free goods The supply of duty-free goods is possible here, contact the customs.
Garbage Many rubbish containers around the harbour.
Chandlery A ships' chandler to NW of the harbour.
Repairs Five shipyards here where engines and hulls can be repaired. Sails and electronic equipment can also be repaired.
Laundrette A laundrette to NW of the harbour.
Post office The PTT is located near the middle of the town.
Yacht clubs Club Nautic Port de Mandelieu-La Napoule (CNPMN) (☎ 93 49 92 91), clubhouse N corner of harbour, showers, bar, etc.
Hotels Two ****, three ***, ten **, three * and some unclassified hotels.
Restaurants Three at the harbour and forty-nine nearby, also a number of café/bars.
Showers Showers and WCs near the root of pontoon C on the NW side of the harbour. Open 0800–2000.
Information office The office of the Syndicat d'Initiative is located on the far side of the railway line.
Visits An art display in the château and other exhibitions are held here. A climb to the Piton de San Peyré is worth the effort.
Beach A small sandy beach to the SW of the harbour.
Communications Bus and rail services, also an air service from Cannes airfield 2M away.

South France Pilot

History
The château was built originally in the 14th century as a stronghold but only the towers remained. It was rebuilt in 1919. The area developed by the British into a sporting area in the late 19th century with a golf course, polo field, race track etc., an image that it still retains.

---

115 PORT DU RIOU DE L'ARGENTIERE
06210 Alpes-Maritimes

Position 43°31'·6N 6°57'E
Minimum depth in the entrance 3m (9·8ft)
in the harbour 2m to 1·5m (6·6 to 4·9ft)
Clearance   Road bridge 3·5m (11ft)
Rail bridge 5·5m (18ft)
Foot bridge 2m (6·6ft)
Number of berths 182
Maximum length overall 8·25m (27ft)
Population 1000 (approx)
Rating 4–3–3

General
This harbour for small yachts is located immediately to the N of the Port de Mandelieu-La Napoule in the Rivière l'Argentière to NW of the road bridge. It is approached by a 350m rocky-sided canal which to a large extent eliminates the effects of any swell. Approach and entrance are easy but dangerous with E–SE winds.

Data
Charts, magnetic variations and weather forecasts see Port de Mandelieu-La Napoule page 25.

Speed limit Maximum speed 3·5 knots.

Warning
Depths may vary during and after the river has been in flood. The sides of the river are shallow.

Approach by day
From SW Round the Pointes de la Galère, St Marc and de l'Aiguille at 400m onto a NNW course and approach a conspicuous group of white apartment blocks. In the closer approach the long rocky Jetée Est of the Port de Mandelieu-La Napoule will be identified and the mouth of the river and the road bridge will be seen between the NE corner of the Jetée Est and the group of apartment buildings.

By night
Not advised but experienced navigators using the following lights could enter in calm conditions:
Port de la Galère Q.R.7M
Port de Théoule Oc(2)WR.6s9/6M
Port de la Rague Iso.G.4s10M
Port de Mandelieu-La Napoule Fl(3)G.12s10M
Vieux Port de Cannes VQ(3)R.2s8M
Port Pierre-Canto Oc.WG.4s13/8M
Les Moines beacon tower Q(6)+LFl.W.15s9M
La Garoupe Fl(2)W.10s31M

Anchorage in the approach
Anchor 200m off the mouth of the Rivière la Siagne in 10m, mud and sand. Open to N–NE–E–SE.

Entrance by day
Approach the mouth of the Rivière l'Argentière on a WSW course and enter in midstream.

By night
Not advised due to lack of navigation lights but experienced navigators could enter using the illumination provided by the street lighting.

Berths
Berth in a vacant place bow or stern-to on left (NE) bank with lines to small posts and report to *Bureau de Port*.

Railway bridge

Port du Riou de l'Argentière looking N from road bridge

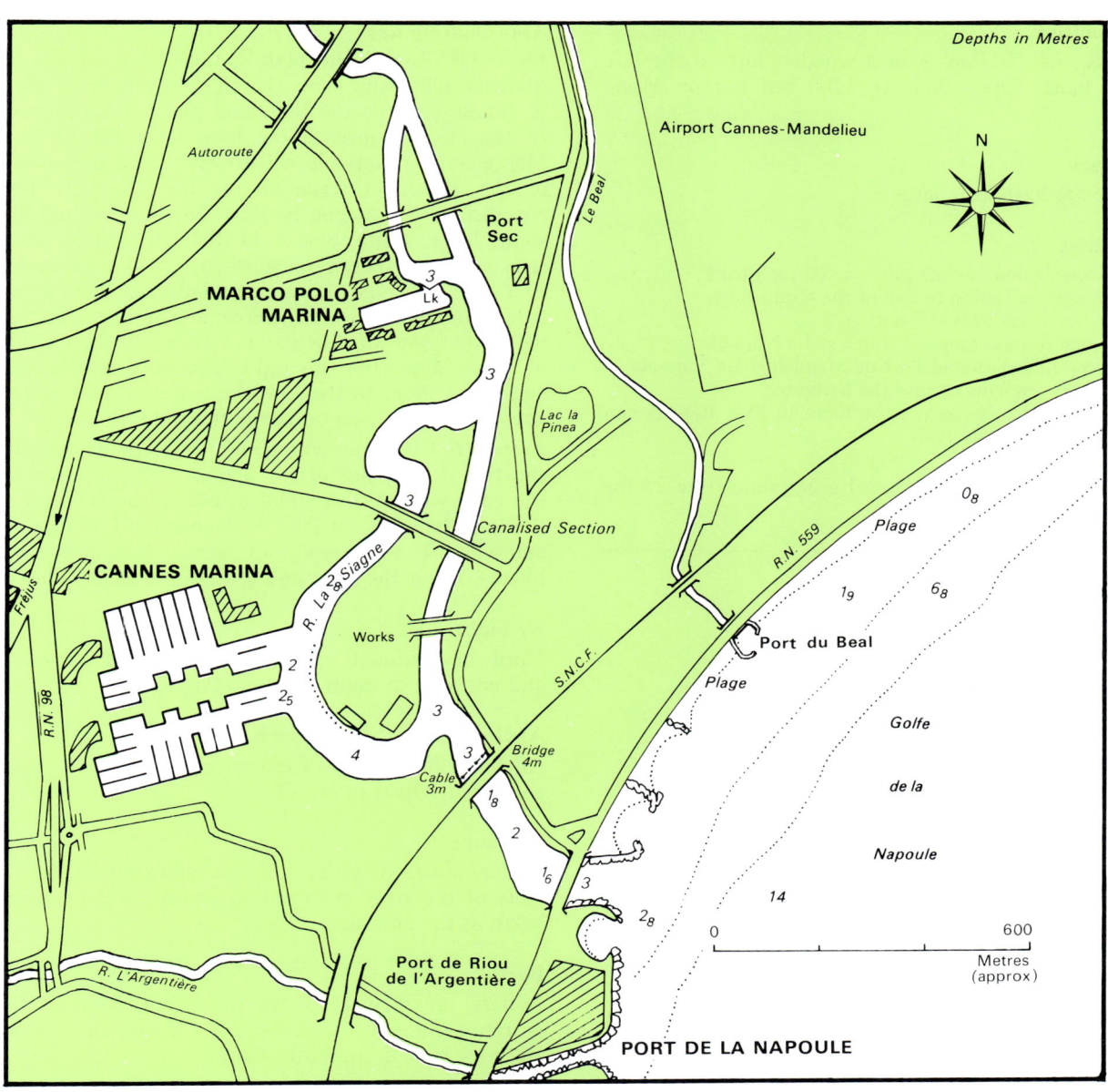

Port du Riou de l'Argentière

Rivière la Siagne

Port du Riou de l'Argentière, entrance looking NW

South France Pilot

Formalities
The *Bureau de Port* is in a wooden hut on the left (NE) bank. Open 0800 to 1200 but not on Mondays.

Charges
There are harbour charges.

Facilities
Slip Two shallow (0·5m) slips one on each bank.
Fuel A service station to SW of the road bridge.
Electricity A few 220v AC outlets.
Provisions A good range of shops at La Napoule.
Ice From fuel station at Port de Mandelieu-La Napoule.
Garbage A few bins around the harbour.
Chandlery Shop on coast road 200m to SW. Repairs can be carried out locally.

See also Port de Mandelieu-La Napoule page 25 for further facilities.

---

116 PORT DE CANNES-MARINA
06210 Alpes-Maritimes

Position 43°32'·3N 6°56'·5E
Minimum depth in the entrance 1·5m (4·9ft)
                in the harbour 4 to 2·5m (13 to 8·2ft)
Width of the entrance 60m
Maximum length overall 12m (39ft)
Bridge clearance 4m (13ft)
Number of berths 1769
Population 2000 (approx)
Rating 4-4-4

General
A major marina development for small craft which is situated about 500m up the Rivière la Siagne. The entrance to the river mouth is only possible in calm weather or with offshore winds. Good facilities for yachtsmen are being provided. This harbour is only suitable for craft drawing 1·5m or less and not more than 4m high.

Data
Charts Admiralty 2166, 2167
       French 5113
       Spanish 121
       ECM 501

Magnetic variation 1°19'W (1990) decreasing by about 8' each year.

Speed limit 3 knots in the river and basins.

Weather forecasts Posted on *Bureau de Port*; also automatic tape-recorded service (*Navimet*).

Warning
Any wind or swell from SE-E causes the sea to break over the bar at the mouth of the river. The Rivière la Siagne has been diverted and its banks straightened. The work is almost complete. Pay attention to the passenger ferry which crosses the river close to the NW side of the rail bridge.

Approach by day
From SW Round the high reddish rocky Point St Marc at 400m and cross the Golfe de Napoule on a N course towards the flat flood plain of La Siagne. In the closer approach the long Jetée Est of Port Mandelieu-La Napoule will be seen with the mouth of the Rivière l'Argentière at its NE end. The entrance to La Siagne is 300m further NE beyond some large white blocks of flats. Enter in midstream, it is shallow to starboard, and pass under first a road bridge, keeping mid-stream, then a rail bridge under its E arch, buoys are hung under this bridge to show shallow patches. Keep to the outside of bends. 50m after this rail bridge turn hard to port and some 300m further on, the two entrances to the harbour will be seen on the port hand.

From NE Cross the wide Golfe de Napoule towards the flat flood plain of La Siagne. The entrance to the river will be seen 300m to NE of the NE end of the long Jetée Est of Port de Mandelieu-La Napoule and close E to a group of large white apartment blocks. Enter the river and ascend as detailed above.

By night
Until navigational lights are established approach and entrance at night are not advised.

Anchorage in the approach
Anchor 200m to SE of entrance in 10m (33ft) mud and weed. Open to N-NE-E-SE.

Entrance
By day Enter by either entrance allowing for the effects of the river current and secure to the waiting berth at the entrance.

Berths
Report on arrival to the reception area at the entrance for the allocation of a berth and secure stern-to, bow to mooring chain.

River leading to Cannes Marina
New canal leading to Port de Marco-Polo and Port S

Port de Cannes-Marina. Junction of river and new canal looking NW

Port de Cannes-Marina

Centre arch navigable

Route nationale bridge to Cannes-Marina and Marco-Polo Marina

E arch navigable

R. La Siagne. Railway bridge

Port de Cannes-Marina looking NW up R. La Siagne

31

South France Pilot

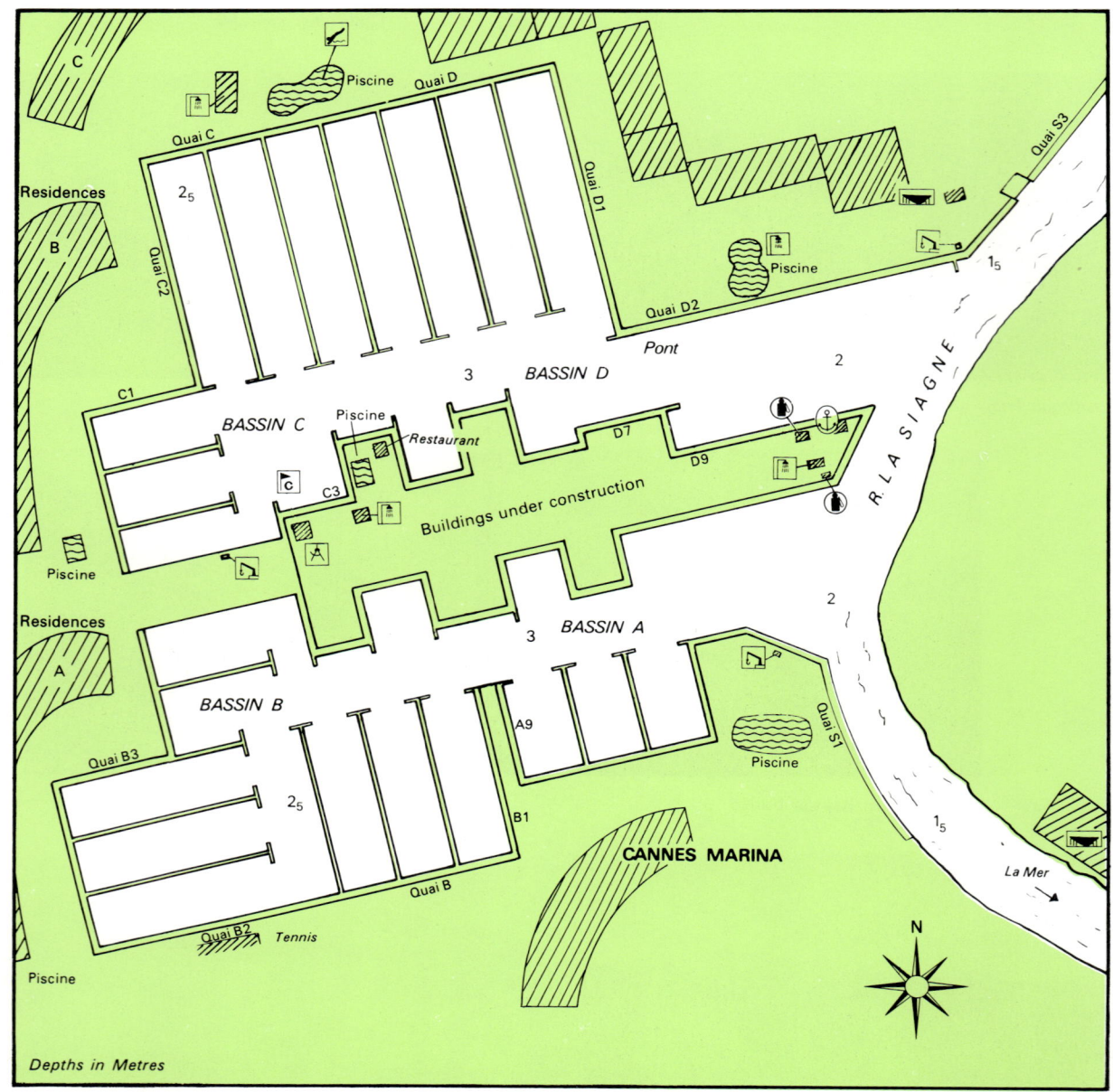

Port de Cannes-Marina

Formalities
Report to the *Bureau de Port* (☎ 93 49 51 27) on arrival. This office is on a small barge which is moved from time to time. Open 0800–1200 and 1400–1800.

Charges
There are harbour charges. The first 24 hours are free.

Facilities
Crane A 5-tonne crane on W side of harbour.
Fuel Diesel (*gasoil*) and petrol from pumps at the entrance.
Water From points on quays and pontoons.
Provisions A large supermarket 300m to W.
Showers Established near harbour.
Chandlers Shop under Residence B.
Repairs A large yacht yard on opposite side of Rivière la Siagne with all facilities.

Electricity 220v AC outlets on pontoons and quays.
Garbage Rubbish containers on the quays.
Yacht club The Club Nautique de Cannes Marina (CNCM) (☎ 93 38 99 72) is being established.

Future developments
This marina is almost completed, some facilities are available and more are planned. Plans are also in hand to construct higher bridges and to dredge the river.

Port de Marco-Polo Marina

Port de Cannes-Marina looking NE. Showing final development

117 PORT DE MARCO-POLO MARINA
06210 Alpes-Maritimes

Position 43°32′·6N 6°56′·7E
Minimum depth in the entrance 1·5m (4·9ft)
in the harbour 2·5m (8·2ft)
Width of the entrance 15m
Bridge clearance 4m (13ft)
Number of berths 239
Population 1000 (approx)
Rating 4-4-4

General
A small marina some half a mile up the Rivière la Siagne for small craft only. Entrance to the river mouth is only possible in calm weather or with offshore winds. Facilities are very limited.

Data
Charts Admiralty 2166
French 5113
Spanish 121
ECM 501

Magnetic variation 1°19′W (1990) decreasing by about 8′ each year.

Speed limit 3 knots.

Warning
The sea breaks on the bar of this river with any wind or swell from SE–S.

Approach by day
From SW Round the high red-coloured rocks of the cliff, Point St Marc, at 400m onto a N course. In the closer approach the Jetée Est of Port de Mandelieu-La Napoule will be seen with the mouth of L'Argentière at its NE end. Beyond this some large white blocks of flats have been built and on the further side is the mouth of La Siagne which can be identified by two bridges. Enter in midchannel, it is shallow to E, and pass under first a road bridge, keeping mid-stream, then a rail bridge, under its centre or E span. Follow the straightened canalised section for about 500m then turn to port into the old river. The entrance will be seen ahead.

From NE Cross the wide Golfe de Napoule towards the flat flood plain at the mouth of La Siagne. In the closer approach the Jetée Est of Port de Mandelieu-La Napoule and the large white blocks of flats will be seen. Proceed as detailed above.

By night
An approach and entrance by night are not advised due to lack of navigational lights.

Anchorage in the approach
Anchor 200m to SE of the entrance to the Rivière la Siagne in 10m (33ft) mud. Open to N–NE–E–SE.

South France Pilot

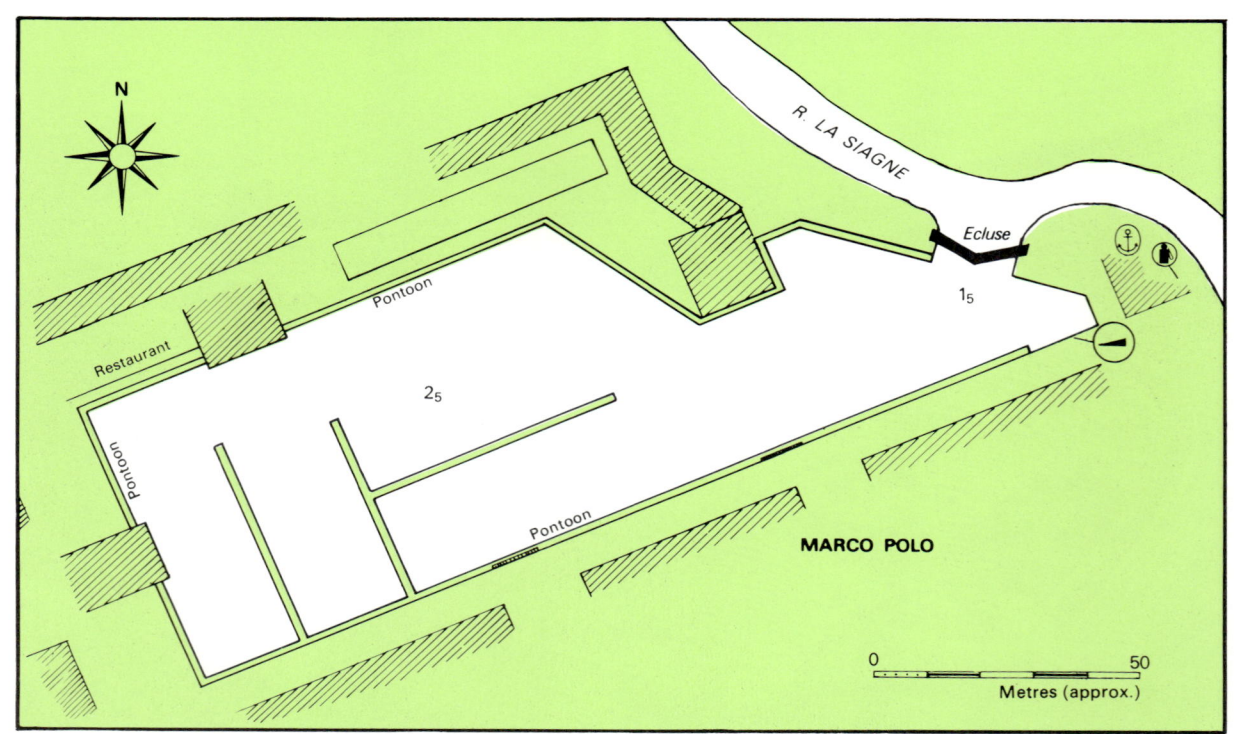

Port de Marco-Polo Marina

Port de Marco Polo Marina, entrance looking W

Entrance
Enter the harbour through a narrow entrance on the port-hand bank, making allowance for the river current. There is a lock which is normally open.

Berths
Secure to any vacant berth and visit the *Bureau de Port* on the S side of the entrance for the allocation of a berth. Secure there stern-to, bow to mooring chain.

Formalities
Report to the *Bureau de Port* (☎ 93 47 28 15) on arrival.

Charges
There are harbour charges.

Facilities
Hard A hard near the entrance.
Fuel Petrol is available at the S side of the entrance.
Water Water points on the quayside.
Electricity Some 220v AC outlets on pontoons and quays.
Provisions Some shops nearby where everyday requirements can be supplied.
Hotels A small hotel in the marina complex.
Restaurants A few restaurants nearby and some café/bars.

Future development
The canalisation of the river and its dredging are almost complete but an increase in the height of the bridges has not yet been accomplished.

Inland Port de la Siagne (Port Sec) looking NE

34

118 PORT DE LA SIAGNE (PORT SEC)
06210 Alpes-Maritimes

Position 43°32'·6N 6°56'·8E
Maximum depth in the entrance 1·5m (4·9ft)
Width of entrance 60m
Maximum length overall 8·5m (28ft)
Number of berths 800
Population 1000 (approx)
Rating 4-3-3

General
This is not a traditional port but a modern equivalent where boats are stored on land when not in use. It was in process of construction and should have been completed by the end of 1989.

Data
See Port de Marco-Polo Marina, page 33, for warnings, approach by day or night and anchorage in the approach.

Warning
This port is in the early stages of construction and changes must be expected.

Entrance by day
This harbour lies on the left (E) bank of the Rivière la Siagne almost opposite the entrance of Port de Marco Polo Marina. The hangers and building are conspicuous. The Aéroport de Cannes-Mandelieu lies on the far side of this port.

Berths
Secure to pontoons on E bank near slip and go to the office for instructions. Smaller boats are stored on racks and larger yachts on hard standing.

Formalities
The office is 100m W of the slip (☎ 92 97 50 10, telex 970 904 F).

Charges
There are charges for parking spaces.

Facilities
Slip A wide slip on E bank of river.
Travel-hoist Travel-hoist and fork-lift trucks.
Fuel At the N side of the slip.
Water Taps to be provided.
Electricity Outlets 220v AC in *carénage* area.
Provisions A supermarket to be built. Les Termes village (1M) has many shops.
Chandlery Shops in NE corner.
Repairs Complete workshop with facilities for repairs.
Yacht club Clubhouse behind the office.
Restaurant Near the office.
Showers May be provided.
Information office At the autoroute exit at Les Termes (1M).
Communications Aéroport de Cannes-Mandelieu (1M).

Future development
Many extra facilities to be provided.

⚓ Off mouth of Rivière la Siagne
An open anchorage 300m E to SE of the mouth of La Siagne in 5m mud and sand. A large white block of flats which lies to S of the river mouth is conspicuous. Coast road and bridge over river. Open to N–NE–E–SE.

119 PORT DU BEAL
06322 Alpes-Maritimes

Position 43°32'·2N 6°67'·4E
Minimum depth in the entrance 2·5m (8·2ft)
 in the harbour 2 to 1·2m (6·6ft to 3·9ft)
Clearance Road bridge 2·6m (8·5ft)
 Road bridge 1·5m (4·9ft)
Width of the entrance 16m (52ft)
Number of berths 120, plus 250 above the road bridge
Maximum length overall 12m (39ft)
Population 1000 (approx)
Rating 4-4-3

General
A small artificial harbour built at the mouth of Ruisseau le Béal only suitable for craft with a draught of less than 1·5m (4·9ft). Open to E winds and swell but otherwise well protected. The harbour is rather noisy because the main coast road runs behind it and it is in line with one of the runways of the Aéroport de Cannes-Mandelieu which is used by light aircraft. Local facilities are limited but excellent facilities and shops exist at Mandelieu-La Napoule (¾M) and Cannes-La Bocca (1M).

Data
For charts, magnetic variation and speed limit see Port de Mandelieu-La Napoule page 25.

Weather forecasts None

Lights None

Buoys A sewage outfall lightbuoy YB (Fl.W.2s) lies ¾M to ESE of this harbour.

Warning
Improvements and changes may be expected. Entrance is not advised with strong E–SE winds. There are several rocky beach breakwaters to the SW of this harbour. Rocks extend at least 10m from the jetties.

Approach by day
From SW Round the Pointes de la Galère, St Marc and l'Aiguille at 400m onto a N course. The long breakwater of Port de Mandelieu-La Napoule, conspicuous group of white apartment blocks and the mouth of Rivière la Siagne will be recognised. The harbour is 700m beyond this river mouth. A long low apartment block lies just to SW of this harbour, which has a line of four balconies.

South France Pilot

From NE Cross the wide Golfe de la Napoule on a west course from a point 1M S of the Vieux Port de Cannes. The industrial area of La Bocca and the large shipyard with a long pier will be recognised. Light aircraft using the Aéroport de Cannes-Mandelieu may assist and the YB sewage outfall lightbuoy (Fl.W.2s) may be seen. The long low apartment block described above may be noticed.

By night
Not advised due to lack of harbour lights and confusing street lights but experienced navigators should easily locate it using the following lights:

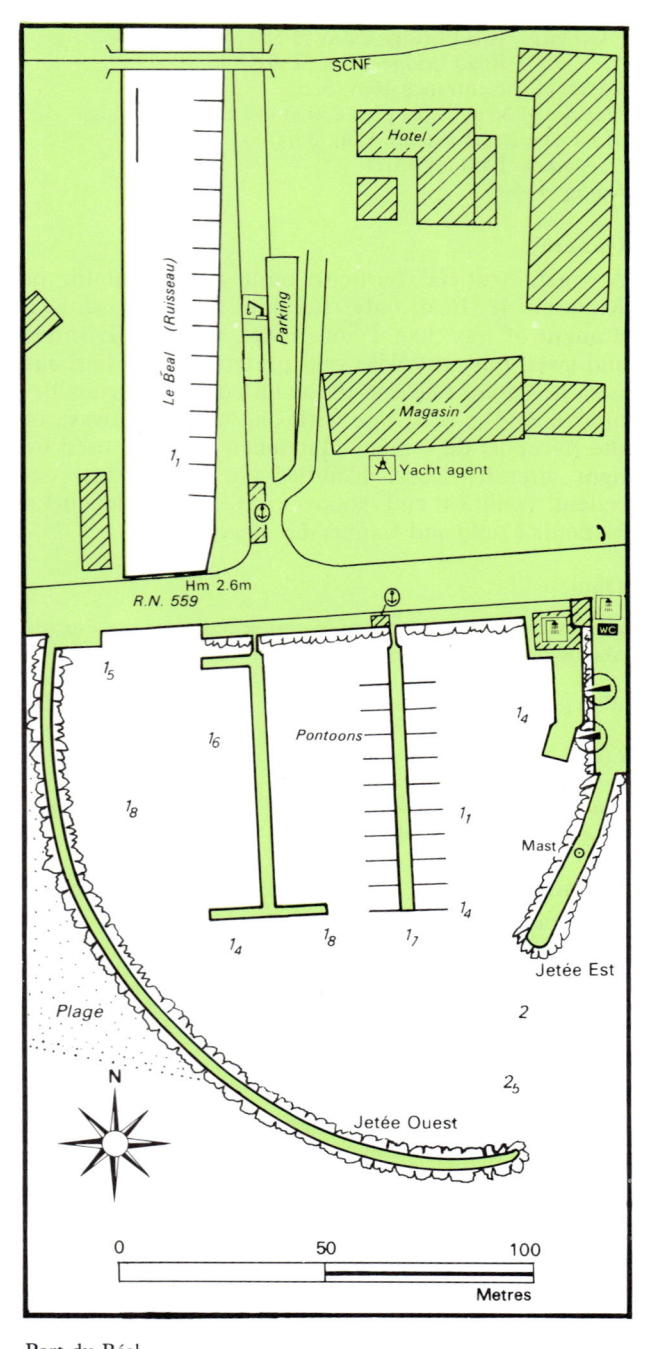

Port de la Galère Q.R.7M
Port de Théoule Oc(2)WR.6s9/6M
Port de la Rague Iso.G.4s10M
Port de Mandelieu-La Napoule Fl(3)G.12s10M
Vieux Port de Cannes VQ(3)R.2s8M
Port Pierre-Canto Oc.WG.4s13/8M
Les Moines beacon tower Q(6)+LFl.W.15s9M
La Garoupe Fl(2)W.10s31M

Anchorage in the approach
Anchor 300m to the S of the harbour entrance in 8m sand and mud. Open to NE–E–SE.

Entrance
By day Approach the harbour on a W course and enter equidistant between the two jetties. There are underwater obstructions projecting from both jetty heads.
By night Not recommended but experienced navigators using the illumination provided by the street lights should experience no difficulty.

Berths
Secure in a vacant berth and report to the *Bureau de Port*. Berths for small craft which draw less than 1·10m and are not higher than 2·6m are available in the Ruisseau le Béal on the far side of the road bridge and below the rail bridge. Even smaller craft drawing less then 1m and not higher than 1·5m can pass under the rail bridge and secure in the first 250m below the junction of a tributary. The left (E) bank has a quay with water and electricity. For permanent berths apply to C.C.I. Aérogare Cannes-Mandelieu (☎ 93 90 40 44).

Formalities
Bureau de Port in a portacabin on the N side of the road (☎ 93 47 21 85). A small day office is also located on the N side of the harbour. Customs at Vieux Port de Cannes.

Charges
There are harbour charges.

Facilities
Slips Two for dinghies on E side of the harbour and one above the rail bridge.
Cranes 3-tonne crane to N of the road.
Water Taps on pontoons and quays.
Electricity 220v AC outlets on pontoons and quays.
Provisions Shops at Mandelieu-La Napoule (¾M) and Cannes-La Bocca (1M).
Garbage A few rubbish containers around the harbour.
Repairs Local yards and specialists can deal with most types of repair.
Yacht clubs The M.J.Club de Cannes (MJC) has an office at 23 Avenue George Picaud in Cannes (☎ 93 39 69 38) and also a small clubhouse Base de Béal (☎ 93 47 40 55) with showers and WC in the NE corner of the harbour, it is primarily a dinghy club.
Communications Bus service along the coast. Rail from La Napoule. Light aircraft from Aérogare Cannes-Mandelieu.

Port du Béal

Port du Béal

Route nationale bridge — *Workshops* — *Showers*

Port du Béal looking W–WNW from the entrance

Port du Béal. Route nationale bridge looking N

Future development
Many extra facilities to be provided.

La Bocca
Shipyard and slipways are conspicuous.

⚓ At head of Golfe de la Napoule
An open anchorage 200m offshore and 400m W of the root of Jetée Ouest opposite a yellow house. Keep to N of cruise ship's anchorage. Open to SE–S–SW–W. Many houses and apartment blocks ashore, also coast road and railway.

120 VIEUX PORT DE CANNES (PORT ST PIERRE)
06400 Alpes-Maritimes

Position 43°32'·7N 7°01'·2E
Minimum depth in the entrance 7m (23ft)
　　　　　　　　in the harbour 6 to 1m (20 to 3·3ft)
Width of the entrance 70m
Number of berths 847
Maximum length overall 60m (197ft)
Population 70,000
Rating 2–2–1

General
An old natural fishing harbour that has been developed into a major yachting centre by the addition of breakwaters and jetties. With the development of tourism, the town and the harbour became a world famous centre for the largest and most expensive yachts. It still has excellent facilities for yachtsmen though the harbour is not quite up to the standard of the more modern ports and some facilities are rather dated and decaying. The harbour is easy to enter and provides shelter from all winds except the SE which makes the harbour uncomfortable despite extensions to the Jetée Ouest. The old parts of the town are very attractive and there is much to see and do ashore.

Data
Charts　Admiralty 2166, 2167
　　　　　French 5113
　　　　　Spanish 121
　　　　　ECM 501

South France Pilot

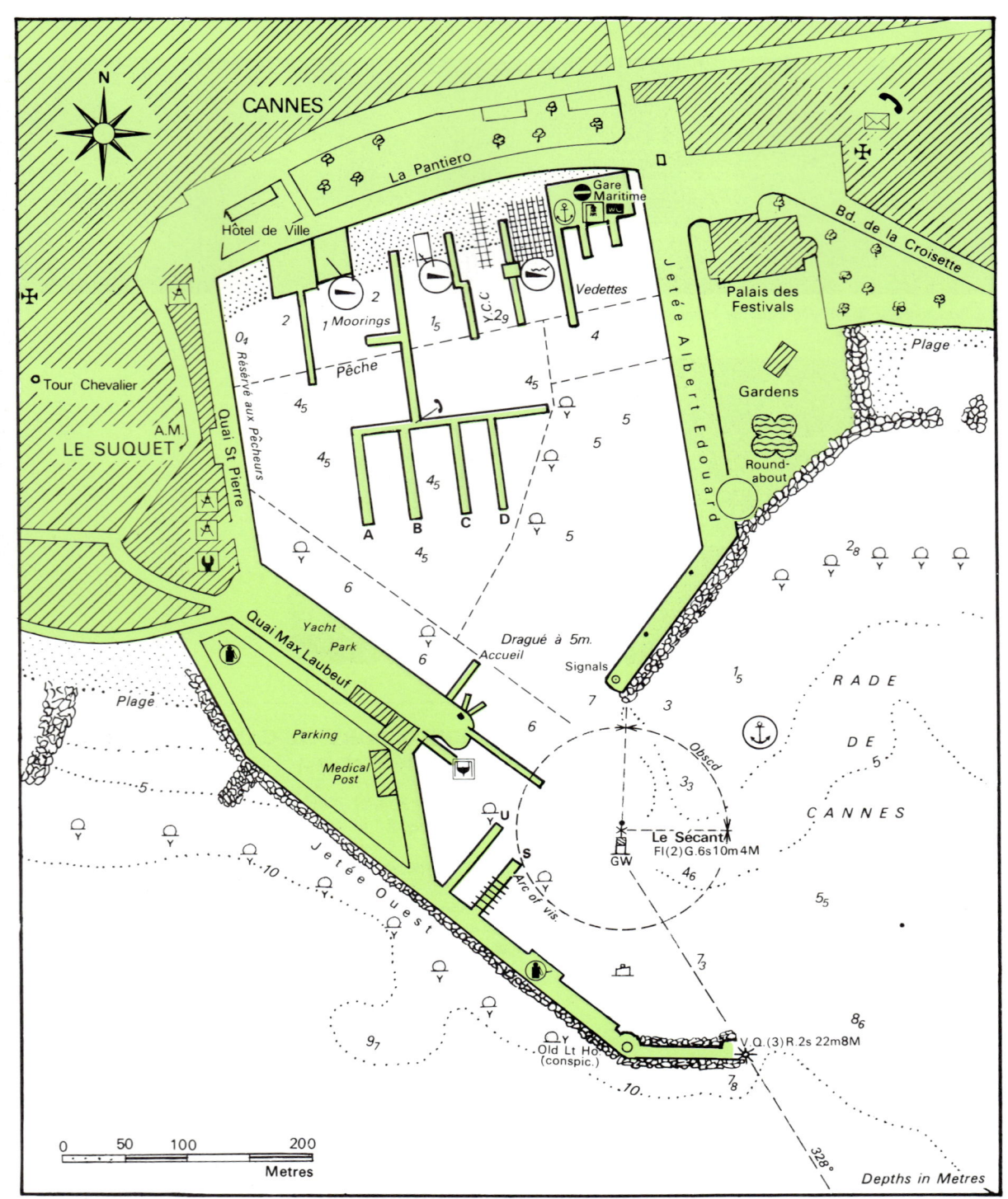

Vieux Port de Cannes

Magnetic variation 1°19′W (1990) decreasing by about 8′ each year.

Port radio Call on VHF Ch 16, work on Ch 12 (English or French), 0800–2130 summer, 0800–1800 winter.

Weather forecast Posted once a day at the *Bureau de Port*. There is also an automatic prerecorded coastal forecast at the same place (*Navimet*). Also ☎ 93 83 00 25.

Speed limit 3 knots inside the harbour and 10 knots between the harbour and Ile Ste Marguerite.

Storm signals A black ball is hoisted on a mast at the head of Jetée Albert Edouard when winds over 35 knots are expected.

Lights
Jetée Ouest Head VQ(3)R.2s22m8M. White tower, red top.
Le Sécant Fl(2)G.6s10m4M. White tower, dark green top. 276°-vis-178°.

Vieux Port de Cannes (Port St Pierre)

Vieux Port de Cannes looking SE (the head of the Jetée Ouest has been extended 130m to E).
Pointe de la Croisette and Les Iles de Lérins in the background

Buoys There is a Y sewage outfall buoy with cross topmark ½M to S of the harbour. Eight Y conical buoys in the harbour mark dredged areas.

Warning

In the harbour and Rade de Cannes, sailing craft do not have an automatic right of way over power craft.

Approach by day

From SW Cross the wide Golfe de Napoule towards the extreme NE corner. The mass of houses, the two towers at Le Suquet and the large white hospital on the skyline are easily seen. In the close approach the white light tower with R top at the end of Jetée Ouest is seen; this in line with *Le Sécant* tower (white with G top) bearing 328° leads to the entrance.

From NE Round the Ile de Lérins outside and to the S of *Les Moines* S Card YB beacon tower topmark, Q(6)+LFl.15s, onto a NNW course leaving the islands 400m to starboard. Passage is also possible either side of Ile Ste Marguerite (see page 48). The mass of houses at Cannes and the two towers at Le Suquet are conspicuous and in the closer approach the light tower at the head of Jetée Ouest and the beacon tower *Le Sécant* will be seen. These last two mentioned towers in line 328° form a safe approach.

Bureau de Port   *Le Sécant   Iles de Lérins*

Vieux Port de Cannes looking SE from Le Suquet

South France Pilot

Old lighthouse *Fuel* *Travel-hoist Le Suquet*

Vieux Port de Cannes, entrance from head of Jetée Ouest looking NW–W

By night
Using the following lights navigate to a position where the entrance lies NE at 300m:
Port de la Galère Q.R.7M
Port de Mandelieu-La Napoule Fl(3)G.12s10M
Port de Pierre-Canto Oc.WG.4s13/8M
La Garoupe Fl(2)W.10s31M

Anchorage in the approach
Anchor 300m to SE of the entrance in 10m (33ft) sand, mud and weed or 150m NE of Le Sécant in 2m sand. Open to SE–S–SW–W.

Entrance
By day Approach the head of Jetée Ouest on a NE course, leaving the white lighthouse with red top 20m to port and then *Le Sécant* beacon tower, white with green top, 20m to starboard onto a NNE course and enter between the heads of Quai Max Laubeuf and Jetée Albert Edouard.
By night Approach VQ(3)R.2s on a NE course and in the closer approach alter to leave this 20m to port and then Fl(2)G.6s 20m to starboard, change course to NNE and enter between the inner pierheads (unlighted).

Berths
Call *Bureau de Port* on VHF Ch 16/12 before entering for allocation of a berth. Secure stern to pontoon that runs across the harbour, bow to chain, and report to *Bureau de Port*. Mooring lines on all berths except head of Jetée Albert Edouard where anchors with trip lines have to be used. If not in contact by VHF secure to pontoon marked 'Accueil' on SW side of the harbour but leave 4 berths near crane vacant.

Formalities
Report to the *Bureau de Port* on first floor (☎ 93 39 61 77) on arrival, open 0800–2130 summer, 0800–1800 winter and not weekends, holidays, or Wednesday afternoons, and if necessary to the customs office (☎ 93 39 22 77) which is on the floor below.

Charges
There are of harbour charges.

Facilities
Slip A slip at the N side of the harbour.
Slipways Five slipways at the NE side of the harbour, some of which can be used by the largest yachts up to 60 tonnes.
Travel-lift A 45-tonne travel-lift to the S of the harbour.
Cranes A 7-tonne crane at the S of the harbour. A mobile crane of 15 tonnes is also available.
Fuel Diesel (*gasoil*) and petrol are available from pumps on the Jetée Ouest 0830–1200 and 1400–1800 hours in summer, 0830–1200 in winter. (☎ 93 39 96 49 and 93 75 63 60).
Water Water points on the quays and pontoons.
Electricity From supply points on quays and pontoons, 220v AC. Jetée Albert Edouard has 380v AC.
Provisions Very many shops of all types near the harbour and a street market to NW of the harbour. There is also a kiosk for small ice.
Ice Delivered to the quays and pontoons in the season.
Duty-free goods Contact the customs for instructions as to the supply of duty-free goods.
Garbage A limited number of rubbish containers on the quays and pontoons.
Chandlery Several shops around the harbour and most types of chandlery items are available.
Repairs A large number of repair organisations and shipyards and all types of repairs can be carried out.
Post office A PTT to NE of the harbour.
Hotels Seven ***** deluxe, five ****, thirty-three ***, forty-eight ** and thirty-four * hotels plus a
Restaurants Over 240 restaurants of all classes and types, also innumerable café/bars.
Yacht clubs The Yacht Club de Cannes (YCC) (☎ 93 43 06 90) has an office, bar, lounge and shower at Palm Beach. The Motor Yacht Club de Côte d'Azur (MYCCA) (☎ 93 43 67 85) has an office and lounge at Palm Beach Casino. There is also the Club Nautique de la Croisette (CNC) (☎ 93 43 09 40) and the Mer et Montagne Club (MMC) (☎ 93 43 92 28).
Showers Three sets of showers and WCs in blocks around the harbour.
Information office The office of the Syndicat d'Initiative is on the sea front to the E of the harbour (☎ 93 39 01 01).
Lifeboat An all-weather lifeboat is stationed here (☎ 93 47 61 11).

Vieux Port de Cannes (Port St Pierre)

e Sécant light tower   *Head of Jetée Albert Edouard*   *Casino (being rebuilt)*   *Anchorage*

Visits The old town, Le Suquet, and the Musée de la Castre are worth visiting also the Observatoire de la Californie for its panoramic views. There are many other interesting places to visit nearby by taxi, rail or bus.

Communications Bus and rail services and also air from the airfield 4M away. Sea services are available to many Mediterranean ports and ferries to the Iles de Lérins. A regular minibus service to Nice airport.

Future development

More electricity points are to be provided on the pontoons and the quays. The shallows around Le Sécant are to be removed and the Jetée Albert Edouard is to be extended.

History

Before the 10th century, Cannes was a small natural fishing harbour with houses collected around Le Suquet, in those days the village was called Canois. Later the area came under the control of the Abbé de Lérins who in 1070 had a watch tower, defensive walls and a refuge built on Le Suquet. In 1834 Lord Brougham and Vaux, the Lord Chancellor of England, was held up in this port on his way to Italy by an outbreak of cholera in that country, he was so delighted with the place that he had a villa built and for the next thirty-four years, until his death, he returned to Cannes each winter. Many English families followed his example and the town developed into a fashionable resort with the railway assisting its rapid growth.

---

121 PORT PIERRE-CANTO
06400 Alpes-Maritimes

Position 43°32′·5N 7°01′·8E
Minimum depth in the entrance 8m (26ft)
                in the harbour 7 to 2m (23 to 6·6ft)
Width of the entrance 110m
Number of berths 650
Maximum length overall 70m (230ft)
Population 70,000 (approx)
Rating 2–2–1

General

A major new artificial yacht harbour which has every conceivable facility available. Approach and entrance are easy and shelter good once inside but it affords little shelter from the NW *mistral* wind itself. Many very large yachts use this harbour.

Data

Charts   Admiralty 2166, 2167
          French 5113
          Spanish 121
          ECM 501

Magnetic variation 1°19′W (1990) decreasing by about 8′ each year.

Port radio VHF Ch 9, French and English.

Weather forecasts Posted twice a day at the *Bureau de Port* and at the yacht club. The forecast is also delivered to yachts. Automatic prerecorded coastal forecast at the *Bureau de Port (Navimet)*. Also ☎ 93 83 00 25.

Speed limit 3 knots.

Lights
Jetée Sud Head Oc.WG.4s11m13/8M. Yellow tower, green top. 010-W-100°-G -010°.
Jetée Ouest Elbow/head Oc(2)R.6s2m6M. Red column, obscured when bearing is less than E.

Warning

In the Baie de Cannes sailing vessels do not have an automatic right of way over power craft. Repairs to the quays and pontoons in progress.

Approach by day

From SW Cross the wide Golfe de Napoule towards Pointe de la Croisette which has a large white building (the casino) on its end. A line of large blocks of flats will be seen on the coast to the NW of it and a tower will be seen on the hill behind the harbour. In the closer approach the Jetée Sud will be seen about 500m to N of this point. Do not mistake it for the smaller jetties immediately N of the point.

South France Pilot

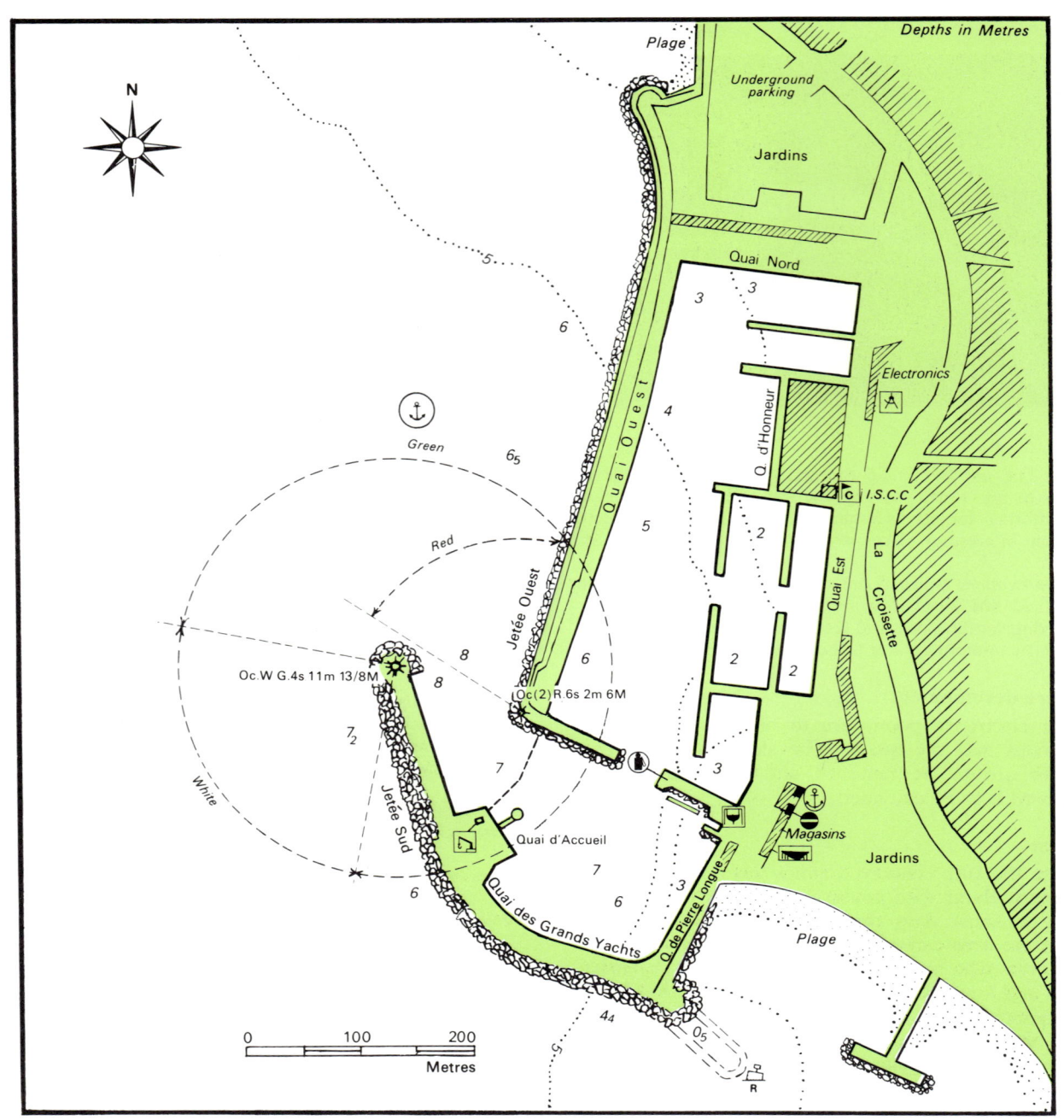

Port Pierre-Canto

Entrance

Port Pierre-Canto, approach looking SE

Port Pierre-Canto

Port Pierre-Canto looking S

From NE Round the Iles de Lérins on the S side outside *Les Moines* S Card YB beacon tower ▼ topmark, Q(6)+LFl.15s. Leave the islands 400m to starboard onto a N course. Some 500m beyond Pointe de la Croisette, which has a large white casino on the point, the Jetée Sud will be seen. Passage is also possible either side of Ile Ste Marguerite (see page 48).

By night
Using the lights listed below, navigate to a position where the entrance lies 300m SE:
Port de Mandelieu-La Napoule Fl(3)G.12s10M
Cannes VQ(3)R.2s8M
La Garoupe Fl(2)W.10s31M

Anchorage in the approach
Anchor 300m to NW of the entrance in 7m (23ft) sand and weed. Open to S–SW–W.

Entrance
By day Round the head of Jetée Ouest at 20m leaving it to starboard and enter on a SE course.
By night Approach Oc.WG.4s on a SE course in the green sector, leave the light 20m to starboard and then Oc(2)R.6s 20m to port.

Berths
Report to the Quai d'Accueil just inside the entrance on the starboard hand for allocation of a berth, usually on the Quai d'Honneur, and secure there stern-to, bow to mooring chain. If the Quai d'Accueil is not manned secure alongside the fuel quay and report to the *Bureau de Port*.

Formalities
Report to the *Bureau de Port* (☎ 93 43 48 66, telex 470 964) on arrival, open day and night. The customs (☎ 93 39 22 77) are in the same building if required. It may also be necessary to report to the office of the clubhouse on arrival if a long stay is intended.

Charges
There are harbour charges.

Facilities
Slipways A floating dock elevator of 70 tonnes capacity.
Cranes A 15-tonne crane and 6-tonne mobile crane are available.
Fuel Diesel (*gasoil*) and petrol pumps at head of spur near the *Bureau de Port* (☎ 93 43 49 00).
Water Water points on all the quays and pontoons.
Electricity Supply outlets of 220v AC are on all quays and pontoons also 380v AC for deep-water berths.

Head of Jetée Ouest   *Palm Beach Casino*

Port Pierre-Canto, entrance looking E–SE

South France Pilot

Provisions Some shops in the harbour and very many in the town and suburbs.
Ice Ice is delivered by van once a day.
Duty-free goods Contact the customs office and yacht club for information about duty-free goods.
Garbage Many rubbish bins around the harbour.
Chandlery Several ships' chandlers in the harbour area and many more in Cannes itself.
Repairs Repairs of all types to hull, engine, sails and electronics are possible at the shipyards and workshops in the harbour.
Laundrette Only in the town.
Post office In the town.
Yacht club The International Sporting Club de Cannes (ISCC) (☎ 93 43 48 65 and 93 43 49 90/1/2) has a modern and luxurious clubhouse alongside the harbour which has lounges, terraces, restaurants, bars, bedrooms, showers and a swimming pool amongst other amenities.
Showers Showers and WCs around the harbour.
Lifeboat A small lifeboat here.
Beaches Sandy beaches either side of the harbour.
Communications Bus service.

See also Vieux Port de Cannes page 37 for details of the town and area.

---

122 LES PORTS DE LA CROISETTE (PORT DE PALM BEACH AND PORT BIJOU)
06400 Alpes-Maritimes

Position 43°32'·5N 7°02'·0E
Minimum depth   in the entrance 2m (6·6ft)
                  in the harbour 2 to 0m (6·6 to 0ft)
Width of the entrance   Port Bijou 15m
                          Port de Palm Beach 120m
Number of berths   Port Bijou 80
                     Port de Palm Beach 120
Maximum length overall 10m (33ft)
Population 70,000 (Cannes)
Rating 4-4-4

General
Two very small shallow harbours side by side. Port de Palm Beach, which lies to the S is managed by the Yacht Club de Cannes (YCC) and has limited facilities; Port Bijou is managed by the public authority of Cannes and is normally reserved for small fishing craft. Approach and entrance are not difficult except in a NW *mistral* when it is dangerous and the harbours become very uncomfortable.

Data
Charts   Admiralty 2166, 2167
           French 5113, 5122
           Spanish 121
           ECM 501

Magnetic variation 1°19'W (1990) decreasing by about 8' each year.

Speed limit 3 knots

Buoys There is a small Y conical buoy marking a sewage outfall just outside the entrance.

Warning
Depths in and around the area are subject to change, sound carefully.

Approach by day
From SW Cross the wide Golfe de Napoule towards Pointe de la Croisette. In the closer approach the Jetée Ouest of Port Pierre-Canto will be seen and the SE end should be left 300m to N. There is foul ground to S of this jetty marked by a small R can buoy square topmark.

From NE Round the Iles de Lérins to S outside *Les Moines* S Card beacon tower YB ▼ topmark, Q(6)+LFl.15s. Follow round onto a N course keeping 400m to W of the islands. When level with Pointe de la Croisette bears E, turn towards it. Passage is also possible either side of Ile Ste Marguerite (see page 48).

By night
Due to the lack of navigational lights a night approach and entrance are not advised.

Anchorage in the approach
Anchor 300m to SW of the entrance in 4m (13ft) sand. Open to SE–S–SW–W.

Entrance
Approach the entrance on a NE course to leave the head of Jetée Ouest 10m to starboard, round it into Port de Palm Beach or proceed in a NE direction to the entrance to Port Bijou.

Berths
Secure stern to quay or pontoon, bow to mooring chain in a vacant place and report, if in Port de Palm Beach, to the yacht club or if in Port Bijou, to the *Bureau de Port* at Port du Mouré-Rouge (which is 1M in a NE direction) for the allocation of a berth.

Entrance   *Casino*

Les Ports de la Croisette, approach looking E

Ports de la Croisette (Port de Palm Beach and Port Bijou)

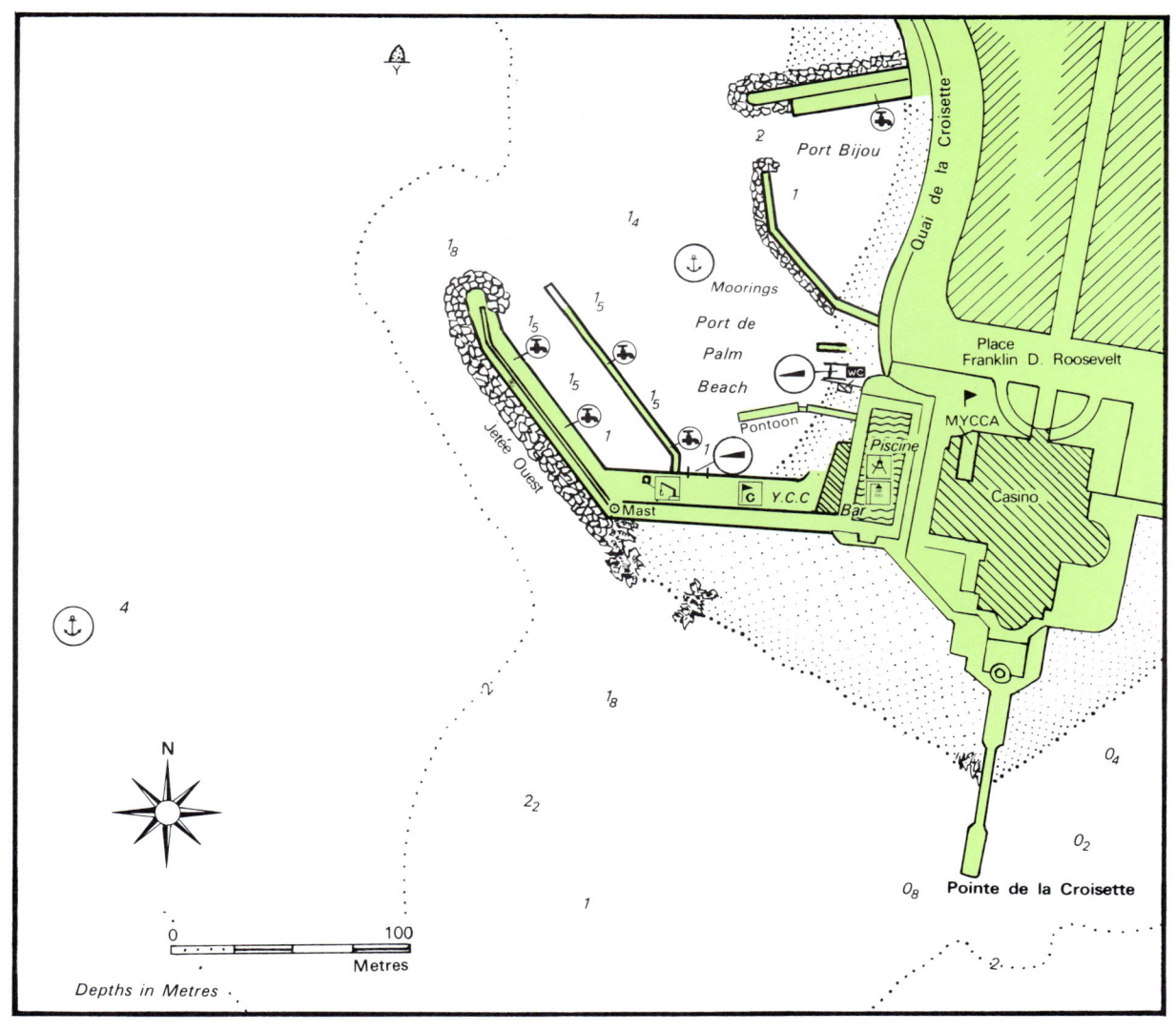

Les Ports de la Croisette

Moorings
There are some private moorings which may be available.

Formalities
On arrival report to the Yacht Club de Cannes (☎ 93 43 05 90) if secured in Port de Palm Beach. If secured in Port Bijou report to the *Bureau de Port* at Port du Mouré-Rouge (☎ 93 68 91 92).

Charges
There are harbour charges.

Facilities
Hard A small hard between the two harbours.
Slips Two slips in Port de Palm Beach.
Crane A 3-tonne crane in Port de Palm Beach.
Water Water points on the quays of both harbours.
Electricity Several outlets of 220v AC.
Provisions Some suburban shops about ½M to the NE.
Garbage A very few rubbish containers.

Yacht club The Yacht Club de Cannes (YCC) (☎ 93 43 05 90) has a small clubhouse in the SE corner of the Port de Palm Beach with a bar, lounge and showers.

Future development
There is a plan for a vast modern yacht harbour and marina complex to be built on the Pointe de la Croisette.

Pointe de la Croisette
A low rock and sand promontory which has a large white casino on its point. A landing pier extends to S. Shoal rocky patches (1·2m) out to 300m between SE and SW. A 10-knot speed limit exists between Ile Ste Marguerite and Vieux Port de Cannes.

South France Pilot

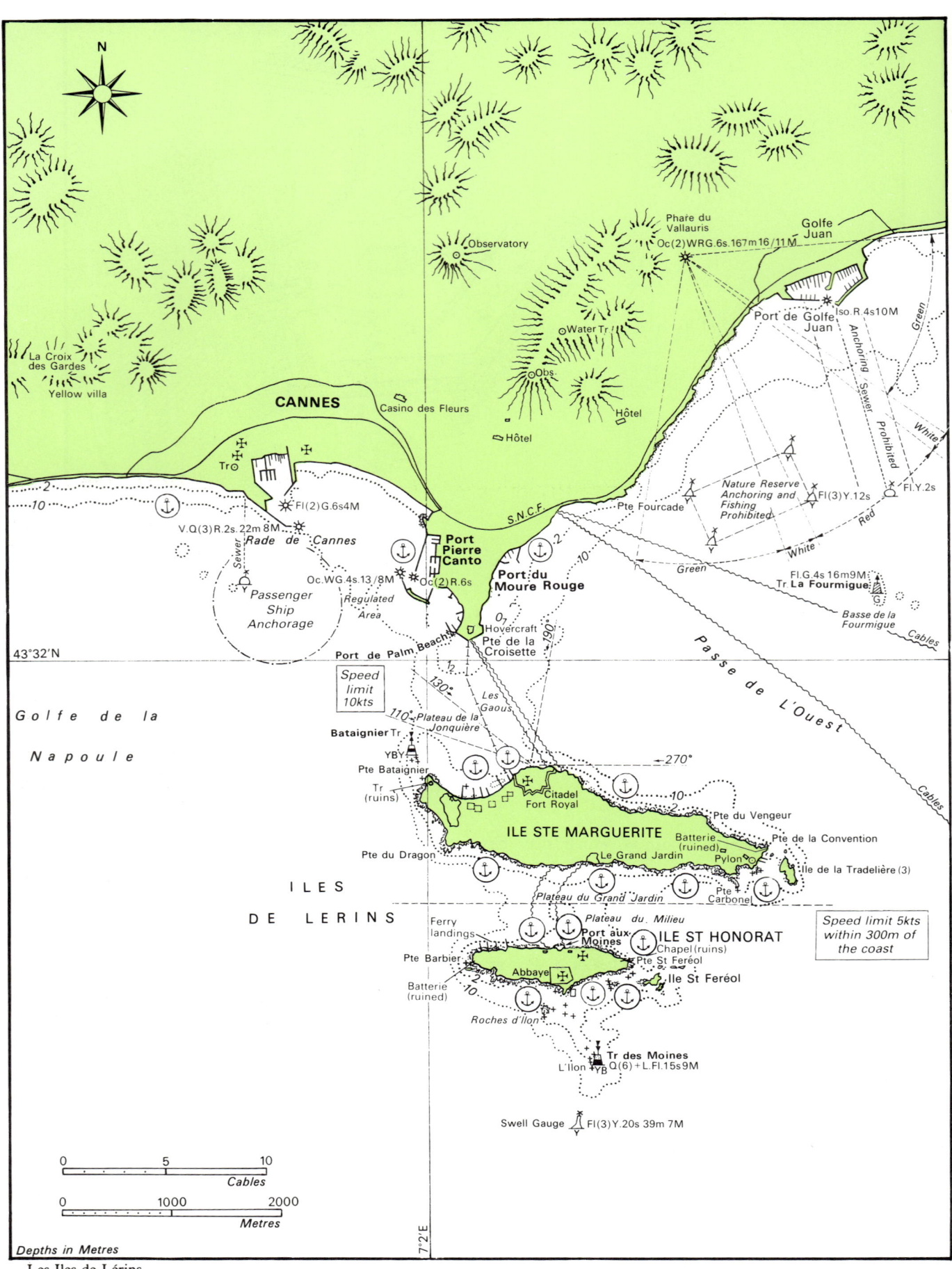

Les Iles de Lérins

Les Iles de Lérins

Ports de la Croisette looking N

Les Iles de Lérins looking E

123 LES ILES DE LERINS

General
The Iles de Lérins consist of two large islands, two small islands and a number of islets and isolated rocks all of which lie just over 1M to S of Pointe de la Croisette. The islands are of low altitude and are tree-covered. The passage between the two main islands and between the mainland and the islands are shallow but it is possible for yachts drawing up to 3m (9·8ft) to traverse them in calm weather.

The islands are virtually deserted except for shipyard workers on one island and some monks on the other. During the day, especially in the season, swarms of tourists are brought over by ferries from Cannes but when they have departed in the late afternoon peace and quiet descend again. Camping ashore is forbidden.

Ile Ste Marguerite
(See also Port de Ste Marguerite, page 51)

This is the largest island being 2M long and ½M wide, it is also the highest (18m). It is tree-covered and it has a very conspicuous château, Fort Royal, 44m (144ft) high, on its N coast and to W a shipyard with four slips, a number of landing piers and a group of houses. There is another small group of houses on the S side of the island. The small Ile de la Tradelière, is joined to the E end of the island by a shallow neck of rock and sand where there is a small pylon. At the W end a shallow sand and rock shoal terminates some 300m to N of beacon tower *Bataignier* (5m) painted as a W Card mark YBY ⚠ topmark.

47

South France Pilot

There are a number of pleasant anchorages along the coast (see chart) and many small sandy coves. There are also some delightful walks around the island and the old Château Fort Royal is of interest.

Ile St Honorat
(See also Port St Honorat (Port aux Moines), p. 49)
This is the second largest island and is only 1M long and 500m wide and is very low (8m) and flat. It is tree-covered with a cultivated area in the middle. On the S side there is a very conspicuous old fortified monastery and an abbey which has a spire. There is a very small harbour on the N side and a few anchorages around the island. A small island, Ile de St Féréol, is joined to the E end of the island by a shallow sandy neck studded with rocks. There is also a foul area to the S of the monastery which tapers away towards the S Card beacon tower, *Les Moines*, YB ▼ topmark, Q(6)+LFl.15s9M. At the W edge of this shoal lies a group of exposed rocks called l'Ilon. Four ferry landing jetties are located near the NW corner of the island.

There are a few sandy coves and the island is pleasant to walk around. The fortified monastery is interesting to visit and there are a number of old remains to see. The new monastery can be visited but women are not allowed inside.

PASSAGES

The passage between Pointe de la Croisette and Ile Ste Marguerite
Minimum depth 4·2m (14ft)

From W to E Approach the N side of the Château Fort Royal on a course between 110° and 130°. To assist, the first bearing is when the trees on Point du Vengeur just clear the foot of the Château Fort and the second is when the corner of the Château Fort is in line with a gable behind it. When shipyards and slips are S change course to E.

From E to W Approach the Château on a course of between 190° and 270°. When 200m from the coast follow it along at this distance until the shipyard and slips are S, then change onto a course between 290° and 310° using the leading marks detailed above as stern marks. When the beacon tower *Bataignier* is S course may be altered as the shallows have been passed.

Les Iles de Lérins. *Les Moines* beacon tower as seen looking S between Ile St Honorat and Ile de St Féréol

The passage between Ile Ste Marguerite and Ile St Honorat
Minimum depth 3m (9·8ft)

From E to W Approach the gap between the two islands on a W course then follow the S coast of Ile de la Tradelière and Ile Ste Marguerite at a distance of 300m. When past the Pointe du Dragon course may be altered as required. There is a speed limit of 5 knots.

From W to E Approach the gap between the islands on an E course and follow the S coast of the Ile Ste Marguerite and Ile de la Tradelière at 300m, when the second island has been passed course can be altered as required.

Ile Ste Marguerite   *Monastère-Fort   Ile St Honorat*

Les Iles de Lérins. Passage between Ile Ste Marguerite and Ile St Honorat looking E

Pte du Vengeur   *Château Fort Royal*   *Chantier*

Les Iles de Lérins. Passage between Pointe de la Croisette and Ile de Ste Marguerite looking SE.

Les Iles de Lérins

Les Iles de Lérins looking N. Ile de St Honorat in the foreground with Ile de Ste Marguerite behind the Pointe de la Croisette with Cannes in the background.

Tour des Moines *Ile de St. Honorat* *Ile de Ste Marguerite*

LES ILES DE LERINS Looking W

History

These two islands were originally called Lero and Lerina before St Honorat founded his monastery in the 4th century, which was one of the first in France. Legend has it that his sister Ste Marguerite founded a nunnery on the other island. The monastery flourished and became a place of pilgrimage second only to the Holy Land. By the 7th century it housed a community of four thousand monks and was very rich, possessing vast estates on the mainland and one of the finest libraries in Europe. In the 11th century Cannes was fortified by the Abbé de Lérins and the fortified monastery built to discourage the frequent raids by the Saracens and other pirate bands. Over the centuries this community produced more than twenty saints and six hundred bishops, amongst whom was St Patrick who spent nine years here. The Spanish attacked the islands in the 17th century and by the end of the 18th century the monastery was closed and eventually confiscated during the Revolution.

More recently, after a number of owners, including a famous actress Mlle Sainval, the abbey was bought by the Cistercian order and except for the fortified monastery itself, it has been virtually rebuilt.

Meanwhile on Ile Ste Marguerite a large fort had been built under the direction of Cardinal Richelieu, this was improved by the Spaniards in the 17th century and altered by Vauban. This fort has held a number of famous prisoners including the 'Man in the Iron Mask', Huguenot pastors and Marshal Bazaine who surrendered to the Prussians. He was one of the few ever to escape from this fort.

124 PORT DE ST HONORAT (PORT AUX MOINES)

Position 43°30'·6N 7°02'·8E
Minimum depth in the entrance 2·4m (7·9ft)
　　　　　　　 in the harbour 1·8 to 0m (5·9 to 0ft)
Width of the entrance 10m
Maximum length overall 10m (33ft)
Number of berths 15
Population 300 (approx)
Rating 2–4–5

49

South France Pilot

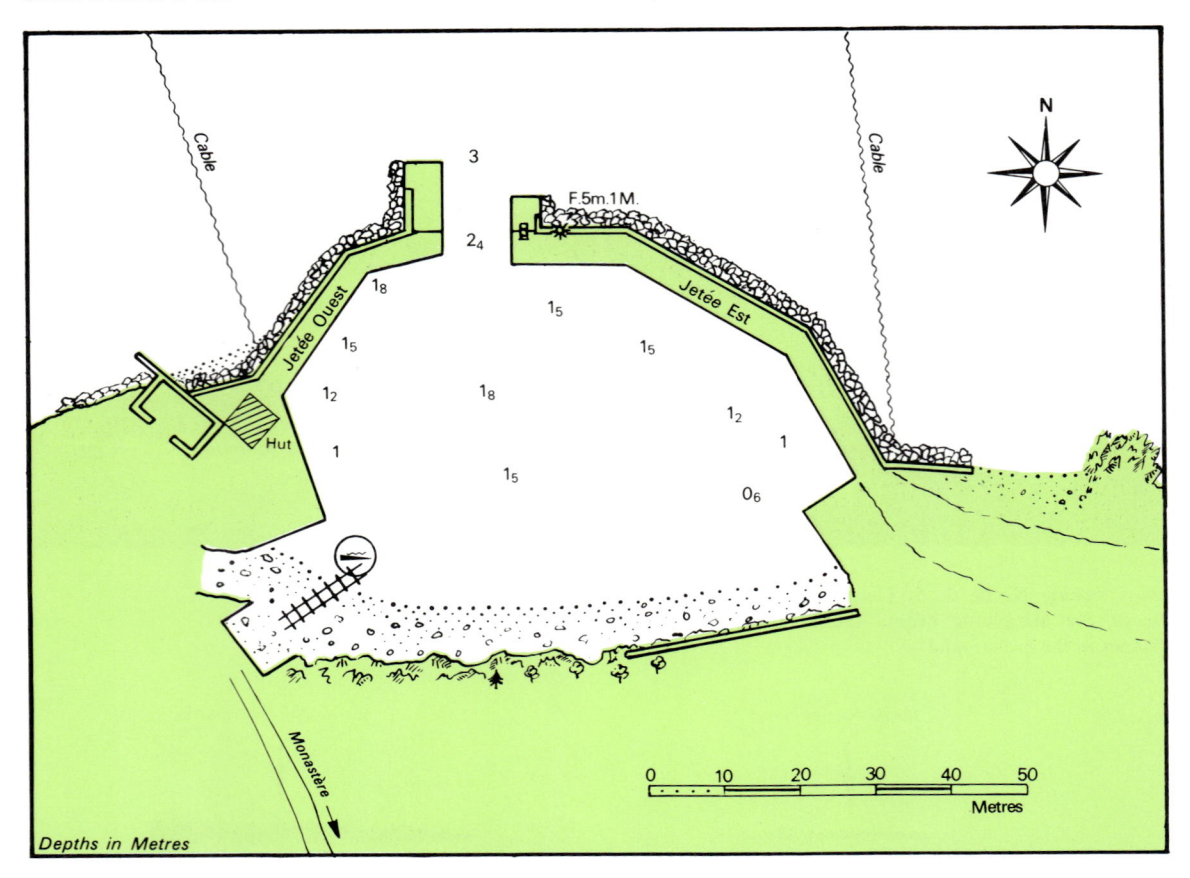

Ile de St Honorat

General
A minute shallow harbour on a beautiful island. Space is severely limited inside the harbour which should only be approached and entered in good weather. The island which is crowded with tourists by day, is deserted at night except for the monks in their abbey. Facilities are virtually nonexistent.

Data
Charts   Admiralty 2167
French 5122
Spanish 121
ECM 501

Magnetic variation 1°19′W (1990) decreasing by about 8′ each year.

Current There is usually a wind-induced current of up to 2 knots running between the islands.

Speed limit 5 knots.

Lights
Jetée Est Head F.W.5m1M. Post

Buoys A Y swell-gauge lightbuoy, Fl(3)Y.20s, is moored 400m to S of *Les Moines* beacon tower.

Warning
In the NW *mistral* dangerous seas form very quickly in the channel and the E-going current becomes strong.

Approach by day
From SW Cross the wide Golfe de Napoule towards the low tree-covered mass of the two islands and when halfway across, the channel between them will be seen. Follow round the N shore of Ile St Honorat at 200m until the entrance to the harbour is SE.

From NE Cross the deep Golfe Juan towards the islands. Round the low Ile de la Tradelière onto a W course leaving the island and the coast of Ile Ste Marguerite 300m to starboard. Keep on the same course until the harbour is SE then turn onto this direction and approach.

By night
Night approach using the lights listed below is possible but care is needed as the islands obscure the lights at times. Navigate to a position where the harbour lies SE at 500m:

Port de la Mandelieu-La Napoule Fl(3)G.12s10M
Pointe de l'Ilette Oc(2+1)WRG.12s13-8M
La Fourmigue Fl.G.4s9M

Anchorage in the approach
Anchor 200m to WNW of the harbour in 4m (13ft) mud and weed. Open to E and W.

Port de Ste Marguerite

Facilities
Hard A sandy hard at the S side of the harbour.
Slipway A slipway (in need of repairs) in the SW corner of the harbour.
Water Water from the restaurant.
Restaurant A restaurant about 500m away by the ferry pier to W of the harbour which caters for the tourists.
Ice In summer ice from a boat.
Visits The old fortified monastery and the new abbey can be visited. There are excellent walks around the island.
Beaches A number of sandy coves around the island.
Communications There are frequent ferries to Cannes and Golfe Juan during day.

Spire (behind trees)

Port aux Moines, Ile de St Honorat, entrance looking S

Port aux Moines, Ile de St Honorat looking NW. Ile de Ste Marguerite is in the background.

Entrance
By day Approach the entrance on a SE course, with great care and at slow speed. Round the head of Jetée Ouest and enter on a S course through the very narrow entrance.

Berths
Berth stern-to quay to suit draught in a vacant space, anchor in the centre of the harbour.

Prohibited anchorages
Cables run across the channel on both sides of this harbour.

Formalities
There is a local official who meets visiting yachts and assists their berthing.

125 PORT DE STE MARGUERITE

Position 43°31'·4N 7°02'·5E
Minimum depth in the entrance 2m (6·6ft)
 in the harbour 2 to 1m (6·6 to 3·3ft)
Population 300 (approx)
Rating 3–4–3

General
This harbour is really only a series of landing piers, moorings and slips along the N coast of the island and is completely open to NW–N–NE winds which make berths untenable. The approach requires some care owing to shallow water and cannot be undertaken in any rough weather. The island and its Château Fort are most attractive with woods and sandy coves and when the tourists go home in the late afternoon it is almost deserted. Facilities are very limited.

South France Pilot

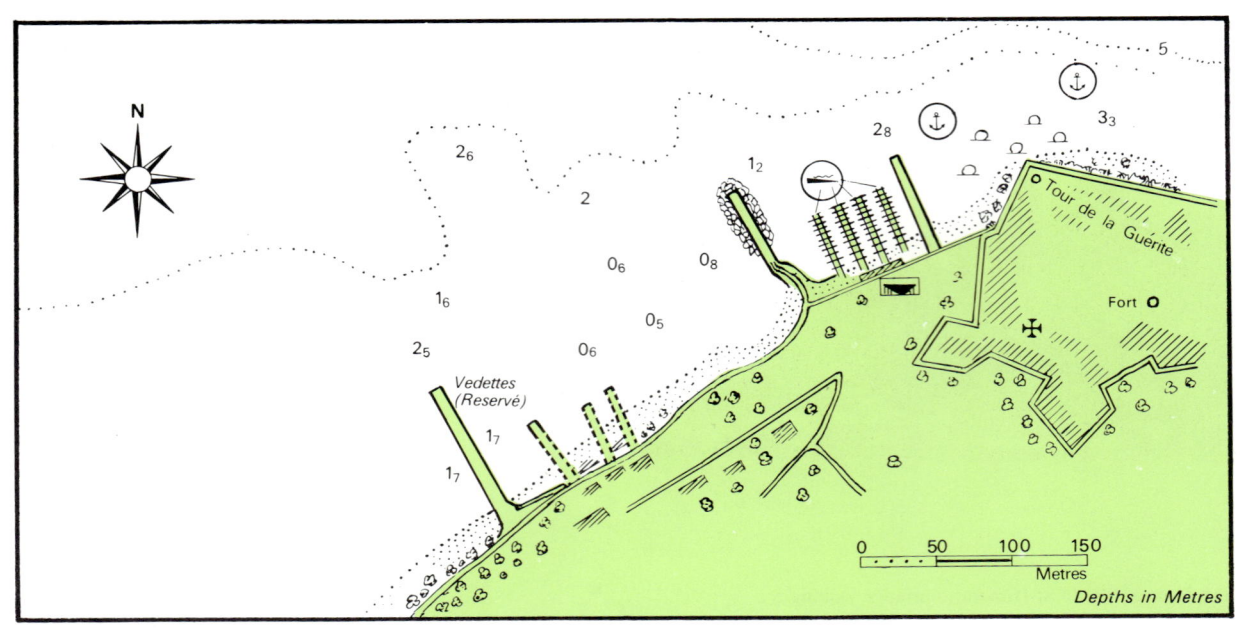

Port de Ste Marguerite

Cap d'Antibes   Château   Fort Royal

Ile de Ste Marguerite. Piers on N coast looking E

Data

Charts Admiralty 2167
French 5122
Spanish 121
ECM 501

Magnetic variation 1°19′W (1990) decreasing by about 8′ each year.

Currents Wind-induced currents of up to 2 knots can flow in the channels to the N and S of this island.

Beacon A W Card YBY beacon tower, *Bataignier*, X topmark, lies to the NW of the island and marks outlying dangerous rocks. A pylon stands in Pointe de la Convention.

Warning

There is a constant stream of fast ferry boats plying between this island and Cannes harbour which take the shortest route possible and should not be followed. Dangerous seas can quickly get up in the channels either side of this island in a NW *mistral*. There is a 10-knot speed limit between Cannes and Ile Ste Marguerite.

Approach by day

From SW Cross the wide Golfe de Napoule towards the low tree-covered mass of this island which lies just S of Pointe de la Croisette and the hills to the N of this point. Ile St Honorat appears to blend into Ile Ste Marguerite from this direction and the channel between them only shows when halfway across the Golfe. In the closer approach the W Card YBY beacon tower, *Bataignier*, ⊥ topmark, will be seen. This tower must be rounded at a distance of over 400m and left to starboard. When the N edge of the Château is bearing 110° or more, approach on this course until the piers are S, then approach the harbour.

From NE Cross the deep Golfe Juan avoiding *La Fourmigue*, G beacon tower ▲ topmark, Fl.G.4s. Approach the N side of the Château Fort on a course between 210° and 290°. When 200m from it follow the coast along at this distance until the piers are S when turn and approach.

By night

Night approach is not recommended due to lack of navigational lights.

Anchorage in the approach

Anchor 300m to N of the landings in 6m (20ft) mud. Open to E and SW–W.

Entrance

By day Approach the piers on a S course with care while sounding all the way.

Berths

Berths may be available alongside any of the piers except the outer end of the largest and most westerly pier which is reserved for the ferries. The jetty just to the W of the slips has a rocky foot.

Moorings

There are some private moorings which might be free near the Château Fort and Point Bataignier about 200m offshore but careful sounding is necessary.

Anchorage

It is possible to anchor in suitable depth between the Château Fort and Point Bataignier about 200m offshore but careful sounding is necessary.

Prohibited anchorage

Cables run from Pointe de la Croisette to a point just E of the Château Fort and a pipe to a point just W. Anchorage is forbidden anywhere near them.

Facilities

Slipways Four slips just to the W of the Château Fort with a capacity of up to 180 tonnes, but one may be out of use.
Water From shipyard or restaurant.
Provisions Limited amount of rubbish containers around the island.
Repairs The local shipyard can repair hulls and engines.
Restaurants A few restaurants and café/bars catering in the main for tourists.
Visits The Château Fort Royal should be visited to see its Musée de la Mer. There are also some pleasant walks around the island.
Beaches Many sandy coves round the island.
Communications Frequent ferry services to Cannes and Golfe Juan during daylight hours.

---

126 PORT DU MOURE-ROUGE
06400 Alpes-Maritimes

Position 43°32'·5N 7°02'·5E
Minimum depth in the entrance 2m (6·6ft)
　　　　　　　in the harbour 1·75 to 0m (5·7 to 0ft)
Width of the entrance 30m
Number of berths 400
Maximum length overall 8m (26ft)
Population 70,000 (Cannes)
Rating 4–3–4

General

A very small shallow harbour mainly used by dinghies and runabouts. Approach and entrance are easy except for winds and swell from E–SE–S which make it dangerous and very uncomfortable inside the harbour. Facilities are very limited.

Data

Charts　Admiralty 2167
　　　　　French 5113, 5122
　　　　　Spanish 121
　　　　　ECM 501

Magnetic variation 1°19'W (1990) decreasing by about 8' each year.

Weather forecasts Posted outside the *Bureau de Port* each day and an automatic tape-recorded forecast (*Navimet*).

Speed limit 3 knots.

Warning

The depths inside this harbour are subject to change, sound carefully.

Approach by day

From SW Round the Iles de Lérins to the S and E, outside *Les Moines* S Card YB beacon tower ▼ topmark, Q(6)+LFl.15s. Keep 400m from the islands and when the Ile de la Tradelière has been rounded proceed on a NW course for 2M when the low harbour breakwater will be seen lying about ½M to N of Pointe de la Croisette. Behind this harbour the high tree-covered hills slope down to the flat Pointe de la Croisette. Passage is also possible either side of Ile Ste Marguerite (see page 48).

From NE Cross the deep Golfe Juan, leaving *La Fourmigue* G beacon tower ▲ topmark, Fl.G.4s, 300m to starboard, towards Pointe de la Croisette. Direct course in the closer approach to ½M to N of this point where the harbour breakwater will be seen.

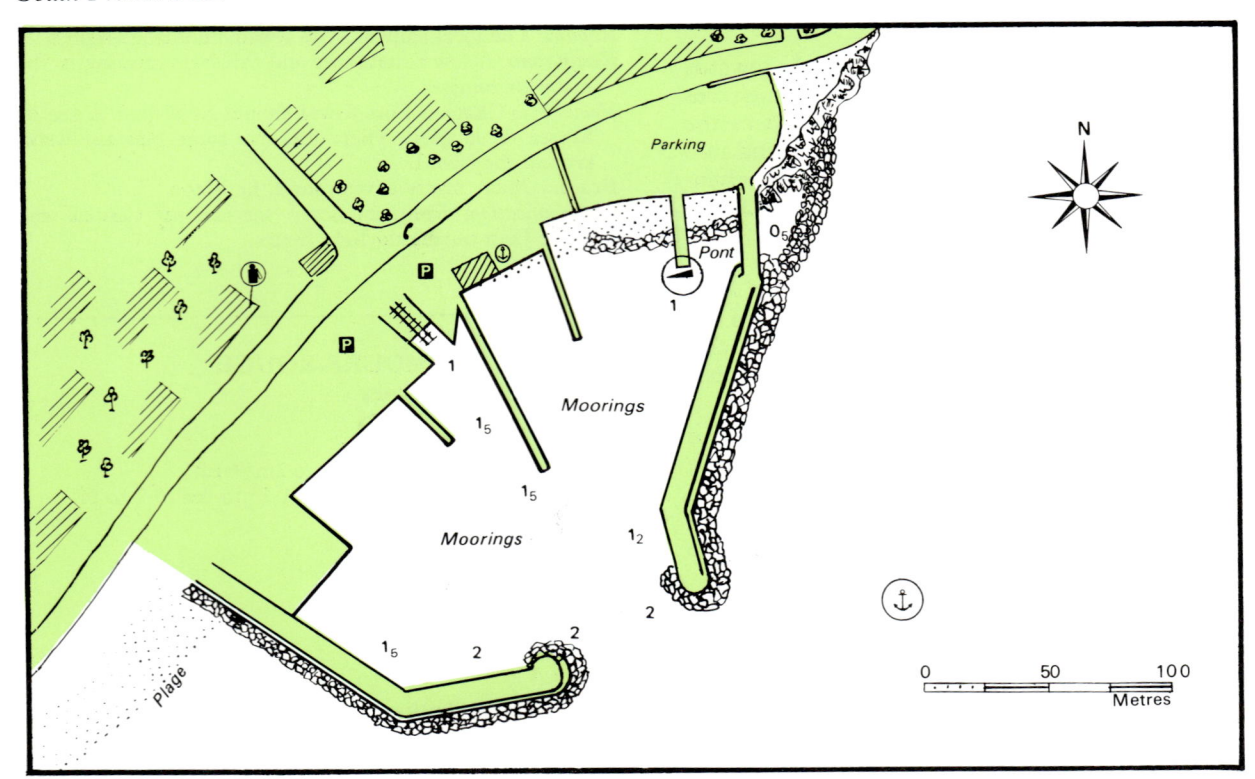

South France Pilot

Port de Mouré-Rouge

Port de Mouré-Rouge looking N

54

Port de Golfe-Juan (Vallauris)

Bureau de Port

Port de Mouré-Rouge looking W–NW–N from entrance

By night
Night approach and entrance are not recommended due to the lack of navigational lights.

Anchorage in the approach
Anchor 100m to E of the entrance in 4m (13ft) sand and mud.

Entrance
By day Approach the entrance on a NW course and enter in mid-channel.

Berths
Secure stern to quay or pontoon, bow to mooring chain in a vacant space and report to the *Bureau de Port* for the allocation of a berth.

Moorings
Some private moorings which may be free.

Formalities
Report to the *Bureau de Port* (☎ 93 38 12 40 and 93 68 91 92 ext 387) on arrival.

Charges
There are harbour charges.

Facilities
Slipway A 10-tonne slipway.
Crane A 14-tonne mobile crane is available.
Fuel Petrol is available from a garage close to the harbour.
Water Water points on the quay and pontoons.
Electricity Some 220v AC outlets on quays and pontoons.
Provisions A few shops inland from the harbour.
Ice Delivered each day by van in the season.
Garbage Some rubbish containers near the road.
Chandlery A small stock of ships' chandlery is kept at the garage.
Repairs A local mechanic can repair engines.
Post office Not far inland from the harbour.
Beaches Sandy beaches either side of the harbour.

⌳ E of Port de Mouré-Rouge
An open anchorage in 5m sand and mud 300m to E of the Port de Mouré-Rouge open to NE–E–SE. Pay attention to cables which come ashore 500m to NE of this harbour. Main coast road and many houses ashore.

---

127 PORT DE GOLFE-JUAN (VALLAURIS)
06350 Alpes-Maritimes

Position 43°33'·8N 7°04'·7E
Minimum depth in the entrance 3·5m (11ft)
in the harbour 3 to 1m (9·8 to 3·3ft)
Width of the entrance 65m
Number of berths 830 plus 1500
Maximum length overall 22m (72ft) and one berth of 60m (197ft)
Population 6000
Rating 3–2–3

General
An old artificial yacht and fishing harbour which has had many new pontoons installed and now it has been more than doubled in size by the construction of a new breakwater to E of the old harbour. Approach and entrance are easy in all conditions except strong E–SE winds which make it difficult. There are good facilities for yachtsmen and an attractive and as yet unspoilt old town.

Data

Charts Admiralty 2167
French 5122
Spanish 121
ECM 501

Magnetic variation 1°19'W (1990) decreasing by about 8' each year.

Weather forecasts The forecast is published once a day at the *Bureau de Port*. Also an automatic prerecorded forecast (☎ 93 83 00 25) (*Navimet*).

South France Pilot

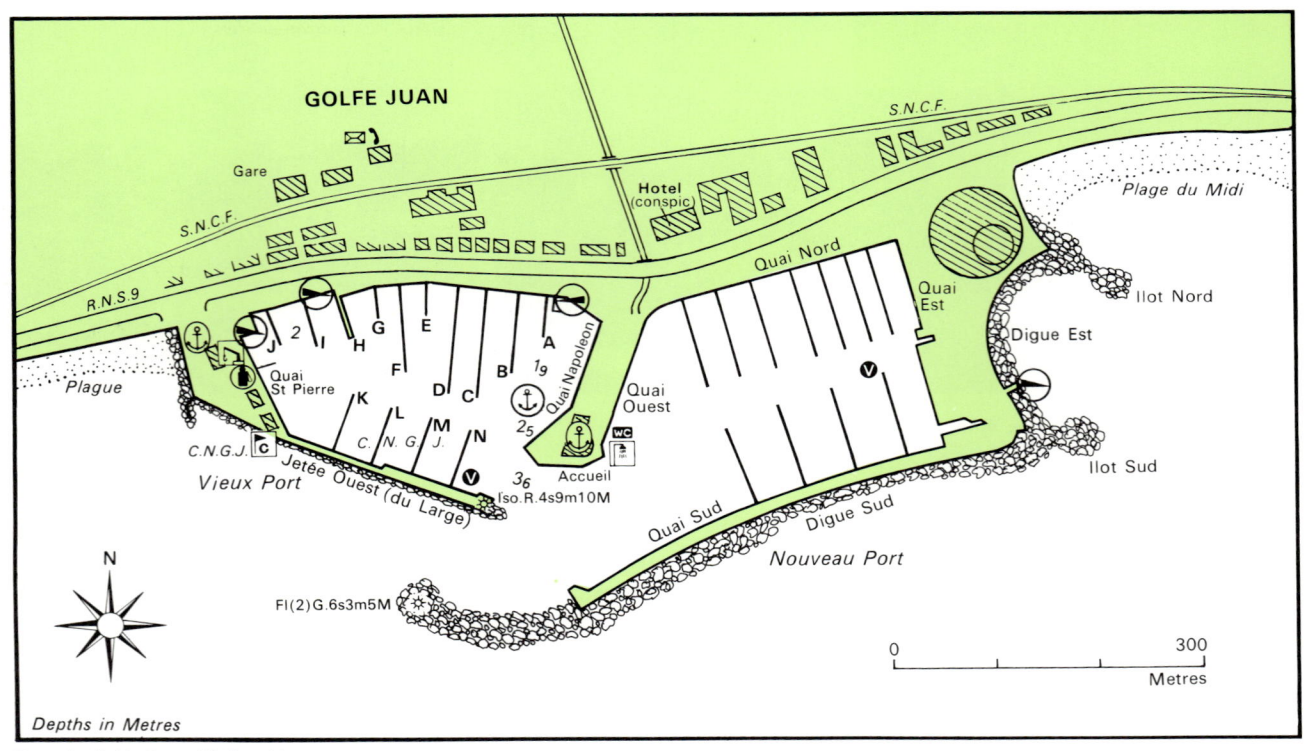

Port de Golfe-Juan (Vallauris)

Speed limit 3 knots.

Port radio VHF Ch 9.

Lights

Vallauris lighthouse Oc(2)WRG.6s167m16-11M. White square tower, black top. 265°-G-305°-W-309°-R-336°-W-342°-G-009°.
Jetée Ouest (du Large) Head Iso.R.4s9m10M. White column, red top.
Jetée Est Head Iso.G.4s2m. Strip light.
Digue Sud Head Fl(2)G.6s3m5M.

Beacon La Fourmigue G beacon tower ▲ topmark, Fl.G.4s16m9M, marks some above-water rocks and a shoal area (5–8m).

Buoys Le Sécanion R pillar buoy square topmark, marks the NE side of a shoal patch (5·2m).

Warning

The shoal patch and above-water rocks, Basses de la Fourmigue, in the centre of the Golfe-Juan, marked by a beacon tower, should be avoided. NE of Basses de la Fourmigue is a marine reserve area marked by Y buoys on the four corners. The SE buoy shows Fl(3)Y. N of Basses de la Fourmigue is a Y buoy marking a wreck (0·6m).

Approach by day

From SW Round the Iles de Lérins to the S outside *Les Moines* S Card YB beacon tower ⚑ topmark, Q(6)+LFl.15s. Passage either side of Ile Ste Marguerite is also possible (see page 48). Enter Golfe-Juan on a N course leaving *La Fourmigue* beacon tower 200m to starboard. The houses of the town of Golfe-Juan will be seen ahead together with a large high-rise yellow-coloured hotel which is near the entrance. In the closer approach the Jetée Ouest (du Large) of the Vieux Port and Digue Sud of the Nouveau Port will be seen.

From NE Round Cap d'Antibes at 500m onto a NW course and leave *Le Sécanion* R pillar buoy 300m to port. The same features are visible in the closer approach as described above. In addition the two small artificial rocky islets to the E of the harbour will be seen.

By night

Using the lights listed below navigate to a position where the harbour entrance is NW 300m. Note that the white sectored lights of Vallauris lead past the Basses de la Fourmigue and the white sectored light of Pointe de l'Ilette leads to the SE of the Iles de Lérins:

Vallauris Oc(2)WRG.6s16-11M
La Garoupe Fl(2)W.10s31M
Pointe de l'Ilette Oc(2+1)WRG.12s13-8M

Anchorage in the approach

Anchor 300m to SE of the entrance in 7m (23ft) mud and weed. Open to SE–S–SW.

Entrance

By day Enter on a NW course between jetty heads. To port is the Vieux Port and ahead is the Nouveau Port.

By night Approach in the W sector of Vallauris light and at 1M turn towards Iso.R.4s. Round it at 20m, leaving it to port onto a NW course and enter.

56

Port de Golfe-Juan (Vallauris)

Port de Golfe-Juan looking N showing old and new harbour. Note several dredgers at work.

Port de Golfe-Juan looking E–SE from the Vallauris lighthouse. Vieux Port in the foreground, Nouveau Port to the left

Port de Golfe-Juan, entrance looking E

Berths

Vieux Port Secure to a vacant berth on first pontoon (N) stern-to, bow to mooring buoy. Report to the *Bureau de Port* at root of Jetée Ouest for the allocation of a berth.

Nouveau Port Secure to Quai d'Accueil beside the fuel berth and report to the *Bureau de Port* nearby for allocation of a berth.

Note The Jetée Est of the Vieux Port is the Jetée and Quai Ouest of the Nouveau Port.

Formalities

Report to the *Bureau de Port* (☎ 93 63 96 25) on arrival open 0800–1900 in summer, 0800–1800 in winter, and if necessary to the customs (☎ 93 63 71 87) which is in the town at Place des Douanes (open Monday, Wednesday, Friday mornings).

Charges

There are harbour charges.

South France Pilot

Outer entrance (to both harbours)

Port de Golfe-Juan, approach looking NW

Hotel   *Outer entrance (to both entrances)*

Port de Golfe-Juan, entrance looking NE

Facilities

Slips Two slips on the W side of the Vieux Port. Two slips on E side of the Nouveau Port.
Slipways Several slips at the N side of the Vieux Port with a maximum capacity of 40 tonnes.
Travel-hoist On E side of Nouveau Port.
Cranes Two cranes at the SW side of the Vieux Port of 5 and 10 tonnes capacity.
Fuel Diesel (*gasoil*) and petrol from pumps to SW of the Vieux Port 0800–1900 in summer, 0900–1100 in winter and also at the head of Jetée Est, Quai Ouest in the Nouveau Port.
Water Water points on the three most E pontoons on both sides of the Vieux Port and all pontoons and quays in the Nouveau Port.
Electricity Supply points for 220v AC on the three most E pontoons on both sides of the Vieux Port and all pontoons and quays in the Nouveau Port.
Provisions A good number of shops of most types in the town.
Ice This is delivered each day in the season to the yacht club.
Garbage Rubbish containers on the quays.
Chandlery Several ships' chandlers to the N of the harbour.
Repairs Nine shipyards and a number of mechanics for the repair of hulls and engines. Sailmaker.

Post office The PTT is located to NW of the harbour near the station.
Hotels One ***, four **, three * and some unclassified hotels.
Restaurants There are nine restaurants and some café/bars.
Yacht club The Club Nautique de Golfe-Juan (CNGJ) (☎ 93 63 83 14) with an office on the Jetée Ouest.
Showers There are six showers and WCs on the N side of the harbour.
Information office The office of the Syndicat d'Initiative is near the station.
Visits Sandy beaches can be found either side of the harbour.
Communications Rail and bus services, ferries to the Iles de Lérins and an airport at Nice.

Future development

Improvement of the facilities offered and completion of the Nouveau Port are in hand.

History

This is the harbour where Napoleon landed on his return to France in 1815 after internment on the island of Elba.

⌱ **Head of Golfe Juan**

An open anchorage in 5m mud and weed 600m off the N shore of this *golfe*, it is very shallow inshore, open to SE–S–SW. Main coast road and railway, a few houses.

---

128 PORT GALLICE, JUAN-LES-PINS
06160 Alpes-Maritimes

Position 43°33'·8N 7°07'·0E
Minimum depth   in the entrance 3m (9·8ft)
                  in the harbour 3 to 1m (9·8 to 3·3ft)
Width of the entrance 40m
Maximum length overall   20m (66ft)
                           43m (141ft) for a few berths
Number of berths 526
Population 6000 (approx)
Rating 2-2-2

General

A medium-sized new artificial yacht harbour built alongside the very small and old fishing harbour of Port du Crouton which has now been considerably enlarged. Easy to approach and enter but care is necessary in strong winds and swell from SW. There are good facilities and the attractive seaside resort of Juan-les-Pins is nearby.

Data

Charts   Admiralty 2167
           French 5122
           ECM 501

Port Gallice, Juan-les-Pins

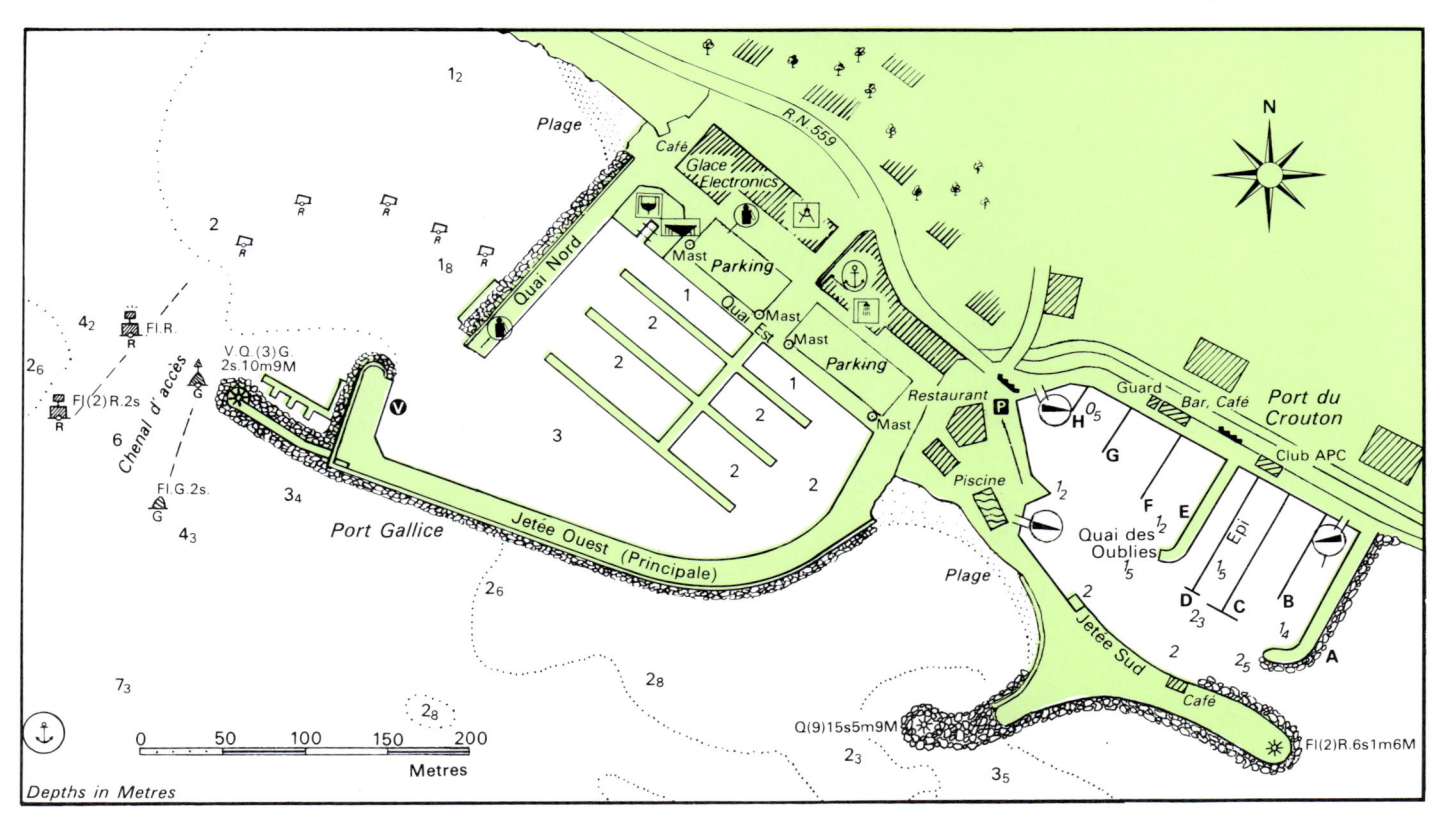

Port Gallice and Port du Crouton

Port Gallice looking NE

South France Pilot

Magnetic variation 1°19′W (1990) decreasing by about 8′ each year.

Radiobeacon
La Garoupe lighthouse GO (— — · / — — —) 294·2 kHz 100M every 6 minutes Seq. 5, 6. Grouped with Punta Revellata (RV).

Port radio VHF Ch 9. Call *Port Gallice* (French and some English).

Weather forecasts Forecasts are posted twice a day outside the *Bureau de Port* and there is also an automatic pre-recorded coastal forecast (*Navimet*).

Speed limit 3 knots.

Traffic signals Displayed from mast at *Bureau de Port*.

Day	Meaning
Red flag	Entry forbidden
Green flag	Exit forbidden
Red and green flags	Entry and exit forbidden

Storm signals Hoisted on mast at *Bureau de Port*. A special light is shown at La Garoupe by day as a storm warning:

Fl(8)W.4s	Force 6 to 7 expected
Q.W	Force 7+ expected

Lights
Jetée Ouest Head VQ(3)G.2s10m9M. White column, green top.
Le Crouton Jetée SE Head Fl(2)R.6s1m6M. Red post on white stand.
W head Q(9)W.15s5m9M. ✗ on yellow tower with black bands.
Ski jump 300m to NW of Jetée Ouest and 350m from the shore. F.Bu & F.Vi, summertime only.

Buoys Two R buoys, the outer one, Fl(2)R.2s, square topmark and the inner, Fl.R. Two G buoys, the outer one, Fl.G.2s, and the inner ▲ topmark, show the port and starboard limits of the entrance channel. Five R can buoys mark shallows to N of the entrance.

Beacon A G beacon tower, *La Fourmigue*, ▲ topmark, Fl.G.4s16m9M, is on the W side of the Basses de la Fourmigue.

Warning
The harbour is uncomfortable during a NW *mistral*. NW of Basses de la Fourmigue is a reserved marine area its four corners are marked by yellow buoys. A water-ski jump is moored 300m to NW of the harbour in summer (2 Bu lights).

Approach by day
From SW Having rounded the Iles de Lérins on the S side outside *Les Moines* S Card YB beacon tower ▼ topmark, Q(6)+LFl.15s9M, cross the deep Golfe-Juan leaving the G beacon tower, *La Fourmigue*, ▲ topmark, 1M to port and the R pillar buoy *Le Sécanion* ¼M to port. On a N course approach the area of the S end of the line of blocks of flats of Juan-les-Pins. The top of the lighthouse La Garoupe which lies to the E of this harbour will be seen above the trees. In the closer approach the Jetée Ouest will be seen, then steer for a position 200m to W of the head of this jetty. Passage is also possible either side of Ile Ste Marguerite (see page 48).

From NE Round Cap d'Antibes at 500m and follow the coast at this distance onto a N heading. Details of the close approach are as described above.

Entrance

Port Gallice-Juan-Les-Pins, approach looking E

By night
Using the lights listed below navigate to a position where the head of Jetée Ouest is 300m NE. Note that the sectored lights lead past the Basses de la Fourmigue and to the S of the Iles de Lérins:

Vallauris Oc(2)WRG.6s16-11M
La Garoupe Fl(2)W.10s31M
Pointe de l'Ilette Oc(2+1)WRG.12s13-8M
La Fourmigue Fl.G.4s9M

Anchorage in the approach
Anchor 300m to SW of the head of the harbour entrance in 6m (20ft) mud and weed. Open to S–SW–W–NW.

Entrance
By day Approach the head of Jetée Ouest on a NE course and enter between two pairs of R and G buoys. Follow them round the head of the jetty onto a SE course leaving the five R can buoys to port and enter between two spurs.

By night Approach VQ(3)G on a NE course and pass between Fl(2)R.2s and Fl.G.2s then leave Fl.R to port and onto a SE course to enter the harbour leaving VQ(3)G 20m to starboard.

Berths
Secure stern-to quay on starboard hand near entrance in a vacant place, bow to mooring chain and report to the *Bureau de Port*.

Port Gallice, Juan-les-Pins

Port Gallice and Port du Crouton looking NE

Conspicuous hotel (Port de Golfe-Juan)

Entrance

Port du Crouton, approach looking NE

Green light tower *La Fourmigue* looking N

Port du Crouton, entrance looking NW–N from new head of Jetée Sud

New head of Jetée Est

61

PORT GALLICE, JUAN–LES–PINS Buoyed entrance looking E

Formalities
Report to the *Bureau de Port* (☎ 93 61 28 64) on arrival and if necessary to the customs whose office is in the same building (☎ 93 33 75 34) and are based in Antibes.

Charges
There are harbour charges.

Facilities
Travel-lift There is a travel-lift of 30-tonnes capacity in the NW corner of the harbour.
Fuel Diesel (*gasoil*) and petrol are available from pumps at the end of Quai Nord (☎ 93 67 36 14). There is another petrol pump in Port de Crouton 0900–1200 and 1500–1800 hours.
Water Water points are on all quays and pontoons.
Electricity Supply points of 220v AC on all pontoons and quays also 380v AC on quays with deep-water berths.
Provisions Excellent shops in the town some ½M away and a self-service shop beside the harbour.
Ice Delivered daily in season to the *Bureau de Port*. Automatic vending machine.
Garbage Rubbish containers around the harbour.
Chandlery Two ships' chandlers to the N of the harbour.
Repairs A shipyard to the N of the harbour where hulls and engines can be repaired. There is also an electronic repair workshop.
Laundrette A laundrette in the town.
Post office Opposite the station in the town.
Hotels Six ****, fifteen ***, thirty-two **, twenty * and some unclassified hotels.
Restaurants Twenty–two restaurants and many café/bars.
Showers Showers near the *Bureau de Port*.
Information office The office of the Syndicat d'Initiative is on the road into the town at 51 Boulevard Guillamont (☎ 93 33 95 64).
Visits The view from La Garoupe lighthouse is worth the climb.
Beaches Excellent sandy beaches either side of the harbour.
Communications Bus and rail services and air from Nice.

Future development
The establishment of a yacht club is planned.

129 PORT DU CROUTON
06160 Alpes–Maritimes

Position 43°33'·5N 7°07'·2E
Minimum depth in the entrance 2·5m (8·2ft)
    in the harbour 2 to 0·5m (6·6 to 1·6ft)
Width of the entrance 25m
Maximum length overall 10m (33ft)
Number of berths 500 (approx)
Population 6000 (approx)
Rating 3–3–3

General
The original little fishing harbour on this part of the coast which had the large yacht harbour Port Gallice built alongside to NW and then had its capacity more than doubled by the construction of a new breakwater to SE. It is used primarily by medium and small-sized yachts and fishing craft. Easy to enter, good protection but some swell from S. Facilities limited but good nearby.

Data
See Port Gallice, Juan-les-Pins, page 58.

Lights
Jetée Sud SE head Fl(2)R.6s1m6M. Small red post.
W Head Q(9)W.15s5m9M. ⚑ on yellow and black tower.

Warning
The new breakwater has only been constructed recently and changes may be expected.

Approach by day
From SW Round the Iles de Lérins on the S side outside *Les Moines* S Card beacon tower YB ⚑ topmark (Q(6)+LFl.15s7M) and cross the wide Golfe-Juan leaving *La Fourmigue* beacon tower G ▲ topmark (Fl.G.4s9M) 1M to port and then *Le Sécanion* a R can buoy ¼M to port onto a N course. La Garoupe lighthouse on the skyline is easily identified, it lies to NE of this harbour. The line of apartment blocks at Juan-les-Pins will also be seen. In the closer approach the breakwater of Port Gallice will be observed, this harbour lies to the S of it.

From NE Round Cap d'Antibes at 500m and follow the coast northwards at this distance. La Garoupe, Juan-les-Pins and Port Gallice will be seen as described above.

By night
Use the following lights to navigate to a position where the harbour lies 500m NE:
Vallauris Oc(2)WRG.6s16-10M
La Garoupe Fl(2)W.10s31M
Port Gallice VQ(3)G.2s9M
Pointe de L'Ilette Oc(2+1)WRG.12s13-8M
La Fourmigue Fl.G.4s9M

Anchorage in the approach
Anchor 500m to SW of the harbour entrance in 8m sand and weed. Open to S–SW–W–NW.

Entrance
By day Approach the S end of the Jetée Sud and round it at 10m leaving it to port and the head of the new jetty to starboard then onto a N course.
By night Approach Fl(2)R.6s on a NE course, round it leaving it 10m to port onto a N course.

Berths
Secure to a vacant berth on the inner side of Jetée Sud and report to the clubhouse.

Formalities
Documentation at clubhouse, customs at Port Gallice (☎ 93 33 37 34).

Charges
There are harbour charges.

Facilities
Slips Three slips around the harbour.
Fuel From Port Gallice, Quai Nord.
Water Several taps around the harbour and on pontoons.
Electricity 220v AC outlets around the harbour and on the pontoons.
Provisions Good shops in Juan-les-Pins (½M).
Ice Small ice from machine at Port Gallice.
Garbage Several containers around the harbour.
Chandlery Shops at Port Gallice and in the town.
Repairs Repairs to hull, engines and electronics by local yards.
See Port Gallice page 58 for details of other facilities in the area.

Future development
Further improvements planned including extra facilities.

⚓ Mouillage du Piton
A semi-open anchorage to S of the Port du Crouton in 3–5m sand. Coast road, large houses and gardens ashore. Open to S–SW–W–NW.

⚓ Port Mallet and Port de l'Olivette
Two small shallow 3·7m bays with moorings, landing stages and several large houses with gardens ashore on the far side of the coast road. Approach with care, there are several rocky heads, and anchor outside moorings. Use an anchor trip-line. Open to SW–W–NW–N. Naval museum ashore.

Pointe de l'Ilette
A low prominent point with conspicuous white lighthouse (9m), several buildings and some trees near the point. To E lies the large Anse de l'Argent Faux.

⚓ Anse de l'Argent Faux
A large well known anchorage in an attractive area with a few large houses and wooded gardens ashore. The centre of the bay is deep (20m) but anchorage can be found in 10m near the shore of low rocky cliffs. Footpath to main coast road. Open E–SE–S–SW.

Cap d'Antibes
A headland (19m) tree covered with low cliffs of white rocks, several large houses and an hotel. A stone pier running down to the water lies at the centre of the Cap inland of which is a large ruined house. There are several awash rocks close inshore.

Cap Gros
A small tree-covered white-cliffed point with 4·6m shallows close off its point.

⚓ Anse de la Garoupe
A popular anchorage in a pleasant deep bay surrounded with large houses and gardens, a sandy beach, beach cafés and road. Anchor in 5m sand and weed. Three awash isolated rocks lie off the beach. Open to N–NE–E–SE.

Anse de la Garoupe looking SW

South France Pilot

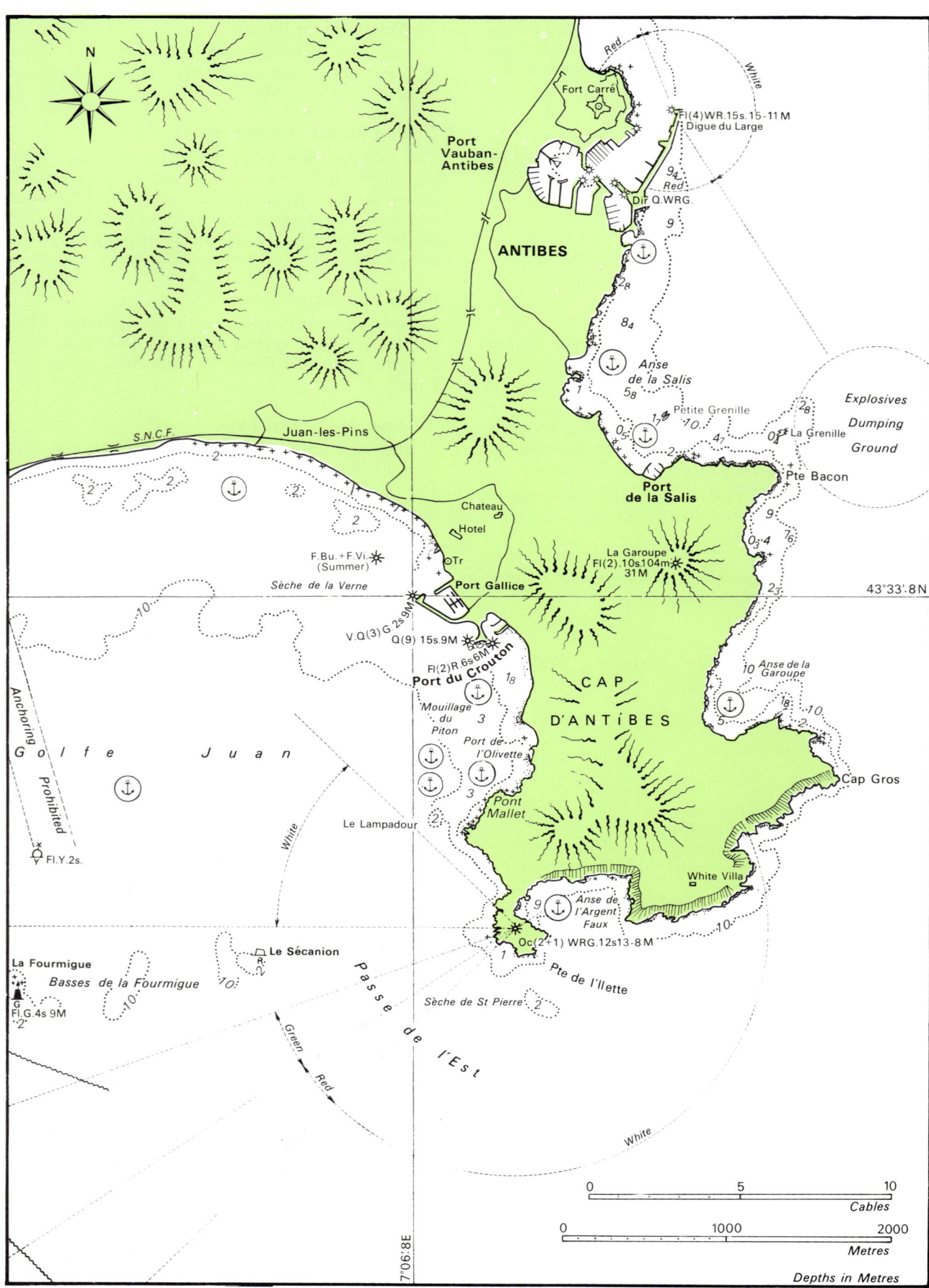

Cap d'Antibes anchorages

Anchorages

Anse de l'Argent Faux looking E

Anse de la Garoupe looking NW

La Garoupe lighthouse

Anse de la Garoupe

South France Pilot

130 PORT DE LA SALIS (ROUS-CHAFFEY)
06600 Alpes Maritime

Position 43°34'·2N 7°07'·9E
Minimum depth in the entrance 2m (6·6ft)
 in the harbour 2 to 0·1m (6·6 to 0·3ft)
Width of the entrance 25m
Maximum length overall 7m (23ft)
Number of berths 200
Population 48,013 (Antibes)
Rating 4-4-4

General
A very small shallow fishing and yachting harbour which is very crowded. The approach and entrance require care and would be impossible in strong winds from N–NE–E. Facilities are very limited.

Data
Charts Admiralty 2167
 French 5122
 Spanish 121
 ECM 501

Magnetic variation 1°19'W (1990) decreasing by about 8' each year.

Radiobeacon
La Garoupe lighthouse GO (— —·/— — —) 294·2 kHz 100M every 6 minutes Seq. 5, 6. Grouped with Punta Revellata (RV).

Speed limit 3 knots.

Warning
The isolated rocky patch, La Petite Grenille, about 300m to the N of this harbour is unmarked. The coast from Antibes to Pointe Bacon is lined with awash and covered rocks close inshore. Keep a good lookout.

Approach by day
From SW Round the low rocky Cap d'Antibes at 500m and follow the coast around at this distance passing outside the Ilot de la Grenille which is located 400m to N of Pointe Bacon. Turn to a W course and when the harbour bears SW approach on this course. The harbour has a block of flats to its NNW.

From NE Cross the wide Baie des Anges towards the lighthouse La Garoupe on Cap d'Antibes. When 1M from it alter course to pass to N of the Ilot de la Grenille and proceed as above.

By night
Night approach and entrance are not advised due to the lack of navigational lights.

Anchorage in the approach
Anchor 300m to NE of the harbour.

Entrance
Enter on a SW course between the heads of the two jetties.

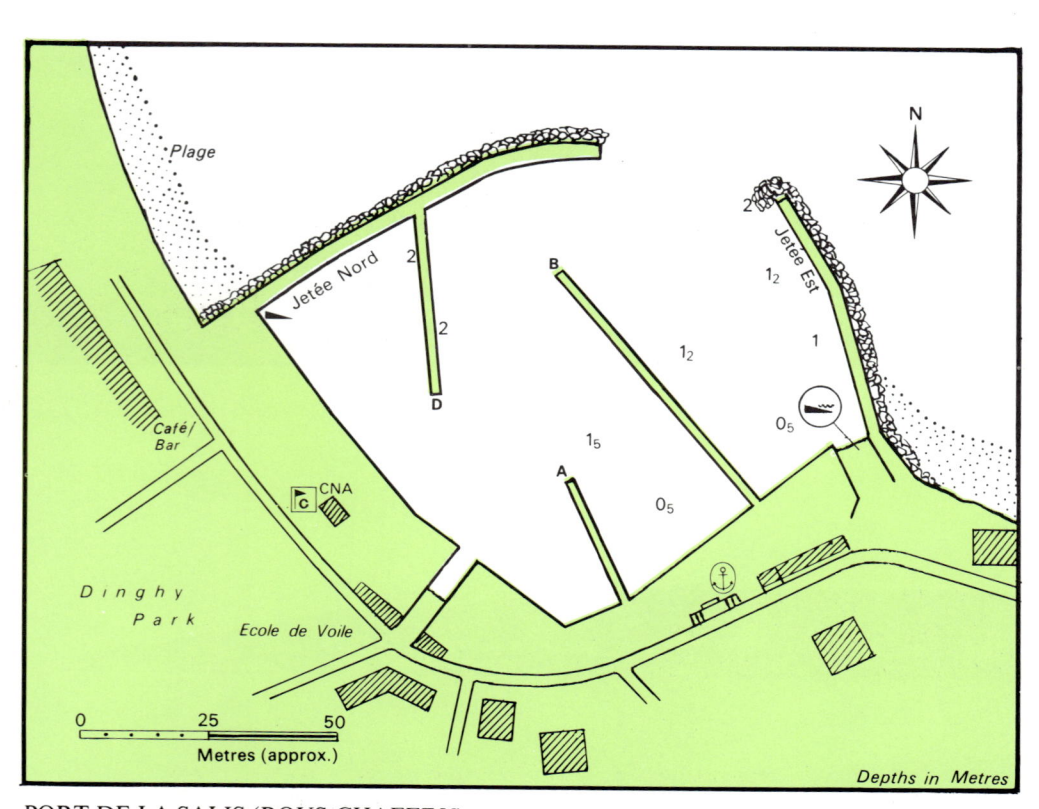

PORT DE LA SALIS (ROUS-CHAFFEY)

Port de la Salis (Rous-Chaffey)

Port de la Salis, approach looking SW

Port de la Salis, entrance looking S

Berths
Secure stern-to in any vacant berth with bow to mooring and report to the *Bureau de Port*.

Formalities
Report to the *Bureau de Port* on arrival.

Facilities
Slips Three slips, one to W one to S and the other to E.
Water A few points for water on the quay and pontoons.
Provisions A few shops about 500m to NW of the harbour.
Restaurants Small café beside the harbour.
Garbage A few rubbish containers on the quay.
Beaches Sandy beaches either side of the harbour.
Communications There is a bus service to Antibes.

⚓ Anse de la Salis
A semi-open anchorage that lies between the Port de la Salis and the old town of Antibes in 3 to 5m sand and mud. There are isolated awash rocks close inshore and a small islet Petite Grenille (300m) to N of the Port de la Salis. A cable is laid from the Pointe des Pendus in an ENE direction. Open to N–NE–E. Road, many houses and shops, etc. ashore.

Port de la Salis looking NW–N–NE

Cap d'Antibes looking N

67

South France Pilot

131 PORT VAUBAN-ANTIBES
06600 Alpes-Maritimes

Position 43°36′N 7°08′·0E
Minimum depth   in the entrance 10m (33ft)
                  in the harbour 8m to 2m (26 to 6·6ft)
Width of the outer entrance 150m
        of the inner entrance 80m
Maximum length overall   65m (213ft) and 19 berths up to 165m (541ft)
Number of berths 1480
Population 70,000; 200,000 in summer
Rating 1–2–1

General
The natural harbour of an ancient and attractive town that has been made into a very large modern yacht harbour by the addition of breakwaters, pontoons and quays. Easy to approach and enter in all weather except NE–E winds and swell which makes the harbour uncomfortable and the approach difficult. Excellent facilities and a good shopping area. Very crowded in season. A considerable number of large and very large motor yachts are based here. This harbour has the greatest tonnage of yachts of any harbour in Europe. The flight path of aircraft landing at Nice airport crosses the harbour at low level and is very noisy.

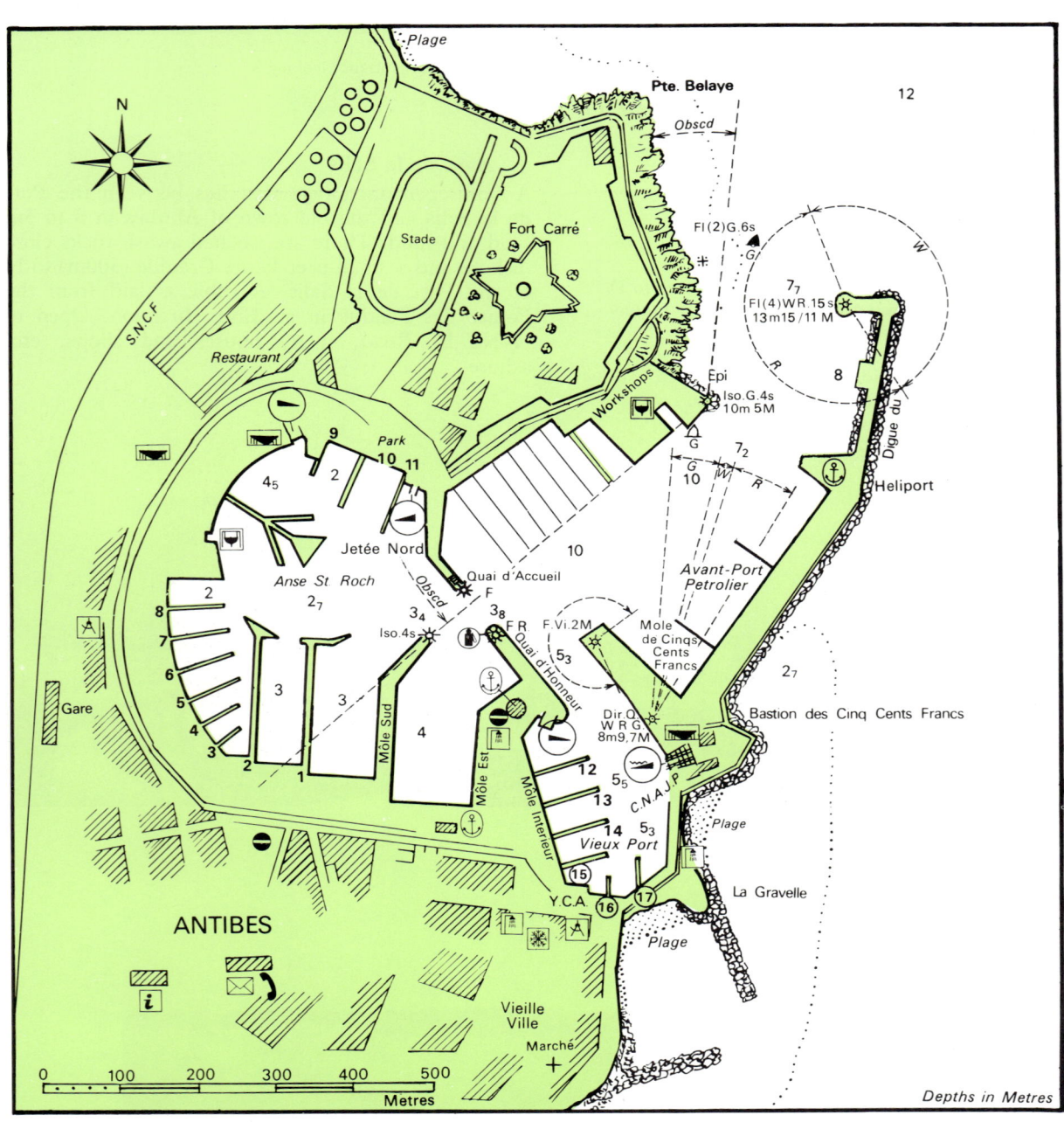

Port Vauban-Antibes

68

Port Vauban-Antibes

Fort Carré   Vieille-Ville

Port Vauban-Antibes looking NE

Port de Vauban-Antibes looking NW

Data

Charts Admiralty 2167
French 6952
Spanish 121
ECM 501

Magnetic variation 1°19′W (1990) decreasing by about 8′ each year.

Radiobeacon

La Garoupe lighthouse GO (— —·/— — —) 294·2 kHz 100M every 6 minutes Seq. 5, 6. Grouped with Punta Revellata (RV).

Air radiobeacon

Nice. Mont Leuza (43°43′·7N 7°20′·2E) LEZ (·—··/·/— —··) 398·5 kHz 75M. Continuous

Port radio VHF Ch 9 (French and English).

69

South France Pilot

Weather forecasts The forecasts are posted twice a day at the *Bureau de Port* and there is also an automatic pre-recorded coastal forecast (*Navimet*). Also ☎ 93 83 91 12, Aéroport Nice-Côte d'Azur.

Speed limit 3 knots.

Traffic signals Shown from a mast at the *Bureau de Port*.

Day	Meaning
Red flag	Entry forbidden
Green flag	Exit forbidden
Red and green flags	Entry and exit forbidden

Storm signals Shown from a mast at the *Bureau de Port* and also a light from La Garoupe lighthouse:
Fl(8)W.4s   Force 6 to 7 expected
Q.W   Force 7+ expected

Lights
Digue du Large Head Fl(4)WR.15s13m15/11M. Tower, white to seaward, yellow to land. Red top.
Digue du Large Spur head Fl.R.2s3m2M. White post, red top.
Epi du Fort Carré head Iso.G.4s10m5M. Orange column, green lantern. Vis 003°-048°, 186°-218° unintens 218°-003°.
Môle de Cinq Cents Francs Root Dir.Q.WRG.8m9-7M. 184·5°-G-194·5°-W- 197·5°-R-211°.
Môle de Cinq Cents Francs Head F.Vi.16m2M. White tower, red top. 335°-vis-232°.
Quai d'Honneur Head F.R
Môle Sud Head Iso.W.4s
Jetée Nord Head F.W

Buoys A G conical lightbuoy, Fl(2)G.6s, ▲ topmark 300m to N of Epi light. A second G conical buoy ▲ topmark 50m to NE of head of Jetée Nord. A Y can buoy 50m to W of Digue du Large level with the heliport.

Warning
Do not mistake the bathing beach, La Gravelle, which has harbour-like breakwaters for the harbour itself which lies further to the N. The yachtyard and workshop areas are being moved to the N side of the harbour.

Approach by day
From SW Round the low rocky tree-covered Cap d'Antibes at 500m following it onto a N course. When Pointe Bacon and its outlying rocky shallows have been passed, the conspicuous Fort Carré and the long high Digue du Large will be seen with the high superstructures of the very large yachts showing above it. Set course for the light tower at the end of this Digue. The two square towers in the Vieille Ville to the S of the harbour are also conspicuous.
From NE Cross the wide Baie des Anges towards Cap d'Antibes which has La Garoupe lighthouse on its summit surrounded by trees. In the closer approach the two towers in the Vieille Ville and Fort Carré are conspicuous. The light tower at the end of the Digue du Large will be seen in the closer approach.

By night
Using the lights listed below, navigate to a position where the head of the Digue du Large (Fl(4)WR.15s15/11M) is WSW at 300m. Note that when approaching from the NE the white sector of the Dir.Q leads to the entrance 194·5°–197·5°.
La Garoupe Fl(2)W.10s31M
Cap Ferrat Fl.W.3s25M
Nice Fl.R.5s20M

Vieille Ville   *Head of Digue du Large*   *Fort Carré*

Port Vauban-Antibes, approach looking SW

Head of Digue du Large   *Inner entrance*   *Fort Carré*

Port Vauban-Antibes, outer entrance looking SSW

Port Vauban-Antibes

Bureau de Port/Yacht club (very large yachts)   *Head of Môle de Cinq Cents Francs*   *Head of Epi*

Port Vauban-Antibes, inner entrance looking SW

Head of Môle de Cinq Cents Francs   *Bureau de Port*   *Fuel station*

Port Vauban-Antibes, approach to *Bureau de Port*

Anchorage in the approach
Anchor 500m to S of the entrance in 10m (33ft) mud and weed. Open to N–NE–E–SE.

Entrance
By day Round the head of the Digue du Large at 20m leaving it to port onto a SSW course and enter between the head of Epi de Fort Carré to port and the Digue du Large spur to starboard. Proceed to the head of Môle Est (Quai d'Honneur) for berthing instructions.

By night Round the Fl(4)WR.15s at 20m leaving it to port and a Fl(2)G.6s to starboard onto a SSW course. Approach Dir.Q in the W sector leaving Iso.G.4s to starboard and Fl.R.2s to port steering towards F.Vi which must be left to port and a turn made towards F.R on the Môle Est (Quai d'Honneur).

Berths
Secure to the Môle Est (Quai d'Honneur) or fuel station. Report to *Bureau de Port* for allocation of a berth. The Vieux Port and Anse St Roch offer better protection from NE–E swell. Secure to quay or pontoon stern-to with bow to mooring chain. It is advised to call the *Bureau de Port* on VHF Ch 9 and reserve a berth when 1M away.

Prohibited anchorage
It is forbidden to anchor inside the harbour to the N and NE of the entrance where cables run.

Formalities
Report to the *Bureau de Port* (☎ 93 34 74 00/03, telex 970 480) on arrival. Open day and night. The customs office (☎ 93 33 75 34) is in the Avenue de Verdun in SW corner of the port.

Charges
There are harbour charges including extra charges for electricity and water.

Facilities
Slips A slip near the *Bureau de Port* and one in the NW corner of the harbour and one outside the Epi.

Slipways A 150-tonne slip in the SE corner of the harbour (to be moved to N side of the harbour).

Travel-lift Two travel-lifts of 45 tonnes in the N corner of the harbour and six mobile cranes of 15-25 tonnes capacity.

Fuel Diesel (*gasoil*) and petrol available from pumps at the head of the Môle Est (Quai d'Honneur) 0800–1900 in summer and 0900–1200 and 1400–1800 in winter (☎ 93 34 03 95).

Water Water points on all quays and pontoons. Use of water is charged.

Electricity Supply points for 220v AC on all quays and pontoons and 380v AC where there are deep-water berths. Use of electricity is charged.

Provisions Many shops of all types just to the S of the harbour including an excellent market.

Ice Delivered by van each day to the harbour in the season and is also available from a shop to the S of the harbour and at fuel station.

Duty-free goods Apply to the *Bureau de Port* for details of merchants who can supply duty-free goods.

Garbage Many rubbish containers all round the harbour.

Vieille Ville   *Fort Carré*   *Entrance*   *Bureau de Port*

Port Vauban-Antibes looking S–SW–W–NW–N from head of Môle de Cinq Cents Francs

Chandlery Several ships' chandlers to the W and SE of the harbour.

Repairs Shipyards (☎ 93 34 27 41) to the N of the harbour where hulls and engines can be repaired. Sails and electronic equipment can also be repaired.

Laundrette Several laundrettes in the town.

Post office The PTT is located to the S of the harbour.

Hotels Five ***, eight **, eight * and other unclassified hotels.

Restaurants Some eighty-three restaurants and very many café/bars.

Yacht club The International Yacht Club d'Antibes (IYCA) (☎ 93 34 30 30) has a clubhouse and office on the Digue du Large with showers and all facilities, services etc. The Club Nautique d'Antibes et Juan-les-Pins (CNA) (☎ 93 34 48 05) has an office to the SE of the harbour. Yacht Club d'Antibes (YCA) (☎ 93 34 20 52) has a clubhouse to SE of the harbour.

Showers Eleven showers are available in the *Bureau de Port* building and to S of the harbour.

Information office The office of the Syndicat d'Initiative is located to the S of the harbour at 11 Place General de Gaulle (☎ 93 33 95 64).

Lifeboat A lifeboat (1st class) is stationed here (☎ 93 33 65 00).

Visits The Château Grimaldi which houses the Musée Picasso and the two other museums in the town should be visited. A walk round La Vieille Ville is rewarding. Excellent view from La Garoupe lighthouse.

Beaches There are a few small beaches either side of the harbour.

Communications Bus and rail services and an airport at Nice.

Future development

It is expected that the N side of the Avant Port will be further developed.

History

Remains of Upper Neolithic and Late Bronze Age occupation have been found nearby. The Phoenicians made use of the natural harbour, the area was then occupied by the Greeks in the 5th century BC. They called the town Antipolis (Antipolitana, Antipolitas) which eventually became Antibes. In due course the Romans took over the town and there are many signs of this occupation in the Vieille Ville. Most of the town was destroyed during the Barbarian invasions. When the frontier between Provence and the Italian states was moved in 1506 to the Rivière le Var, a tower called Tour St Jacques was built on the hill where the Fort Carré now stands. In 1585 it was reconstructed as a fort with 18 guns. Le Maréchal Vauban fortified the town, harbour and rebuilt Fort Carré in 1680. Napoleon was in charge of the coastal defences of the area in 1794 and installed his wife and family in Villa Sabe. It is said that he was later imprisoned in Fort Carré for a short time. When he landed at Golfe Juan in 1815 after his escape from the Isle of Elba he sent General Bertrand on ahead to Antibes to see what his reception would be, the general was captured and confined to Fort Carré. Napoleon therefore decided to advance NW towards Paris. With the expansion of tourism Antibes flourished along with other nearby towns. The harbour has been expanded several times and is now the port with the largest tonnage of yachts in Europe.

⚓ N of Fort Carré

Anchor in 3 to 4m sand and mud 300m offshore with the fort lying S. Open to N–NE–E. Coast road and shingle beach.

Head of Digue du Large   Port Vauban-Antibes

N of Fort Carré looking SE–S

132 PORT DE MARINA, BAIE DES ANGES
06270 Alpes-Maritimes

Position 43°38′N 7°08′·5E
Minimum depth in the entrance 5m (16ft)
in the harbour 5 to 2m (16 to 6·6ft)
Width of the entrance 60m
Maximum length overall 35m (115ft)
Number of berths 589
Population 1000 (approx)
Rating 3–3–3

General
A modern artificial yacht harbour that is a part of a major housing complex consisting of huge S-shaped pyramidal blocks of flats. Approach and entrance are not difficult but in strong winds from E–SE–S can become dangerous. The vast blocks of flats shelter the harbour from NW–N winds, but are rather overpowering and claustrophobic. E winds cause a heavy swell in the harbour.

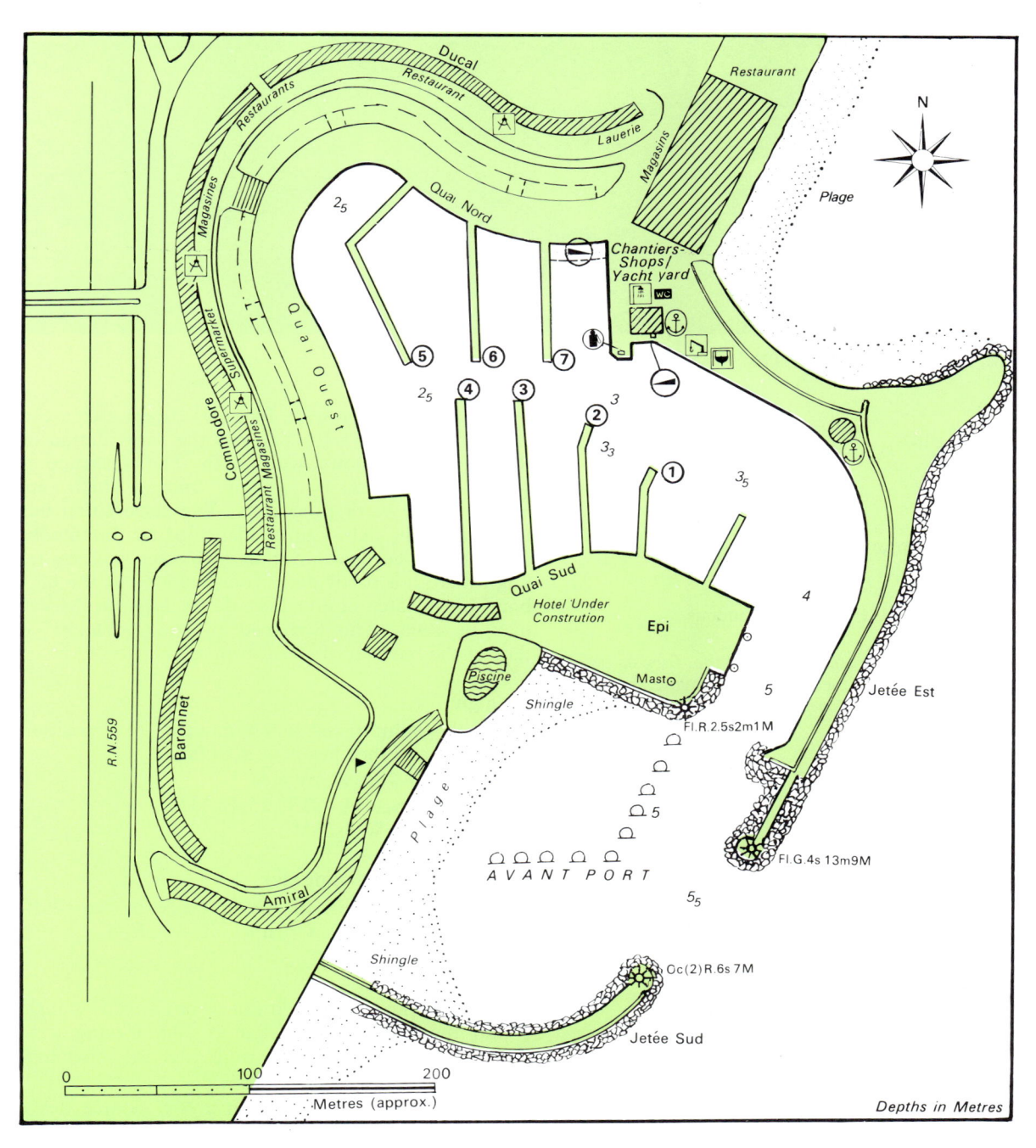

Port de Marina, Baie-des-Anges

South France Pilot

Port de Marina, Baie des Anges looking NW

Data

Charts Admiralty 2167
French 9265
Spanish 121
ECM 501

Magnetic variation 1°19′W (1990) decreasing by about 8′ each year.

Port radio VHF Ch 9, 16 (French). Continuous.

Weather forecasts Forecasts are posted at the *Bureau de Port* twice each day and there is an automatic prerecorded coastal forecast (*Navimet*).

Speed limit 3 knots.

Lights
Jetée Sud Head Oc(2)R.6s6m7M. White tower, red top.
Jetée Est Head Fl.G.4s13m9M. White tower, green top.
Epi elbow Fl.R.2·5s2m1M. Line.

Warning

In strong E winds, a heavy swell finds its way into the harbour.

Approach by day

From SW Round Cap d'Antibes at 500m onto a N course. Pass the conspicuous Vieille Ville d'Antibes with its two towers and large Fort Carré. The coast is then featureless until the high and unmistakable S-shaped pyramidal blocks of flats around this harbour are seen.

From NE Cross the wide Baie des Anges giving the delta of the Rivière Le Var and the construction of the airport extension a wide berth. The construction work is marked by yellow buoys which are moved as the work progresses. The airport that lies to the E of the delta can be identified by the intense air traffic. The concentration of houses at Cros-de-Cagnes are not particularly conspicuous but the harbour breakwater of the Port de St Laurent-du-Var may be seen. The S-shaped pyramidal blocks of flats at the harbour are seen from afar.

By night

Using the lights listed below navigate to a position where the entrance lies NW at 300m:
La Garoupe Fl(2)W.10s31M
Vauban Antibes Fl(4)WR.15s15/11M
Cap Ferrat Fl.W.3s25M

Anchorage in the approach

Anchor 300m to SE of the entrance in 8m (26ft) sand, mud and weed. Open to NE–E–SE–S.

Entrance

By day Approach the entrance on a NW course round the head of Jetée Est at 20m leaving it to starboard onto a NE course and enter the inner harbour.

By night Approach Fl.G.4s on a NW course, leave it 20m to starboard rounding it onto a NE course leaving Oc(2)R.6s and Fl.R to port.

74

Port de Marina, Baie des Anges

Berths
Secure stern to quay, bow to mooring chain in any vacant berth and report to the *Bureau de Port* for the allocation of a berth.

Formalities
Report to the *Bureau de Port* (☎ 93 20 01 60 ext 752 and 751, telex 470 697F) on arrival. Open 0900–1230 and 1430–1830, Saturday 0900–1200. Customs office is at Antibes (☎ 93 33 75 34) also at Marina Baie des Anges (☎ 93 20 01 60 ext 604).

Charges
There are harbour charges.

Facilities
Slip A slip in NE corner.
Travel-lift A travel-lift of 50 tonnes.
Cranes A 3-tonne crane, two mobile cranes of 5 tonnes.
Fuel Pumps for diesel (*gasoil*) and petrol are at the N side of the harbour, 0800–1930 in summer, 0800–1900 in winter. (☎ 93 20 01 60 ext 754, telex 470 679).
Water Water points on all quays and pontoons.
Electricity Supply points for 220v AC are on all quays and pontoons and 380v AC where there are deep-water berths.
Provisions A large supermarket 400m to NW, some shops round the harbour including a small supermarket and many more in Cros-de-Cagnes some 2M away.
Ice Ice is available in season from a shop beside the harbour.
Garbage Rubbish containers around the harbour.
Chandlery Three ships' chandlers beside the harbour.
Repairs A shipyard to the NE of the harbour where normal repairs to hull and engines can be undertaken.
Showers Ten showers and WCs alongside the harbour by the *Bureau de Port*.
Restaurant Several restaurants beside the harbour.
Yacht club Yacht Club International Baie des Anges (YCIBA) (☎ 93 31 56 89 and 93 31 24 45).
Information office At the *Bureau de Port*.
Lifeboats A small lifeboat is stationed here.
Beaches Shingle beaches either side of the harbour.
Communications Bus service, rail and air services at Nice.

Future development
Facilities are to be developed including hotels, more shops and restaurants, etc.

Head of Epi   Head of Jetée Est

Port de Marina Baie-des-Anges, entrance looking NW–N–NE from head of Jetée Sud

133 PORT DE CROS-DE-CAGNES
06800 Alpes-Maritimes

Position 43°39'·4E 7°10'·3E
Minimum depth in the entrance 2m (6·6ft)
in the harbour 1·8 to 1m (5·9 to 3·3ft)
Width of the entrance 30m
Maximum length overall 6m (20ft)
Number of berths 160
Population 22,195
Rating 4–3–4

General
A very small harbour for yachts and fishing craft of shallow draught. It is very crowded in the season. Approach and entry require care because of silting and are dangerous in strong winds from SE–S–SW. Facilities are limited.

Data
Charts Admiralty 2167
French 9265
Spanish 121
ECM 501

Magnetic variation 1°19'W (1990) decreasing by about 8' each year.

Jetée Sud   Entrance and head of Jetée Est

Port de Marina Baie-des-Anges, approach looking W

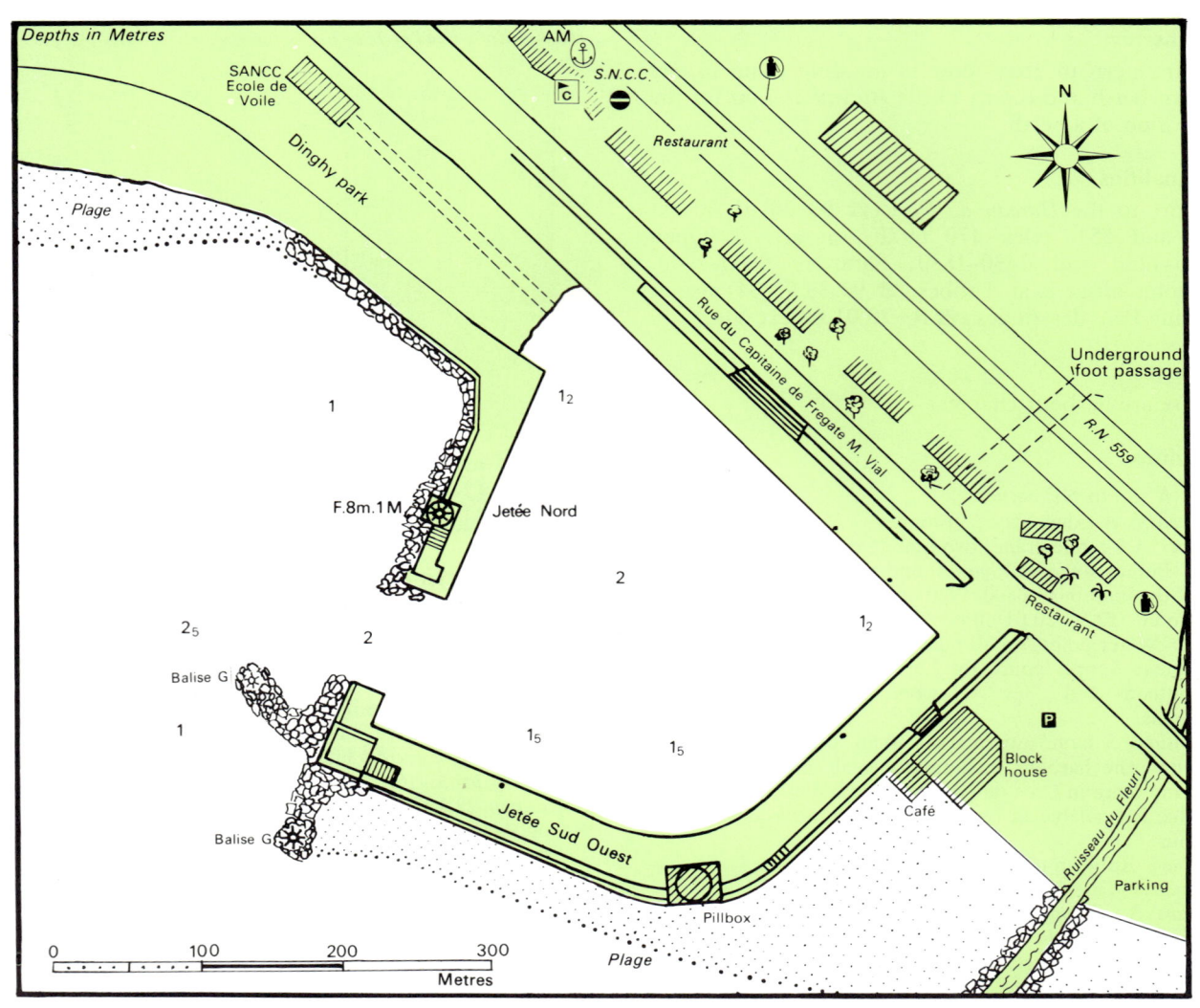

South France Pilot

Port de Cros-de-Cagnes

Weather forecasts The forecasts are posted each day at the Bureau de Port.

Speed limit 3 knots.

Lights
Jetée Nord F.8m1M. Grey-blue concrete pylon.

Marks Two small G beacons, ▲ topmarks, on SW jetty head spurs.

Warning
The depths in this harbour and in the entrance are very uncertain and alter during storms.

Approach by day
From SW Cross the wide Baie des Anges on a N course. The unique S-shaped pyramidal blocks of flats at Port de Marina Baie des Anges are very conspicuous. The coast to the NE is low and flat but the group of houses at Cros-de-Cagnes and the yellow clock tower's pointed roof will be seen. This harbour lies near a group of trees and there is a pale blue-grey light pylon at the entrance.

From NE Cross the Baie des Anges well outside the Var delta and the construction of the airport extension. The area is marked by Y buoys which are moved as work progresses. The airport just to the E of the delta is recognised by the intense air traffic. The group of houses at Cros-des-Cagnes will be seen with the S-shaped blocks of pyramidal flats in the distance. The harbour lies near a group of trees and there is a pale blue-grey light pylon at the entrance.

Entrance

Port de Cros-de-Cagnes, approach looking N

76

Port de Cros-de-Cagnes

Port de Cros-de-Cagnes looking NW

By night
Due to the lack of suitable navigational lights night approach and entry are not advised.

Anchorage in the approach
Anchor 300m to the SW of the entrance in 8m (26ft) sand and weed but take soundings first, because the bottom shelves steeply. Open to E–SE–S.

Entrance
By day Approach the coast about 200m to W of the entrance on a W heading, leaving the two spurs with small G beacons to starboard. When the entrance bears ENE turn to this course and enter.

Berths
Secure stern to the quay, bow to mooring chain in a vacant berth and report to the *Bureau de Port*.

Formalities
Report to the *Bureau de Port* (☎ 93 31 04 72) on arrival. There are customs available if required, contact *Bureau de Port*.

Charges
There are harbour charges.

Facilities
Hard There is a hard for dinghies in the NW corner of the harbour.
Fuel Petrol from garage in the town or service station on RN 559 to SE which has diesel (*gasoil*).
Water Some water points around the harbour.
Provisions A fair number of shops in the town nearby.
Garbage A few rubbish containers around the harbour.
Chandlery Several ships' chandlers in the town.
Repairs Repairs can be undertaken by local craftsmen.
Post office The nearest is about 2M away in Cagnes-sur-Mer.
Hotels Five ★★, seven ★ and several unclassified hotels.
Restaurants Three restaurants and a number of café/bars.
Yacht club The Société Nautique de Cros-de-Cagnes (SNCC) (☎ 93 31 37 09) has a clubhouse to the N of the harbour with bar, lounge, showers.
Information office The Syndicat d'Initiative has an office some 500m along the front in a W direction.
Lifeboats An all-weather lifeboat is stationed here (☎ 93 31 72 28).
Visits The Château-Musée de Cagnes and the Maison de Renoir should be visited.
Beaches Sandy beaches either side of this harbour.
Communications Bus service, rail and air services at Nice.

Future development
Minor improvements planned.

History
The Château de Grimaldi was built in the 14th century and as a centre of society on the coast remained in the family's possession until the Revolution. The artist Renoir spent the last twenty years of his life here.

South France Pilot

⚓ SE of Port de Cros de Cagnes

Sound carefully because it is deep to S and SW of this harbour, anchor in 5–10m sand and mud. Another close by 300–400m to ESE of this harbour. Many houses, shops, etc. ashore on the other side of the busy coast road. Open to SE–S–SW.

134 PORT DE SAINT LAURENT-DU-VAR
06700 Alpes Maritimes

Position 43°39′N 7°11′E
Minimum depth in the entrance 8m (26ft)
in the harbour 6 to 2·5m (20 to 8·2ft)
Width of the entrance 60m (approx)
Maximum length overall 50m (164ft)
Number of berths 1064
Population 15,500
Rating 3–3–3

General

A modern artificial yacht harbour that has been constructed on the W side of the mouth of the Rivière le Var. The harbour is easy to approach and enter but difficult and perhaps dangerous to enter with strong winds from SE–S–SW. Good protection once inside but a swell can be experienced with SW winds and big seas. All normal facilities are provided including shops and nearby is one of the largest hypermarkets in France. On the other side of the mouth of the Var is Nice airport which has frequent air services to many major international airports. The noise created by aircraft taking off and landing is considerable. The harbour is used as a 'garage' for yachts whose owners fly in from Paris and other centres to use them.

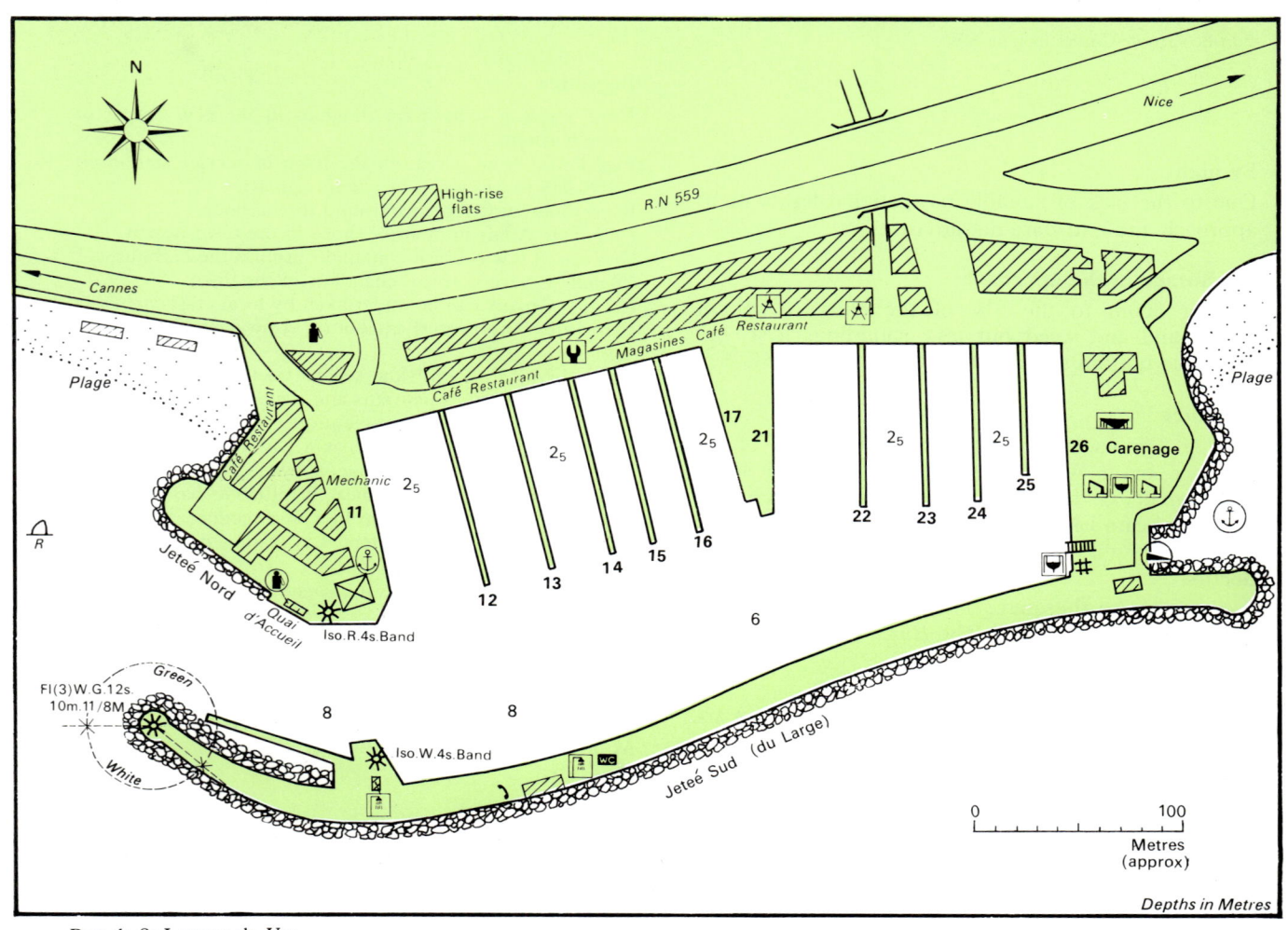

Port de St Laurent-du-Var

Port de St Laurent-du-Var

Port de St Laurent-du-Var looking E

Data

Charts Admiralty 2167
French 6952
Spanish 121
ECM 501

Magnetic variation 1°19′W (1990) decreasing by about 8′ each year.

Port radio VHF Ch 9, 16 (French). Continuous watch.

Weather forecasts Posted each day at the *Bureau de Port*. Automatic prerecorded forecast (*Navimet*) or ☎ 93 72 31 32.

Speed limit 3 knots.

Lights
Jetée du Large Head Fl(3)WG.12s11/8M. White tower, green top. 310°-W-090°-G-310.°
Jetée Nord Head Iso.R.4s (band).
Jetée du Large Spur Iso.W.4s (band).

Warning

It is forbidden to anchor inside the harbour.

Approach by day

From SW Cross the wide Baie des Anges towards the unmistakable 'S' curved pyramid-shaped blocks of flats at Port Marina Baie des Anges and then follow the coast along at 1M towards the E, passing the small town of Cros-des-Cagnes. The rocky breakwaters of this new harbour which are not very conspicuous will be seen short of the wide delta of the Rivière le Var and the airport. A tall block of flats to N of the entrance is conspicuous.

From NE Cross the wide Baie des Anges giving the airport at the E side of the mouth of the Rivière le Var a berth of 1M and passing to S of a line of Y buoys which mark construction work where the airport is being extended. (Note these buoys are moved as the work progresses). When the mouth of the river is N and a large road bridge can be seen, course may be set towards this harbour which can be identified by a long rocky breakwater. Do not muddle the many rocky beach groynes which lie between the harbour and the river mouth with the breakwater. These groynes are not continuous. A high-rise block, glass-faced with two white pillars, in the Var valley and an ordinary high-rise block of flats to N of the entrance will be recognised.

South France Pilot

By night
Using the following lights navigate to a position 2M to S of the harbour and approach Fl(3)WG.12s on a N heading:
La Garoupe Fl(2)W.10s31M
Antibes Fl(4)WR.15s15/11M
Marina Baie des Anges Fl.G.4s9M
Cap Ferrat Fl.W.3s25M

Anchorage in the approach
Anchor about 200m to W of the head of the Jetée du Large in 8m sand and mud. Open to E–SE–S.

Entrance
By day Approach the head of the Jetée du Large on a N course, round the head at 20m and enter on an ESE course.
By night Approach a Fl(3)WG.12s on a N course leaving it to starboard and rounding it at 20m onto an ESE course entering between Iso.R.4s (band) and Iso.W.4s (band).

Berths
On arrival secure to the Quai d'Accueil which is beside the fuel pump just inside the entrance to port for allocation of a berth. Then secure stern to berth as directed.

Formalities
Report to the *Bureau de Port* (☎ 93 07 12 70) on arrival at the Quai d'Accueil, open day and night. Customs at Antibes. (☎ 93 34 33 69 and 93 33 75 39).

Charges
There are harbour charges.

Facilities
Slips One at E end of the harbour.
Cranes Two cranes one of 4 tonnes, another of 6 tonnes at the *carénage*.
Travel-lift A travel-lift of 50 tonnes at the *carénage*.
Fuel Diesel (*gasoil*) and petrol from pumps just inside the entrance to port. Open 0800–2000 hours in summer (☎ 93 07 60 57 and 93 31 24 00).

High block of flats   Entrance

Port de St Laurent-du-Var, approach looking NE

Entrance   High block of

Port de St Laurent-du-Var, approach looking NW

Water Points along the quays and pontoons.
Electricity 220v AC points on quays and pontoons.
Provisions Hypermarket ½M to E can meet most requirements. More shops at St Laurent-de-Var.
Garbage Rubbish bins on the pontoons.
Chandlery Six chandlery shops in the area.
Repairs Sixteen yacht yards, a number of engine mechanics and an electronics mechanic and electrician in the area.
Yacht clubs Cercle Nautique de Port de St Laurent-du-Var (CNPLV) Ave Donaclei (☎ 93 02 53 73).
Post office At St Laurent-du-Var.

Tall block of flats   Bureau de Port

Port de St Laurent-du-Var, entrance looking N–NE

Port de St Laurent-du-Var

Fuel   Bureau de Port

Port de St Laurent du Var. Inside entrance looking N–NE–E

Aéroport buildings

Showers Three shower/WC blocks around the harbour.
Hotels Two **, one * and some pensions.
Restaurants Some restaurants and cafés near to the harbour, others at St Laurent-du-Var and at the airport.
Beach Sandy beach to E and W of the harbour.
Communications Rail, bus and air services nearby. Ferry service in season to and from Aéroport Nice-Côte d'Azur (☎ 93 21 30 83).

Future development
More service buildings and shops still to be constructed.

Aéroport Nice-Côte d'Azur looking SW

Delta du Rivière le Var
An important river which delivers much silt into the Baie des Anges. The road/rail bridge ½M inland and three chimneys are conspicuous as is a large glass-faced high-rise building of unique design beyond.

Aéroport Nice-Côte d'Azur
A very busy airport which is low lying and has been built out from the coast on the deposits brought down by the Rivière le Var. It is marked by a line of round Y buoys with a Y beacon ▼ topmark at each end of the line. It is prohibited to enter between the buoys except near the SW end where there is a landing pier for air passengers to be collected or put ashore. Areas at both ends of the runways are forbidden to yachts with masts higher than 4m (13ft). A small harbour is under construction near the NE end of the area.

Aéroport Nice-Côte d'Azur

Entrance   Port de Nice   Cap de Nice   Rade de Villefranche   *Cap Ferrat lighthouse*

Port de Nice approach

81

South France Pilot

135 PORT DE NICE
06000 Alpes-Maritimes

Position 43°41'·5N 7°17'·5E
Minimum depth in the entrance 10m (33ft)
                 in the harbour 7 to 2m (23 to 6·6ft)
Width of the entrance 63m
Maximum length overall 137m (449ft)
Number of berths 420
Population 400,000
Rating 1–2–2

General
An old natural port that is used by fishing boats, yachts and commercial craft, which has been improved by the construction of jetties, quays and pontoons. Nice is the largest town and port on this part of the coast but there is little accommodation for yachts. Approach and entrance are not difficult and good shelter is obtained, though swell in the outer harbour is uncomfortable in strong SE–S–SW winds and the seas may break in the entrance. There are good facilities and an attractive old town nearby.

Data
Charts Admiralty 149, 2167
        French 4708, 5176
        Spanish 121
        ECM 500, 501

Magnetic variation 1°14'W (1990) decreasing by about 8' each year.

Sea level In E–SE winds the sea level can rise up to 1m (3·3ft) under exceptional conditions.

Current A weak current flows out of the harbour.

Air radiobeacon
Nice. Mont Leuza (43°43'·7N 7°20'·2E) LEZ (·—··/·/———··) 398·5 kHz 75M Continuous.

Port radio VHF Ch 8, 12, 16 (French and English). Continuous

Weather forecasts Posted at 0835 each day outside the *Bureau de Port* also automatic prerecorded coastal forecast (*Navimet*) or ☎ 93 72 31 32.

Speed limit 3 knots.

Port de Nice looking NW

Port de Nice

Port de Nice

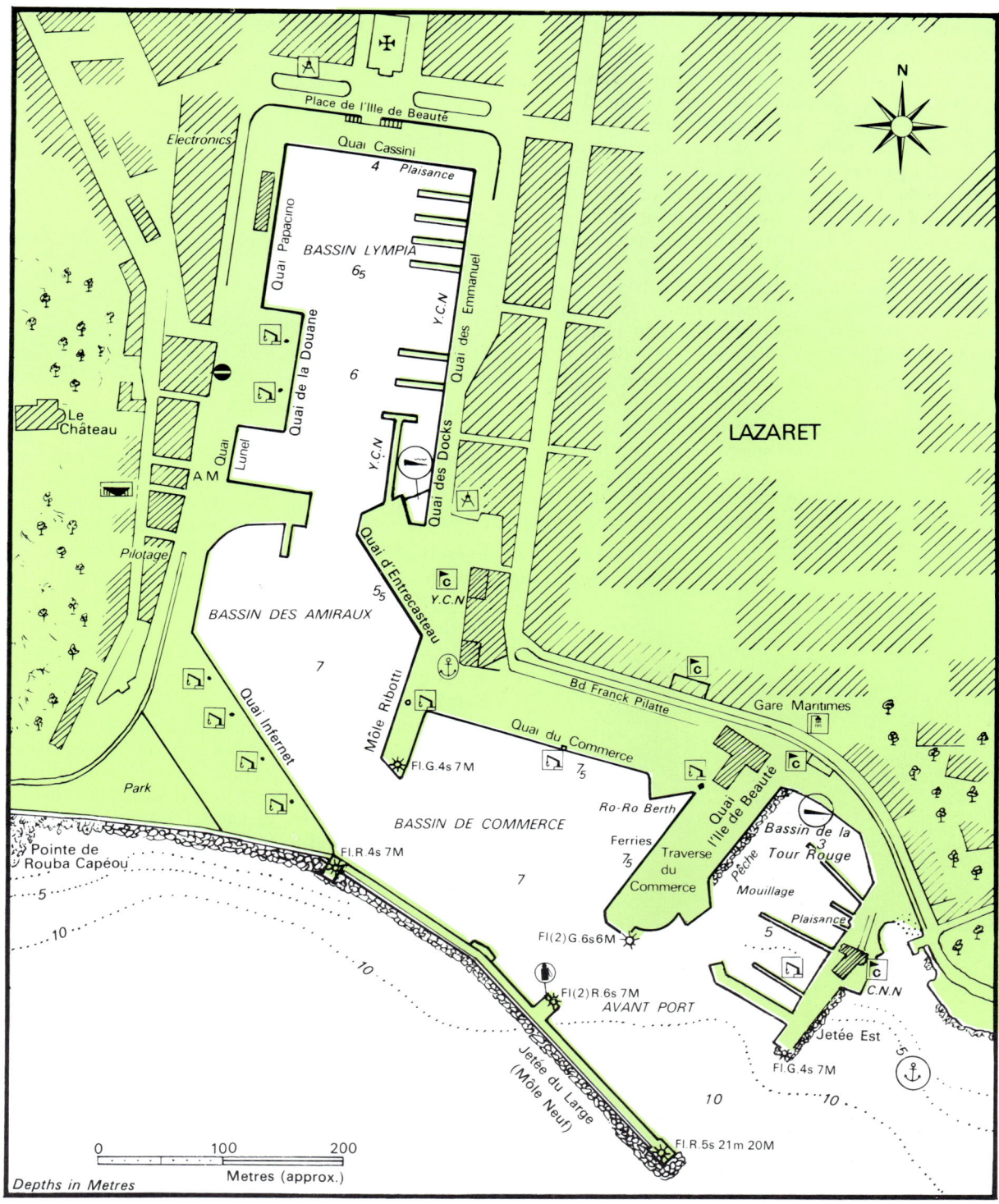

Lights
Jetée du Large Head Fl.R.5s21m20M. White square tower, red lantern.
Môle Neuf Spur Fl(2)R.6s6m7M. White column red top.
Root Fl.R.4s6m7M Red column.
Jetée Est Head Fl.G.4s5m7M. White column, green top.
Traverse du Commerce Head Fl(2)G.6s6m6M. White column, green top.
Môle Ribotti Head Fl.G.4s6m7M. White column.

Warning
Because commercial craft have right of way in this harbour and must not be obstructed, entrance and exit should not be attempted when large craft are manoeuvring. Sailing craft do not have automatic right of way over power craft in the area.

South France Pilot

Approach by day
From SW Cross the wide Baie des Anges to S of a series of Y buoys which mark the airport extension under construction, keeping well clear of the delta of the Rivière le Var. The airport just E of the mouth of the river will be located by the considerable air traffic. From this area a solid line of buildings on the coast stretch to Nice harbour with the exception of a small tree-covered break at Mont de le Château just W of the port. This hill has a large monument carved into its S face. Beyond the port, Mont Boron is high and steep-sided and has a large pink-coloured building, Château Smith (Smythe), on its face. In the closer approach the light tower at head of Jetée du Large is easily seen.

From NE Round the sloping promontory of Cap Ferrat which has a conspicuous signal station, lighthouse and hotel. Cross the deep Rade de Villefranche and round the steep-sided Pointe des Sans-Culottes at the SE end of Mont Boron, this hill has a large pink house and many blocks of flats on its SW face. The harbour mouth opens up when this feature has been passed.

Le Château   Entrance

Port de Nice, approach looking NE

Monument   Le Château   Entrance   Cap de Nice

Port de Nice, approach looking NW

By night
Using the lights listed below navigate to a position where the head of Jetée du Large is N 300m:
La Garoupe Fl(2)W.10s31M
Cap Ferrat Fl.W.3s25M

Anchorage in the approach
Anchor 500m to NE of the head of Jetée du Large in 5m (16ft) mud and weed. Open to SE–S–SW–W.

Entrance
By day Approach the head of Jetée du Large and round it at 30m leaving it to port and continue on a NNW course up the harbour parallel to the jetty. After 400m change to a N course into the inner basins.

By night Approach Fl.R.5s on a N course and leave it 30m to port, changing to a NW course leaving Fl.G.4s to starboard. Pass between Fl(2)R.6s and Fl(2)G.6s lights and then between Fl.R.4s and Fl.G.4s. On passing the last Fl.G.4s alter to a N course.

Berths
Quai des Emmanuel Secure stern to pontoon bow to mooring buoy in a vacant space and report to *Bureau de Port*.

YCN pontoon Secure stern to pontoon, bow to chain in a vacant space. If there are no spaces secure temporarily to a commercial quay. Yachts on this quay must leave a crew on board who can move the yacht if required. In all cases report to the *Bureau de Port* at once and to the Yacht Club de Nice.

Moorings
There are yacht moorings in the Bassin de la Tour Rouge which may be vacant, apply to the Club Nautique de Nice on quay to SE of the Bassin.

Formalities
Report to the *Bureau de Port* (☎ 93 89 50 85), open day and night in summer on arrival and if on a yacht club pontoon or on a mooring to the yacht club concerned. If arriving at night in winter when the *Bureau de Port* is closed a plan will be found outside showing when commercial craft are due to berth on the various quays. There is a customs office to NW of the port (☎ 93 55 42 42) at 4 Quai de la Douane.

Charges
There are harbour charges.

Facilities
Slipway There is a 3-tonne slipway in the Avant Port.
Slips There are small slips in the Avant Port and another behind the YCN pontoon.
Cranes There are six cranes of 6 tonnes and one of 12 tonnes around the harbour.

Port de Nice

Bureau de Port

Port de Nice looking N–NE–E–SE

Fuel Diesel (*gasoil*) and petrol are available from pumps on the spur of the Digue du Large or by tanker lorry (☎ 93 01 70 70) 0800–1700 hours.
Water Some water points around the harbour.
Electricity A few 220v AC supply points on the quays and on the pontoons.
Provisions Very many shops of all types and quality nearby and also a market and fish market.
Ice From Albertini, a grocer, close to the NW corner of the harbour.
Duty-free goods It is possible to obtain duty-free goods here by applying to the customs.
Garbage A very limited number of rubbish containers around the port.
Chandlery Several ships' chandlers round the port.
Repairs Many shipyards and mechanics can repair hulls, engines and electronic gear, also a sailmaker.
Laundrette Several in the town, one is to SE of the railway station at 16 rue d'Angleterre.
Post office The PTT is some distance away to S of the railway station.
Showers 4 showers and 6 WCs.
Hotels Three *****, nine ****, forty ***, ninety **, sixty-nine * and many unclassified hotels.
Restaurants Over 173 restaurants and many café/bars of all types and quality.
Yacht clubs The Yacht Club de Nice (YCN) (☎ 93 89 44 17) has an office to the E of the harbour and a pontoon with limited services on it including showers. The Club Nautique de Nice (CNN) (☎ 93 89 39 78) has a clubhouse with a restaurant, bar, lounge, showers, etc. to the E of the entrance at Blvd Frank-Pilatte where they have a basin with moorings. There are several other clubs including La Mouette ASCE (☎ 93 88 59 26) and Cercle du Yachting Léger International de la Côte d'Azur (☎ 93 88 89 82).
Information office The office of the Syndicat d'Initiative is some way away located at Acropolis d'Esplanade Kennedy to the N of the Casino Municipal (☎ 93 92 82 82). There is another next to the railway station (☎ 93 87 07 07) and at the airport (☎ 93 83 32 64).
Lifeboats A small 2nd-class lifeboat stationed here.
Visits Very many interesting places to visit including no less then seven museums. Many Roman ruins and some fine gardens round Le Château.
Beach A long beach to the W of the harbour.
Communications Rail, bus and air services. There are also sea services to North and South America and Mediterranean ports. A ferry service in season from the harbour to a landing pier at Nice-Côte d'Azur airport (☎ 93 21 30 83).

Future development
A new commercial harbour is to be developed at the airport extension that is under construction. When completed it will be fully developed into a yacht harbour.

History
This harbour was first developed by the Greeks as an outpost of their colony at Marseille (Nikiai) in the 4th century BC and they called their village at the foot of Mont de Château 'Niki' (Victory). The Romans arriving in the 2nd century BC established Cemenlum a mile inland which is now Cimiez and together with Niki, were destroyed in the Barbarian invasion. In the 11th century the town, now Nice, became a free town but in 1388 it became part of Savoy (Savoie) which lasted until 1860. In the 18th century Le Château was razed to the ground and in the next century the harbour was expanded as the town developed into a famous resort.

Cap de Nice
A conspicuous headland (178m) surmounted by Mont Boron (191m). The lower part of Cap de Nice is covered with large apartment buildings. This headland is steep-to with a few small rocks close inshore.

⚓ W side of the Rade de Villefranche
Anchor in 5–6m mud and rocks close inshore 1M to N of the Pointe des Sans-Culottes which lies to the head of the Rade open to S with swell from both SE and SW. Steep cliffs and hills ashore with the coast road halfway up, many houses near the N point.

South France Pilot

Port de Villefranche Rade looking N   *Entrance*   *Citadelle*

Port de Villefranche looking NW

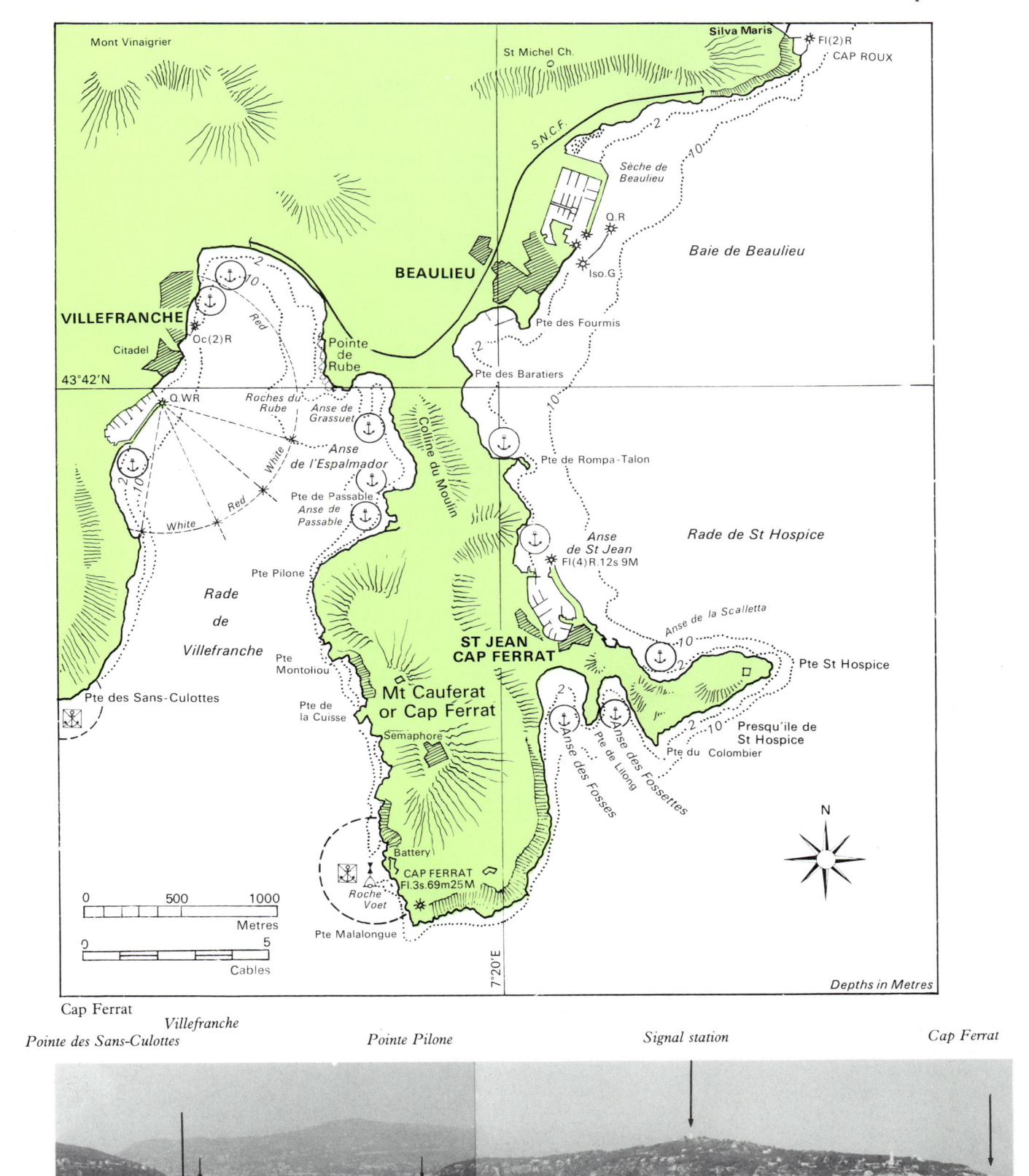

Cap Ferrat

Port de Villefranche-sur-Mer, entrance to Rade de Villefranche looking NNE–NE

South France Pilot

136 PORT DE VILLEFRANCHE-SUR-MER
06230 Alpes-Maritimes

Position 43°42'·0N 7°18'·7E
Minimum depth in entrance 5m (16ft)
 in harbour 4 to 1m (13 to 3·3ft)
 in Darse Nord 0·7 to 0·5m (2·3 to 1·6ft)
Width of the entrance 30m
Maximum length overall 60m (197ft), visitors 16m (52ft)
Number of berths 400
Population 7500
Rating 1–1–2

General
A very attractive old town and surroundings with two harbours, one small shelter-type harbour the Darse Nord (or de la Santé) to the N of the Citadelle, normally used by fishing craft, and a larger yacht harbour, the Darse Sud to the S of the Citadelle. The facilities and protection offered by the Darse Sud are excellent, the Darse Nord offers some protection but very few facilities. Approach and entrance to both harbours is simple though in strong winds from S–SW the Rade can be rough. Both harbours are very crowded in the season.

Data
Charts Admiralty 149, 2167
 French 4708, 5176
 Spanish 121
 ECM 500, 501

Magnetic variation 1°14'W (1990) decreasing by about 8' each year.

Air radiobeacons
Nice. Mont Leuza (43°43'·7E 7°20'·2E) LEZ (·—··/·/——··) 398·5 kHz 75M Continuous.

Weather forecasts Posted daily and an automatic pre-recorded coastal forecast at the *Bureau de Port* (*Navimet*) or ☎ 93 83 00 25.

Speed limit 3 knots.

Port radio VHF Ch 9 (French).

Lights
Darse Sud Môle Est head Q.WR.8m12/8M. White hut, red lantern, white cupola. 009°-R-286°-W-311°-R-335°-W-009°
Darse Nord Môle de la Santé head Oc(2)R.6s10m7M. White column, red top and base.

Warning
There are a number of large unlit mooring buoys in the Rade. Sailing vessels do not have their normal right of way over power craft when in the Rade. The head of the bay is marked off for bathers in the season. Anchorage off the town is deep with indifferent holding. There are two areas NW of Cap Ferrat where anchorage and fishing are prohibited and one off the Pointe des San-Culottes also near a small isolated rock, La Roche Voet. It lies close inshore to W of Cap Ferrat and is marked by a W Card YBY beacon ⚑ topmark. (See chart page 87).

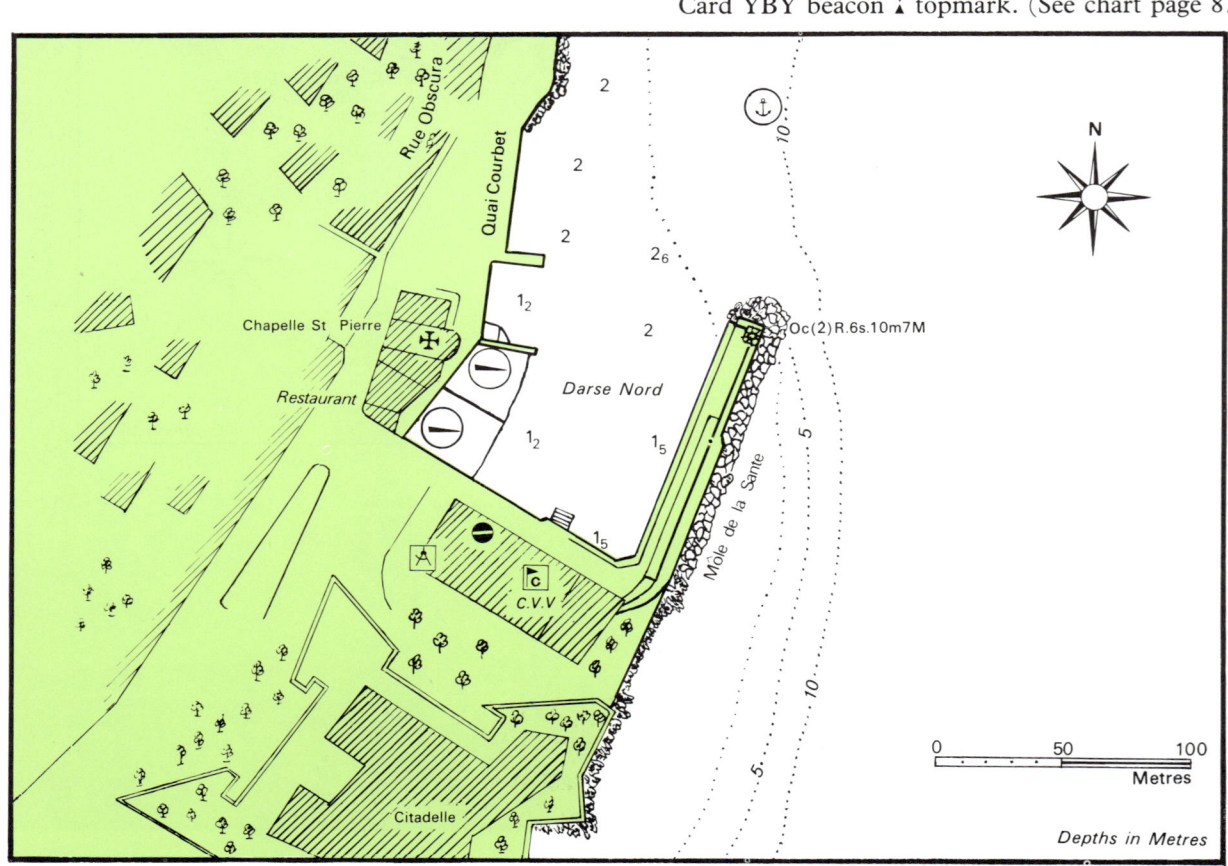

Port de Villefranche-sur-Mer (Darse Nord)

Port de Villefranche-sur-Mer

Entrance to Darse Sud   Citadelle   Entrance to Darse Nord

Port de Villefranche-sur-Mer, approach looking NW

Approach by day
From SW Cross the wide Baie des Anges towards Cap Ferrat, passing the entrance to Nice and rounding Pointe des Sans-Culottes at the SE corner of Mont Boron, a high hill with a conspicuous large pink house, Château Smith (Smythe) and many blocks of flats on its SW face. Follow the coast around onto a N course. The Darse Sud lies 1M from the point and has a very conspicuous Citadelle just beyond its entrance. The Darse Nord is located to N of the Citadelle.

From NE Cross the mountain-lined Baie de Beaulieu and round the low tree-covered Pointe St Hospice which is followed by the higher sloping Cap Ferrat with signal station and lighthouse on its summit, a large hotel on its S face and a lighthouse on its SW point. Follow the coast in a NNW direction. The town of Villefranche will be seen from a distance and the Citadelle is conspicuous in the closer proach. The entrance to the Darse Sud lies just S of of the Citadelle and the Darse Nord to N of it.

By night
Using the lights listed below navigate to a position from where the entrance to the Darse Sud lies 200m to N. Note the sectored light on the Môle Est head which may assist:
Cap Ferrat Fl.W.3s25M
Nice Fl.R.5s20M
Môle de la Santé Oc(2)R.6s7M

Anchorage in the approach
Anchor 150m to S of Môle Est head in 10m (33ft) mud, sand and weed, open to SE–S–SW, or on the opposite side of the Rade de Villefranche, open to S–SW.

Port de Villefranche-sur-Mer, entrance to Darse Sud looking S

Entrance
Darse Sud
By day Approach the head of Môle Est and round it at 20m leaving it to port on the SW course.

By night Approach Q.WR on a N course and leave it 20m to port, rounding it onto a SW course. The sectored light will assist navigation.

Entrance
Darse Nord
By day Round the head of Môle de la Santé at 20m to port into the harbour.

By night Round Oc(2)R.6s at 20m to port.

Berths
Darse Sud Secure in a vacant berth and report to the *Bureau de Port* which is located at the head of Darse Sud, for the allocation of a berth.

Port de Villefranche-sur-Mer, Darse Nord looking NE–E

Darse Nord Secure in a vacant berth on inner side of Môle de la Santé and apply to harbourmaster at head of the Darse (only short-term berths available).
Quai Courbet Short-term berths, stern to road to NW of Darse Nord using the yacht's anchor with a trip-line.

Anchorages

Anchor to N of Darse Nord about 100m from the shore in 10m mud and sand, holding unreliable. Open to SE–S–SW.

Citadelle

Port de Villefranche-sur-Mer. Darse Sud looking N

Formalities

Report to the *Bureau de Port* at Darse Sud (☎ 93 01 70 70) on arrival. Open 0700–1900 in summer, 0730–1800 in winter, or to harbourmaster at Darse Nord. Customs (☎ 93 01 71 21) at Darse Nord if necessary.

Charges

There are harbour charges.

Facilities

Slip A slip to the W of both harbours.
Slipway Three slipways of 20 to 40 tonnes on the W side of Darse Sud.
Dry dock A dry dock at the S end of the Darse Sud which will take 150-tonne vessels up to 65m long, 8·25m beam and 3·5m draught.
Cranes There are two cranes to the S of the Darse Sud one of 6 tonnes and the other of 1 tonne. A 1-tonne crane at Darse Nord and a mobile crane of 25 tonnes.
Fuel Diesel (*gasoil*) and petrol are available from pumps at the head of a pontoon in the Darse Sud.
Water Water points on all quays and CMV pontoons.
Electricity Supply points 220v AC are available on quays and CMV pontoons.
Provisions Many shops in the town nearby.
Ice Available in summer at the Quai de la Corderie.
Duty-free goods Apply to the customs at the Darse Nord. There is a supply shop close by.
Garbage Some rubbish bins around the harbour.
Repairs Major repairs to large yachts can be undertaken here and there is an electrician and radio mechanic in the town.
Laundrette Several laundrettes in the town.
Post office The PTT is to the NW of the Citadelle in Avenue Albert 1er.
Hotels Seven ***, eleven **, three * and many unclassified hotels.
Restaurants Over thirty-five restaurants and many café/bars.
Yacht clubs The Club de la Mer de Villefranche (CMV) (☎ 93 01 84 18 and 93 01 72 16) has a clubhouse to NW of the Darse Sud with restaurant, bar, lounge, terrace, showers, etc. The Club de la Voile de Villefranche (CVV) has a clubhouse to S of Darse Nord with similar facilities.
Information office The Syndicat d'Initiative has an office just NE of the sports stadium in Jardin Franco Binon (☎ 93 01 73 68).

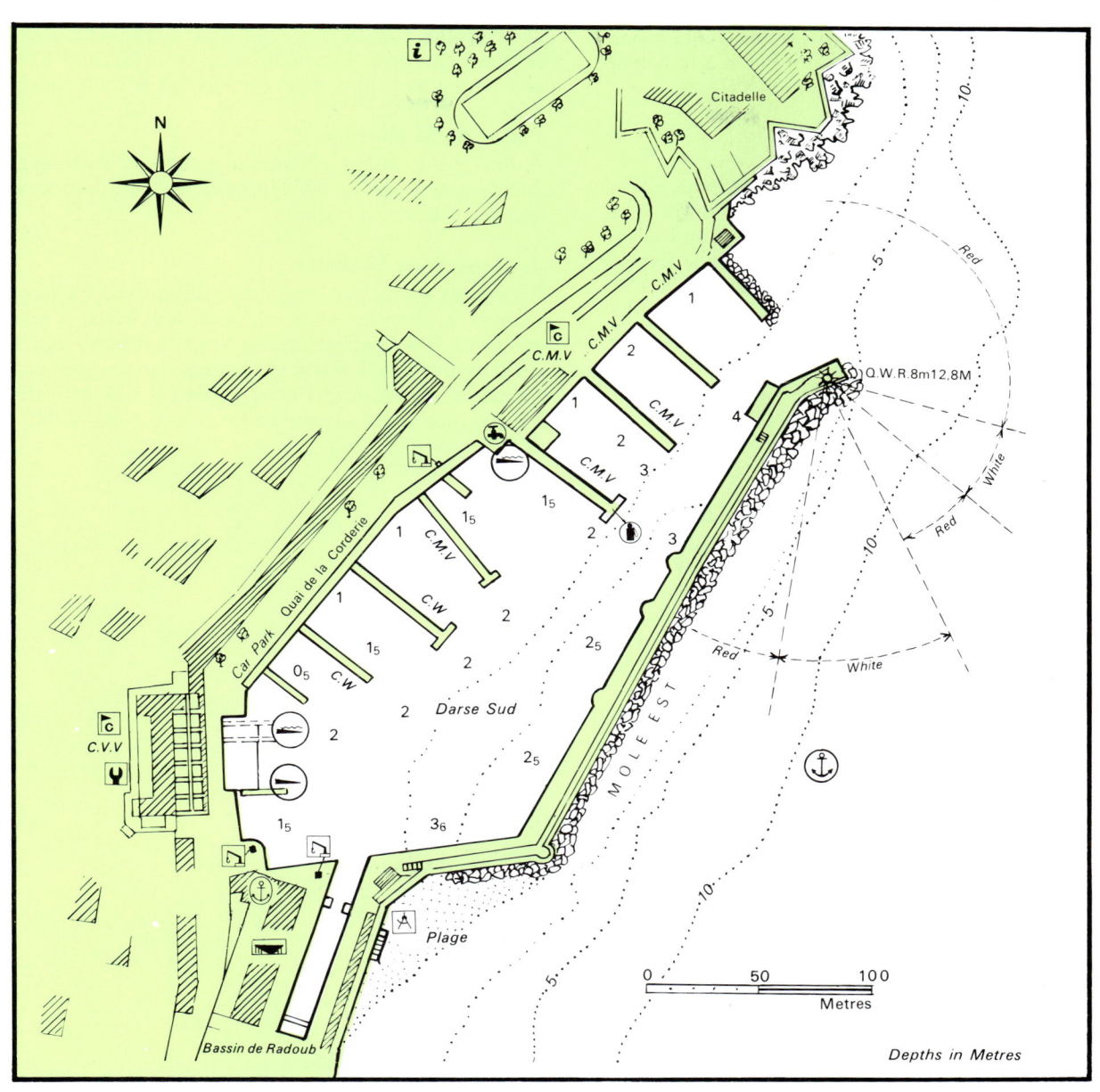

Port de Villefranche-sur-Mer (Darse Sud)

Visits The old town near the church with its narrow streets and stairways should be visited also the Chapelle St Pierre which has been decorated by Jean Cocteau. The Citadelle is worth a visit as is the medieval underground road – La rue Obscure.

Beach A nice little pebble beach near the root of Môle Est.

Communications Rail and bus services, air services at Nice.

Future development

There are plans for the development of a new and separate yacht harbour.

History

First recorded in the year 130 BC Villefranche remained a small fishing harbour until in the 14th century it became a 'Freeport' during the time of Charles II of Anjou. The Citadelle was built in 1557. The Rade has been used as a fleet anchorage by the French and other nations for hundreds of years.

⚓ Head of the Rade de Villefranche

A large area with a bottom of mud and weed covering the upper third part of the Rade offers a good anchorage in 2–3m surrounded by high hills covered with houses. Open to S. There are two large mooring buoys in the area, anchorage is not permitted between them.

⚓ E side of the Rade de Villefranche

Three anchorages are available in 5m mud and weed, the first off Pointe du Rube in Anse de Grasseut. Look out for shallows and rocks off the Pointe du Rube. Some 300–400m further S in the Anse de l'Espalmador is the second and S of Pointe de Pass-

South France Pilot

able in the Anse de Passable is the third. The coast near these anchorages is lower and has a number of large houses with gardens. Open to S–SW.

Cap Ferrat
A conspicuous high (132m) promontory with a distinctive tall (32m) white eight-sided light tower with a green band located on its SW extremity and a signal station at the highest point. Anchoring, fishing and diving are forbidden 2M to W and S of Cap Ferrat and a similar area exists 200m off Pointe des Sans Culottes. A W Card YBY beacon topmark marks Roche Voet 300m to NW of the lighthouse and near a battery position, diving fishing and anchoring are also forbidden here. (See plan page 87).

⚓ Les Fosses and les Fossettes
Two pleasant and popular anchorages divided by the thin promontory of Pointe de Lilong which has a high wall at its head and is surrounded by low rocky cliffs with large houses, pine woods and gardens. Both bays have shingle beaches. Les Fosses has two rocks near its head, and four large blocks of a ruined jetty on W side. Anchor in 4–5m sand and weed with Pointe de Lilong bearing E. Les Fossettes has a rock close inshore on its E side and also off Pointe du Colombier. Anchor 100m to S of the head of the bay in 5m sand and weed. These anchorages are open to S with swell from SE and SW, and have a road to St Jean-Cap Ferrat at their head.

Pointe de St Hospice
A low rocky-cliffed promontory covered with trees and several large houses and gardens. On its summit is a low tower and chapel.

⚓ Anse de la Scalletta
A popular semi-open anchorage often used by large yachts. Anchor in 3–5m in sand and weed. There are rocks close inshore off the head of the bay which is surrounded by a few large houses and gardens and a road to St Jean-Cap Ferrat. There is a beach café, a restaurant and a shingle beach. Open NW–N–NE.

Anse des Fossettes   *Cap d'A*

Pointe de St Hospice looking NE

Signal station

Cap Ferrat looking E

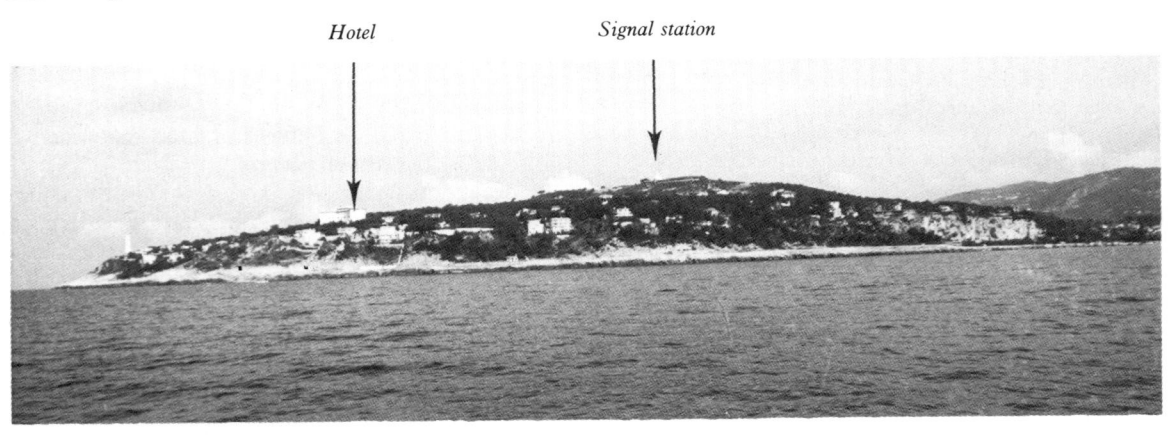

Hotel   *Signal station*

Cap Ferrat looking W

92

Cap Ferrat anchorages

Pointe de Lilong

Anse des Fossettes

⚓ *Espalmador* *Pointe de Passable* ⚓ *S of Pointe de Passable*

Espalmador and S of Pte de Passable looking E

Pointe du Rube ⚓ *Grassuet* ⚓ *Espalmador* *Pointe de Passable*

Anse de Grasseut and Anse de l'Espalmador looking E

Pointe du Rube

Anse de Grasseut looking E

South France Pilot

Les Fosse et Fossettes

Anse de la Scalletta looking NW

137 PORT DE ST JEAN-CAP FERRAT
06230 Alpes-Maritimes

Position 43°41′·4N 7°20′·2E
Minimum depth in the entrance 4·5m (15ft)
in the harbour 4·5 to 2·5m (15 to 8·2ft)
Width of the entrance 50m
Maximum length overall 28m (92ft)
Number of berths 560
Population 2300
Rating 2–3–3

General
An old and small fishing harbour in attractive surroundings that has been considerably enlarged and turned into a major yachting harbour. Approach and entrance need care especially in NE–E–SE winds and swell. A pleasant harbour to visit. Facilities are fair and everyday supplies are available.

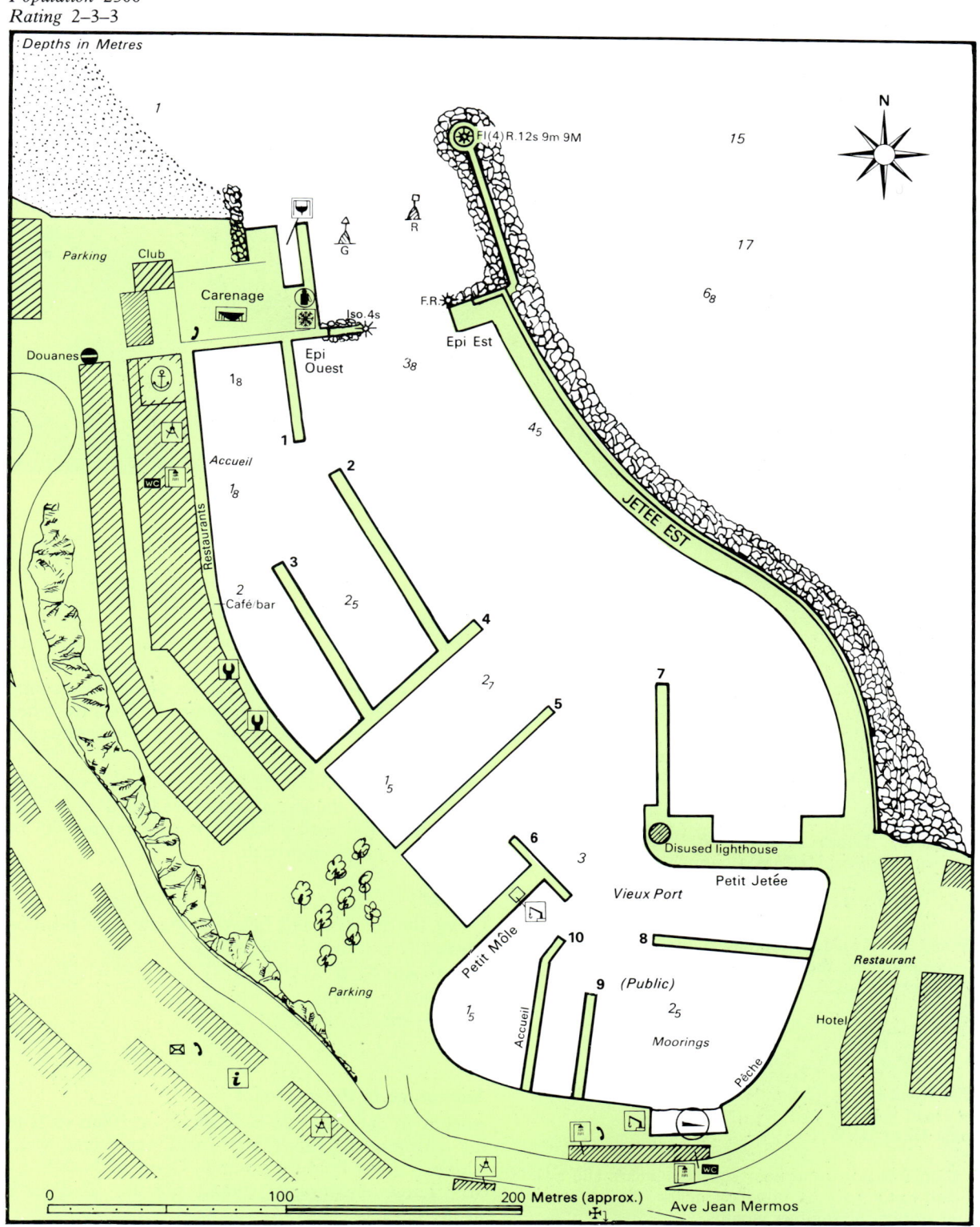

Port de St Jean-Cap Ferrat

South France Pilot

Port St Jean-Cap Ferrat looking N

Data

Charts Admiralty 2167
French 5176
Spanish 121
ECM 500

Magnetic variation 1°14′W (1990) decreasing by about 8′ each year.

Air radiobeacon
Nice. Mont Leuza (43°43′·7N 7°20′·2E LEZ (·—··/·/——··) 398·5 kHz 75M. Continuous.

Port radio VHF Ch 9 (French).

Weather forecasts Posted once a day at the *Bureau de Port* and also automatic prerecorded coastal forecast (*Navimet*) or ☎ 93 83 00 25.

Speed limit 3 knots.

Lights
Jetée Est Head Fl(4)R.12s9m9M. White column, red top.
Epi Est Head F.R
Epi Ouest Head Iso.W.4s

Buoys A small R port-hand buoy square topmark and a G starboard-hand buoy ▲ topmark mark the entrance channel during the summer months.

Approach by day

From SW Round the high sloping Cap Ferrat which has a conspicuous signal station on top and a lighthouse with a large hotel at its point. Also round the low tree-covered rocky Pointe St Hospice when the rocky Jetée Est will be seen with a light tower at the entrance.

From NE Cross the wide Baie de Beaulieu on a SW course towards the signal station at Cap Ferrat. The rocky Jetée Est with a light tower at its end will be seen in the closer approach.

By night

Using the lights listed below navigate to a position where the entrance is 300m to W:
Cap Ferrat Fl.W.3s25M
Beaulieu Q.R.10M
Silva Maris Fl(2)R.6s8M

Anchorage in the approach

Anchor in the Anse de la Scalletta or 200m to E of the entrance in 8m (26ft) rock, sand and weed which is poor holding ground. Open to N–NE–E–SE. These anchorages should not be used in a strong E wind.

Port de St Jean-Cap Ferrat

Entrance   Signal station

Port de St Jean-Cap Ferrat, approach looking SSW

Port de St Jean-Cap Ferrat entrance

Entrance

By day Approach the head of Jetée Est on a W course, round it at 20m leaving it to port and enter the harbour in mid-channel between a R and G buoy (summer).

By night Approach Fl(4)R.12s on a W course, leave it 20m to port and round it onto a S course, enter the harbour in mid-channel leaving F.R to port and Iso.W (line) to starboard.

Berths
Proceed to berths Nos 322–331 marked 'Accueil' in the Nouveau Port and secure stern-to. Report to the *Bureau de Port*. A call on VHF Ch 9 from 1M off is advised.

Formalities
Report to the *Bureau de Port* (☎ 93 76 04 56) on arrival open 0600–2200. Customs are at Beaulieu-sur-Mer (☎ 93 01 16 00) and a sub-office to N of harbour.

Charges
There are harbour charges.

Facilities
Slip A slip at the S end of the harbour.
Travel-lift A travel-lift near the entrance of 38 tonnes.
Cranes A crane of 15 tonnes near the clubhouse.
Fuel Diesel (*gasoil*) and petrol are available from pumps at the Epi Ouest just inside the entrance 0830–2000 hours in summer and 0830–1300 out of season and at weekends (☎ 93 01 47 47).
Water Water points are to be found on all quays and pontoons.
Electricity Supply points are to be found on all quays and pontoons of 220v AC also 380v AC on the berths with deep water.
Provisions There are some shops in the village and many more in Beaulieu about 1M away.
Ice Ice is delivered by van to the harbour during the season, also from fuel station.
Garbage Rubbish containers are established around the harbour.
Chandlery Three ships' chandlers to SW of the harbour and in the village.
Repairs A small shipyard where all normal repairs can be carried out established near the entrance.
Laundrette A laundrette in the village.
Post office A PTT is in the village.
Hotels One ****, one ***, three **, two * and ten unclassified hotels.
Restaurants Nine restaurants and a number of café/bars.
Yacht club The Sociétés Régates de St Jean-Cap Ferrat, Centre Municipal Sportive, Place G.Clemenceau (☎ 93 01 38 65) and the International Sporting Club de St Jean-Cap Ferrat (ISCSJCF) (☎ 93 06 58 37) has a small office to the W of the harbour. The Club Nautique TSC (☎ 93 06 55 10). Base Nautique St Jean-Cap Ferrat.
Showers Showers are at the S and W sides of the harbour. Keys from the *Bureau de Port*.
Lifeboat A small lifeboat is stationed here.

Tête du Chien   Bureau de Port   Fuel   Visitors' berths

Port de St Jean-Cap Ferrat looking N–NE–E–SE

South France Pilot

Information office The Syndicat d'Initiative has an office in the village.
Visits In addition to some excellent coastal walks there is a zoo and a museum.
Beaches Sandy and pebble beaches to NW of the harbour.

Future development
Facilities to be improved.

⚓ N of Pointe Rompa-Talon

A shallow anchorage in 2–3m rock, weed and sand, to be used with care. Low rocky cliffs, a footpath to Beaulieu/St Jean-Cap Ferrat and a few houses. Open to N–NE–E.

---

138 PORT DES FOURMIS
06310 Alpes-Maritimes

Position 43°42'·3N 7°20'·0E
Minimum depth in the entrance 1·5m (4·9ft)
in the harbour 1·5 to 0·5m (4·9 to 1·6ft)
Width of the entrance 20m
Number of berths 60
Population 4300 (Beaulieu)
Rating 3-4-4

General
A very small fishing and yachting harbour only suitable for shallow-draught craft. Approach and entrance would be difficult and dangerous in winds and seas from NE–E–SE. Facilities are very limited but the surroundings are very attractive.

Data

Charts   Admiralty 2167
French 5176
Spanish 121
ECM 500

Magnetic variation 1°14'W (1990) decreasing by about 8' each year.

Air radiobeacons
Nice. Mont Leuza (43°43'·7N 7°20'·2E) LEZ (·—··/·/———··) 398·5 kHz 75M. Continuous.

Speed limit 3 knots.

Warning
The sea bed in and around the entrance is very uneven and a good lookout should be kept from the bow for underwater obstructions and rocks.

Approach by day
From SW Round the low rocky tree-covered Pointe St Hospice and cross the Rade on a NNW course towards a conspicuous house on Pointe des Fourmis, Villa Kerylos, which has a flat roof and stands to the E of this harbour.

Entrance   *Villa*

Port des Fourmis, approach looking NW

From NE Cross the Baie de Beaulieu on a SW course. The Villa Kerylos referred to above will be seen to the S of the town of Beaulieu with the harbour backed by some ornamental public gardens just W of the Villa.

By night
Approach and entry at night are not recommended due to the lack of navigational lights, and dangerous rocky shallows.

Anchorage in the approach
Anchor 400m to SE of the entrance in 6m (20ft) sand, rock and weed, but the holding is not good. Open to NE–E–SE.

Entrance
By day Approach the entrance with care on a NW course and round the head of Jetée Sud at 10m onto N course.

Berths
Secure stern to pontoons or quay with anchor from bow in a vacant space and report to the *gardien* for the allocation of a berth.

Formalities
Report to the *gardien* on arrival.

Charges
There are harbour charges.

Facilities
Slip A small slip in the E corner of the harbour.
Slipway A small slipway in E corner of the harbour.
Crane A 2-tonne crane on the central pontoon.
Fuel From a garage nearby.
Water Supply points on the quays and pontoons.

Port des Fourmis

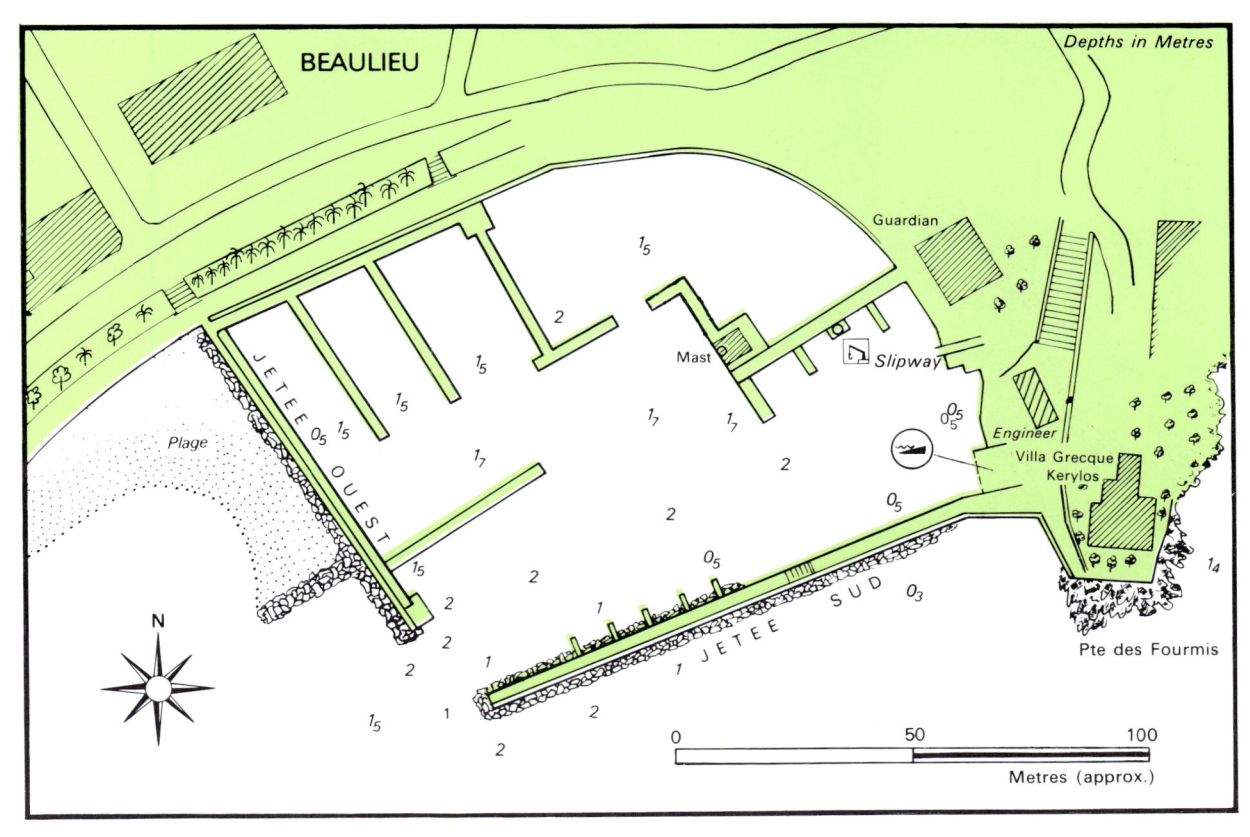

Port des Fourmis (Rough sketch. Not to scale)

Villa Kerylos   *Pointe St Hospice*

Port des Fourmis looking E–SE–S

Electricity Supply points of 220v AC on quays and pontoons.
Provisions Many shops in the town of Beaulieu nearby.
Repairs Limited repairs to wood hulls and engines can be carried out by a local shipwright.
Yacht club Club Nautic de Beaulieu-sur-Mer (☎ 93 01 12 41) has a branch here.
Visits The Villa Kerylos should be visited, it is a copy of an antique Greek palace of the time of Pericles, it is open 1400–1800 (not November and Mondays) and 1500–1900 in summer.

Remaining facilities are as for the Port de Beaulieu-sur-Mer, below.

Future development
Improvements planned including mooring chains for berths, and dredging.

139 PORT DE BEAULIEU-SUR-MER
06310 Alpes-Maritimes

Position 43°42'·6N 7°20'·5E
Minimum depth in the entrance:
    Passe Principal 8m (26ft)
    Passe Secondaire 3·5m (11ft)
    in the harbour 7 to 1·5m (23 to 4·9ft)
Width of the entrance 40m
Maximum length overall 45m (148ft)
Number of berths 776
Population 4304
Rating 3–2–2

South France Pilot

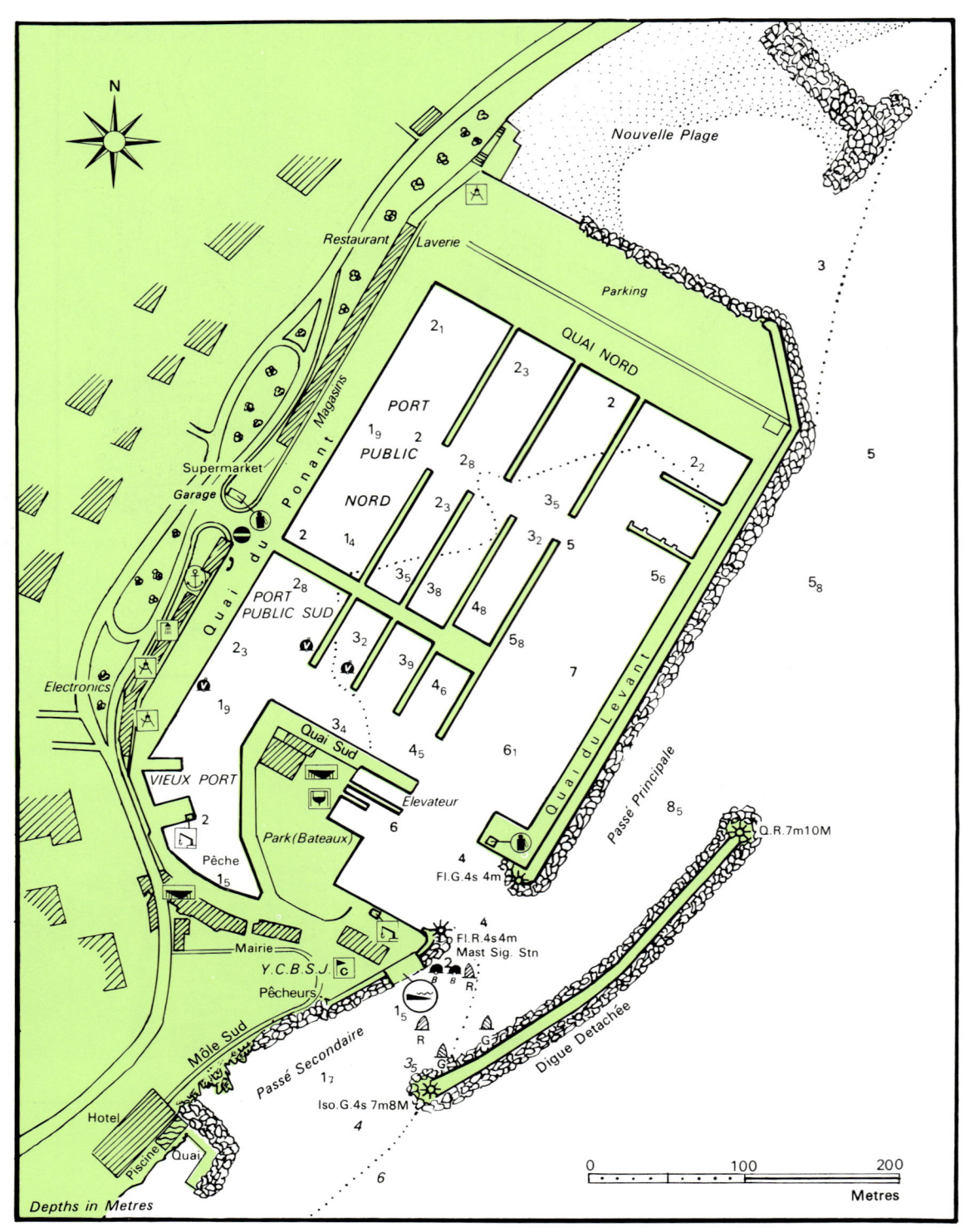

Port de Beaulieu-sur-Mer

General

The old, natural and originally very attractive harbour of Beaulieu situated in spectacular mountainous surroundings has had a very large artificial yacht harbour built outside it which has all possible facilities. Approach and entrance are easy and good shelter obtained once inside. The pleasant 'Victorian' seaside town nearby provides a good shopping centre.

Data

Charts Admiralty 2167
French 5176
Spanish 121
ECM 500

Magnetic variation 1°14′W (1990) decreasing by about 8′ each year.

Port de Beaulieu-sur-Mer

Port de Beaulieu looking NW

Air radiobeacon
Nice. Mont Leuza (43°43'·7N 7°20'·2E) LEZ
(·—··/·/——··) 398·5 kHz 75M. Continuous.

Port radio VHF Ch 9 (French, some English).

Weather forecasts Forecasts are posted once a day at the *Bureau de Port* and there is also an automatic pre-recorded coastal forecast (*Navimet*) or ☎ 93 01 10 49.

Speed limit 3 knots

Traffic signals Shown from a flagstaff on S side of the inner entrance.

Day	Meaning
Red ball	Entry forbidden
Green ball	Exit forbidden
Red and green balls	Entry and exit forbidden

Storm signals Hoisted on a flagstaff at S side of the inner entrance.

Lights
Digue Detachée N head Q.R.7m10M. White tower, red top.
S head Iso.G.4s7m8M. White tower, dark green top.
Quai de Levant Head Fl.G.4s4m. White column, green top.
Môle Sud Head Fl.R.4s4m. White column, red top.

Buoy Passe Secondaire is marked by two small R can buoys, two small G conical buoys and two spherical B buoys.

Warning
The Passe Secondaire should only be used by craft drawing less than 3m (9·8ft) maximum length overall 18m (59ft) due to silting. Anchoring and fishing is forbidden up to 250m to E of both entrances and also in an area ½M ESE of this harbour marked by four Y buoys, one at each corner.

Approach by day
From SW Round the large high sloping Cap Ferrat that has a conspicuous signal station at its top, a lighthouse on its SW point and an hotel on its S side. Next round the low rocky tree-covered Pointe St Hospice onto a NNW course towards some high hills which have the autoroute cut into its face. Houses and blocks of flats, a part of the town, will be seen at the foot of the hills. In the closer approach the digue and harbour walls will be seen. An archway near the S end of the harbour is conspicuous.

From NE From Cap d'Ail, a very high promontory with a rocky outcrop (Tête de Chien) on top, follow the coast passing several minor points as far as Cap Roux which rises nearly vertically from the sea and has a viaduct to its W. The coast road is undercut into its face with a tunnel on the SE side. The town of Beaulieu with the harbour walls below is easily seen in the close approach. An archway near the S end of the harbour is conspicuous.

South France Pilot

S end of Digue Detachée   *N end of Digue Detachée*   *N head of Digue Detachée*

Port de Beaulieu-sur-Mer, approach looking NW

Port de Beaulieu-sur-Mer, Passe Principale looking S

By night
Using the lights listed below navigate to a position where the entrance to the Passe Principale lies W at 300m:
Cap Ferrat Fl.W.3s25M
St Jean Fl(4)R.12s9M
Silva Maris Fl(2)R.6s8M

Anchorage in the approach
Anchor 300m to the E of the entrance to the Passe Principale in 10m (33ft) mud, weed and rock. Open to NE–E–SE–S.

Entrance
Passe Principale
By day Approach the N end of the Digue Detachée on a W course. Round it leaving it 20m to port onto a SSW course for 150m, then turn to starboard and leave the S head of the Quai du Levant 20m to starboard rounding this and the fuel station onto a N course into the harbour.

Passe Secondaire
By day If drawing 3m or less (max LOA 18m) approach the S end of the Digue Detachée on a W course and round it leaving it to starboard onto a NE course and pass between two sets of R and G buoys, then turn to a NW course and enter the harbour leaving two B spherical buoys to port.
By night Approach Q.R on a W course, leave it 20m to port turning onto a SSW course and then round a Fl.G.4s at 20m onto a N course, leaving a Fl.R.4s to port.

Berths
The number of the berth to occupy, normally in the S part of the harbour, will be announced by loudspeaker or by the *gardien* from the head of Quai du Levant, or call on VHF Ch 9 when 1M from the harbour, otherwise secure at the fuel station and report to the *Bureau de Port*. Secure stern to pontoon with bow to mooring chain.

Formalities
Report to the *Bureau de Port* (☎ 93 01 10 49) open day and night, on arrival and if necessary to the customs (☎ 93 01 10 00) in their office next door.

Charges
There are harbour charges.

Facilities
Slip A slip just to S of the entrance.
Travel-lift A travel-lift of 40 tonnes and a lifting dock of 150 tonnes near the entrance.
Cranes Two cranes of 5 tonnes in the Vieux Port, also a mobile crane.
Fuel Diesel (*gasoil*) and petrol are available from pumps at the head of Quai de Levant, 24 hours in summer. (☎ 93 01 41 22).
Water Water points on all quays and pontoons.
Electricity Supply points of 220v AC on all quays and pontoons and 380v at deep-water berths.
Provisions Some shops beside the harbour and many more in the town.
Ice The teashop Le Clipper just W of the harbour has ice for sale in the summer (☎ 93 01 06 20).
Duty-free goods Apply to the *Douane* for information about duty-free goods.
Garbage Many rubbish bins around this harbour.
Chandlery Several ships' chandlers beside the harbour.
Repairs Six yards for repairs to hulls and engines. Electronic equipment can also be repaired. A sailmaker and electrician are available.
Laundrette To the N of the harbour.
Post office The PTT is located on the far side of the railway station 400m to W.
Hotels Two ****, two ***, four **, six * and five unclassified hotels.
Restaurants Fifteen restaurants and some café/bars.
Yacht club The Yacht Club de Beaulieu-St Jean (YCBSJ) (☎ 93 01 14 44) has a small clubhouse to S of the harbour with lounge and showers.
Showers Ten showers and WCs beside the *Bureau de Port*.

Passe Secondaire   *Chantier Naval*   *Port de Silva-Maris (Port d'Eze-sur-Mer)*
Head of Digue du Levante (Fuel station)

Port de Beaulieu-sur-Mer, inner entrance looking SW–W–NW

entrance   *S entrance*   *N entrance*

Port de Beaulieu-sur-Mer looking NW–N–NE–E–SE

Information office The Syndicat d'Initiative is located at the far side of the station.
Visits The Villa Kerylos, a reproduction Greek house, the Musée Ile de France and the 11th-century Roman chapel are worth a visit.
Beach A beach to the N of the harbour.

140 PORT DE SILVA MARIS (PORT D'EZE-SUR-MER)
06360 Alpes-Maritimes

Position 43°43'·0N 7°21'·2E
Minimum depth in the entrance 3m (9·8ft)
                in the harbour 3 to 0·5m (9·8 to 1·6ft)
Width of the entrance 30m
Number of berths 58
Population 1400
Rating 3–3–4

General
A very small artificial harbour built just N of Cap Roux as part of a housing estate. Approach and entrance require care and would be dangerous in strong winds from SE–S. Facilities are very limited.

Data
Charts   Admiralty 2167
         French 5176
         Spanish 121
         ECM 500

Magnetic variation 1°14'W (1990) decreasing by about 8' each year.

Air radiobeacon
Nice. Mont Leuza (43°43'·7N 7°20'·2E) LEZ (·—··/·/—··) 398·5 kHz 75M. Continuous.

Speed limit 3 knots.

Lights
Jetée Est Head Fl(2)R.6s6m8M. White column, red lantern and base.

Buoys A small R buoy marks the shoal extension of Jetée Est and a G buoy the starboard side of the entrance.

Warning
This harbour is near a river mouth and silting may take place. Rocks project from the foot of the quays.

Approach by day
From SW Cross the Baie de Beaulieu towards the very conspicuous Cap Roux which has a high almost vertical rocky point. The harbour lies just beyond the point with a large block of flats with red balconies behind it.
From NE Follow the coast along from Cap d'Ail which is a very high promontory with an isolated rocky outcrop, Tête de Chien, on top. There are three smaller promontories before the Mer d'Eze is

South France Pilot

Port de Silva-Maris looking N

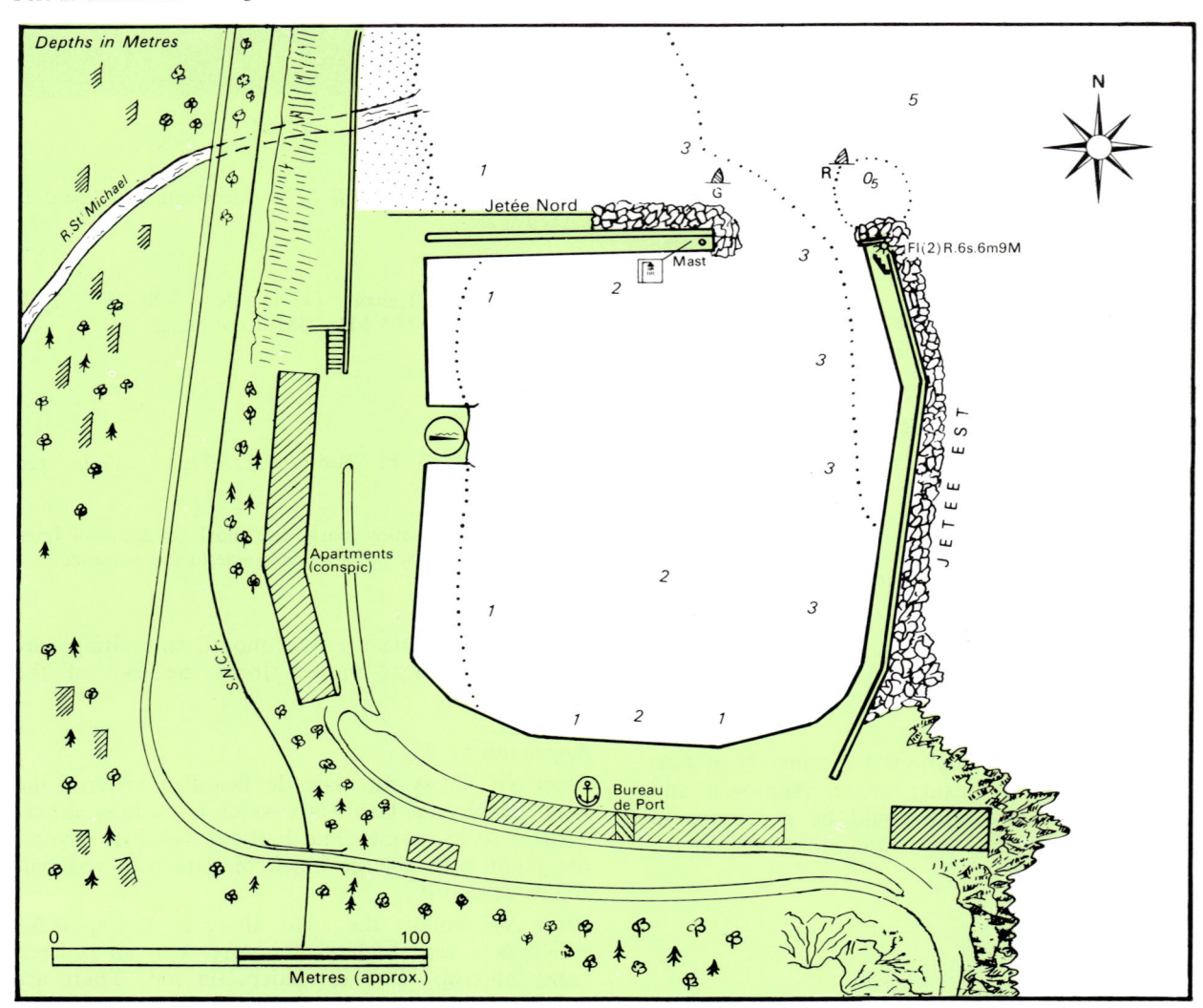

Port de Silva-Maris (Port d'Eze-sur-Mer) (Rough sketch. Not to scale)

Port de Silva-Maris (Port d'Eze-sur-Mer)

Entrance

Port de Silva-Maris (Port d'Eze-sur-Mer), approach looking SW

Port de Silva-Maris looking SE–S

reached when this harbour will be seen at the foot of the high vertical cliffs of Cap Roux with a large bock of flats with red balconies behind it.

By night
Using the lights listed below navigate to a position where the entrance is 300m to W:

Cap Ferrat Fl.W.3s25M
Beaulieu Q.R.10M
Monaco Oc.R.4s11M

Anchorage in the approach
Anchor 300m to E of the entrance in 10m (33ft) sand, gravel and weed. Open to E–SE–S.

Entrance
By day Approach the entrance on a W course and round onto a S course leaving the small R buoy to N of Jetée Est to port, enter leaving a small G buoy to starboard.

By night Using care, approach Fl(2)R.6s on a W course. When 50m away alter course to leave this light 30m to port. When the light is S change onto this course and approach very slowly to locate the small unlit R buoy which has to be left to port and a small G buoy to starboard. Enter in mid-channel.

Berths
Secure stern to quay, bow to mooring chain in a vacant berth. Report to the *gardien* for the allocation of a berth.

Formalities
Report to the *gardien* on arrival at the *Bureau de Port*.

Charges
There are harbour charges.

Facilities
Hard A small hard at the W side of the harbour.
Fuel From a service station about ½M away.
Water Points around the harbour.
Electricity Electric supply points 220v AC around the harbour.
Provisions From the village of Eze-sur-Mer some ½M away, and from Beaulieu 1M away.
Garbage A few rubbish bins around the harbour.
Showers Near head of Jetée Nord.
Post office The PTT is in the village of Eze-sur-Mer.
Hotels One ****, two **, one * and three other hotels.
Restaurants Two in the village and several café/bars.
Information office A Syndicat d'Initiative in the village.
Beach A long beach to the NE of the harbour.
Visits The medieval hill-top village of Eze (427m) should be visited, a path from E edge of Eze-sur-Mer.
Communications Bus and rail service at Beaulieu, air service from Nice.

Cap Roux
An exceptional high headland of vertical reddish-yellow rock (268m) with the coast road partially undercut into the rock at the bottom.

⚓ N of Cap Roux
An anchorage 200m to NE of the entrance to Port de Silva-Maris in 4m sand and rock, sandy beach coast road with high hills behind. Village shops, hotel, restaurants at Eze-sur-Mer. Open to NE–E–SE with swell from S.

Eze
A very good example of a *village perché*, a very old village conspicuous on the crest of a sugar loaf hill (427m).

105

South France Pilot

Eze-sur-Mer

To N of Cap Roux looking NE from Port Silva-Maris (Eze-sur-Mer)

Baie de St Laurent looking N

Cap Mala

Baie de St Laurent looking N

⚓ **Baie de St Laurent**
A pleasant anchorage in 5–10m sand, sheltered by Cap Mala which has a lone rock close to its point. Beach, beach huts, cliff roads and houses ashore, a conspicuous wall supports the railway. Open to S–SW. There are four old stone warping bollards near the entrance.

⚓ **W of Cap d'Ail**
A semi-open anchorage between Cap d'Ail and Cap Rognoso. Rocky cliffs with rocks close inshore, a few houses and road. Anchor in 8m sand and rock. Open to SE–S–SW.

141 PORT DE CAP D'AIL
06320 Alpes-Maritimes

Position 43°43'·5N 7°25'·0E
Minimum depth in the entrance 20m (66ft)
in the harbour 20 to 5m (66 to 16ft)
Width of the entrance 75m
Number of berths 254
Maximum length overall 35m (115ft), 10 berths 50–60m (164–197ft)
Population 23,000 (Monaco)
Rating 3–2–3

General
A small deep artificial yacht harbour just on the French side of the boundary with Monaco, built as part of a vast housing complex. Easy approach and entrance. Good protection from E but subject to swell from SW. With heavy swell from SE–S–SW the entrance can be difficult.

Data
Charts Admiralty 2167
French 6863
Spanish 120
ECM 500

Magnetic variation 1°14'W (1990) decreasing by about 8' each year.

Speed limit 3 knots.

Port radio VHF Ch 9 (French).

Weather forecast Posted at *Bureau de Port* daily. Automatic prerecorded forecast (*Navimet*) or ☎ 93 72 31 32.

Lights
Digue du Large SW head Fl.G.4s11m10M. Green concrete pedestal. 262°-vis-172°.
NW Elbow Fl.G.4s7m6M. Green structure, synchronised with SW head. 172°-vis-262°.

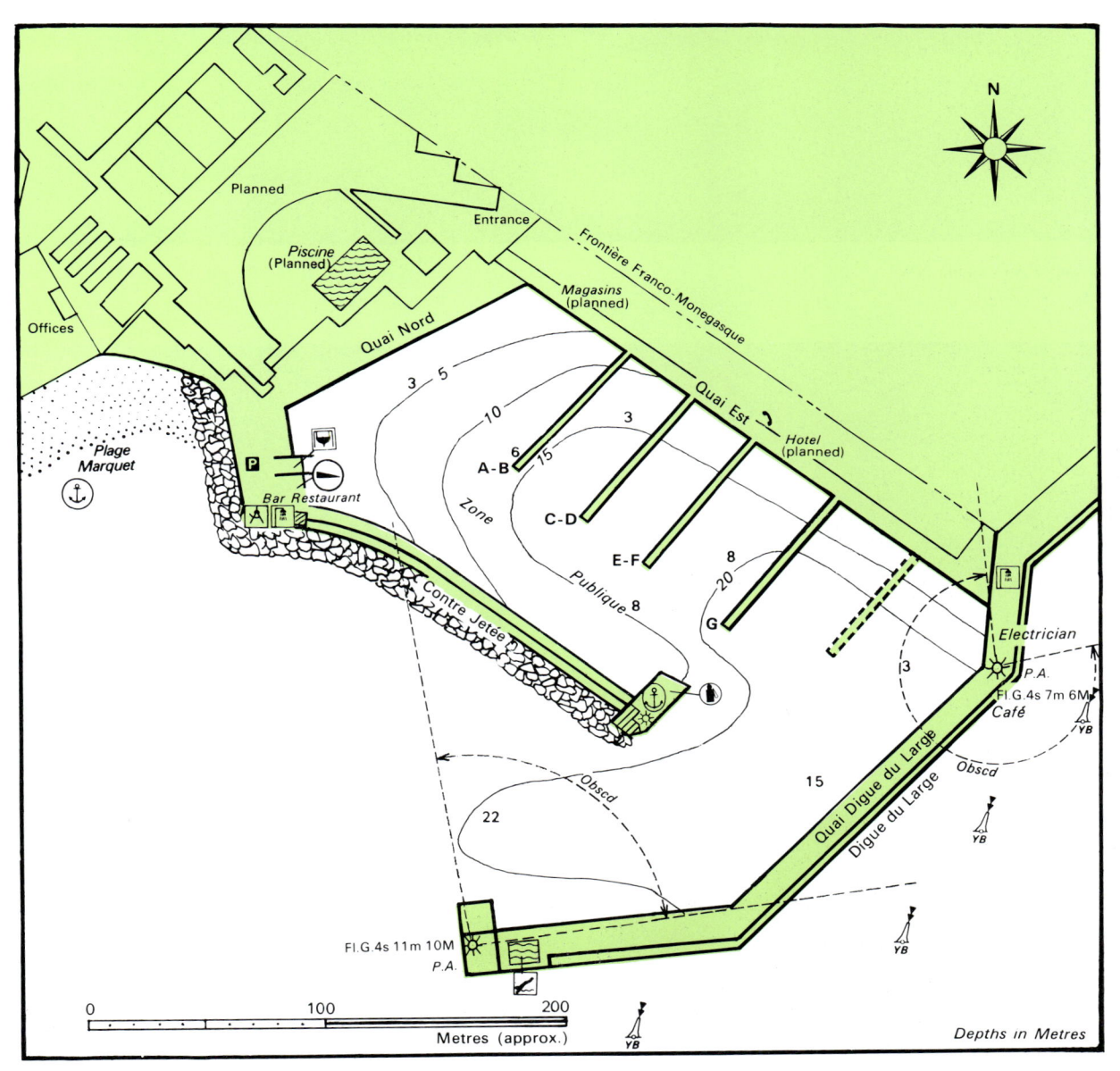

Port de Cap d'Ail

South France Pilot

Port de Cap d'Ail looking NW

Port de Cap d'Ail looking NW

Port de Cap d'Ail

Jetée Ouest Head Fl.R.4s5m5M. Red framework tower.
Heliport 4·8M WSW Digue Sud Fontvieille Aero Mo MC (— —/— · —·) 30s. Occas.

Buoys A red conical buoy (Fl.5s) lies 800m to SE of this harbour on the boundary of France and Monaco. A line of small S Card YB buoys ⚑ topmarks, lie outside the Digue du Large marking area where navigation is forbidden.

Warning
As the facilities of this harbour are not yet fully constructed, alterations can be expected to the data and charts. Berths are subject to swell from W and SW. Rocky foot to quays project several metres. In rough weather keep well clear (at least ½M) of the outer breakwater which reflects the waves. Do not confuse Pointe St Martin with Cap Martin.

Prohibited area
A 150m strip, forbidden to navigation, lies outside the breakwater and between the Ports of Cap d'Ail and Fontvieille, and is marked by 6 S and 1 W Card buoys. There is a heliport ashore between the two ports, which has a building behind it shaped like three white tents.

Approach by day
From SW Cross the wide Baie de Beaulieu and round the very high Cap d'Ail which has a rocky outcrop on its summit, the Tête de Chien, and a low projecting point. The long high breakwater, the Digue du Large, will be seen at once and the entrance lies inshore of it.

From NE Follow the coast at 600m passing the concentration of houses and high-rise buildings of Monaco. Round the vertical cliffs of Pointe St Martin that has a tall grey-coloured building, Musée d'Océan, on its face. The long high concrete breakwater, the Digue du Large, will then be seen. Pass entrance to Port de Fontvieille. The entrance to Port de Cap d'Ail lies at the far end of the Digue du Large.

Port de Cap d'Ail, approach looking N

Port de Cap d'Ail, approach looking W

Port de Cap d'Ail, entrance looking NE

South France Pilot

By night
Using the following lights navigate to a position ½M to S of a Fl.G.4s10M:
Menton VQ(4)R.3s10M
Cap Ferrat Fl.W.3s25M
Beaulieu Q.R.10M

Anchorage in the approach
Anchor off the Plage Marquet in 4m sand and rock. Pay attention to a submerged breakwater off the SW end of the beach. Do not use in rough weather.

Entrance
By day Approach the W end of the long Digue du Large on a N course. Leave it 20m to starboard and round it onto an E course and enter the harbour.
By night Round Fl.G.4s leaving it 50m to starboard onto a NE course and enter leaving Fl.R to port.

Berth
Secure alongside the fuel berth and report to *Bureau de Port* for allocation of a berth. Berth stern to pontoon and secure to bow mooring chain.

Formalities
Report to the *Bureau de Port* at the head of the Contre Jetée on arrival (☎ 93 78 28 46 and 93 78 40 80) open day and night. Customs office in Monaco (☎ 93 30 26 00).

Harbour charges
There are harbour charges.

Facilities
Travel-lift A travel-lift of 40 tonnes in the *carénage* area.
Crane A crane of 10 tonnes.
Slip A slip in the NW corner of the harbour.
Fuel Diesel (*gasoil*) pumps and petrol near *Bureau de Port* at head of Contre Jetée (☎ 93 78 28 46). Open 0900–1200 and 1400–1900.
Water Water points on all quays and pontoons.
Electricity 220v AC and 380v AC on pontoons and quays.
Provisions Shops to be established to E of harbour, very many shops in Monaco, ½M away.
Ice Automatic machine for small ice.
Garbage Rubbish containers round the harbour.

Heliport *Bureau de Port*

Port de Cap d'Ail looking S–SE

Port de Cap d'Ail looking N–NE–E from head of Digue Sud

Chandlery A number of shops in Monaco and one in NW corner of the harbour.
Repairs A shipyard to N of the harbour where hulls and engines can be repaired.
Yacht club Club Nautic de Cap d'Ail (CNCA) has a small clubhouse on the Plage Marquet.
Restaurants Many in Monaco, a café/snack bar in E corner of the harbour.
Showers Available in two sanitary blocks with 12 showers and WCs, one in the NW corner and the other in the E corner.
Communications A heliport is established alongside the harbour, taxis available, bus and rail services in Monaco.

For other facilities see Port de Monaco, page 114.

Future development

Hotel and shops to be constructed, possible change in the layout of pontoons (one extra). Establishment of clubhouse, swimming pool and restaurant at head of Digue du Large.

---

142 PORT DE FONTVIEILLE

Position 43°43'·8N 7°25'·7E
Minimum depth in the entrance 16m (52ft)
in the harbour 13 to 1m (43 to 3·3ft)
Width of the entrance 60m
Number of yacht berths 150
Population 23,000 (Monaco)
Rating 3–2–3

General

A modern artificial yacht harbour built outside a small old harbour and surrounded by a vast housing complex and a cliff. Easy to approach and enter. Facilities are limited. and are being improved. A harbour with good shelter but difficult to enter in strong E–SE winds.

Data

Charts Admiralty 2167, 149
French 6863
Spanish 121
ECM 500

Magnetic variation 1°09'W (1990) decreasing by about 8' each year.

Speed limit 3 knots.

Port radio VHF Ch 9. Cal *3AP* (0800–1900).

Weather forecast Automatic prerecorded forecast (*Navimet*) or ☎ 93 88 17 24.

Lights
Jetée Extérieure Head Oc(2)R.6s10m10M. White column, red top.
Môle Contre Jetée Head Fl.G.4s5m7M. Green lantern.
West side Fl.R.4s3m4M. White post, red top.
Heliport 4·8M WSW of Digue Sud Head. Aero Mo MC (— — / — · —)30s. Occas.

Warning

In rough weather keep well clear (at least ½M) of the outer breakwater which reflects waves.

Prohibited area

A strip forbidden to navigation 150m from the breakwater between the Ports of Cap d'Ail and Fontvieille is marked by 6 S and 1 W Card buoys. There is a heliport ashore between the two ports, which has a building behind it shaped like three tents.

Approach by day

From SW Round the high Cap d'Ail which has a rocky outcrop at its summit, the Tête de Chien. Ahead will be seen the long high outer breakwater, the Digue du Large, follow this along outside the line of small S Card buoys and the entrance will be found at its E end just before the high cliffed Pointe St Martin is rounded.

From NE From Cap Martin, with its conspicuous signal tower (disused) with TV/radio tower on top and a large hotel, follow the coast along at 500m. Monaco is easily recognised by reason of its skyscrapers. Round Pointe St Martin close inshore. This point has a vertical cliff face with a conspicuous grey building built into it, the Musée d'Océan. Once round the point the harbour entrance will open up ahead.

By night

Use the following lights to navigate to a position ½M S of conspicuous Musée d'Océan:
Menton VQ(4)R.3s10M
Cap Ferrat Fl.W.3s25M
Beaulieu Q.R.10M

Entrance

By day Approach the entrance on a NW course and round the head of the Digue du Large at 20m leaving it to port and the head of the *môle* to starboard. Follow round to starboard once inside.

By night Approach Oc(2)R.6s on a NW course, round it at 20m and leave it to port and a Fl.G to starboard.

Berths

Secure to first pontoon for allocation of a berth, then secure stern to pontoons or quay where instructed and report to *Bureau de Port*. Berths are possible inside the *môle* but there is no access except by dinghy and no facilities.

Formalities

Report to the *Bureau de Port* on arrival (☎ 93 50 80 99), open 0830 to 2030 in summer, 0830 to 1900 in winter.

Harbour charges

These are very expensive.

South France Pilot

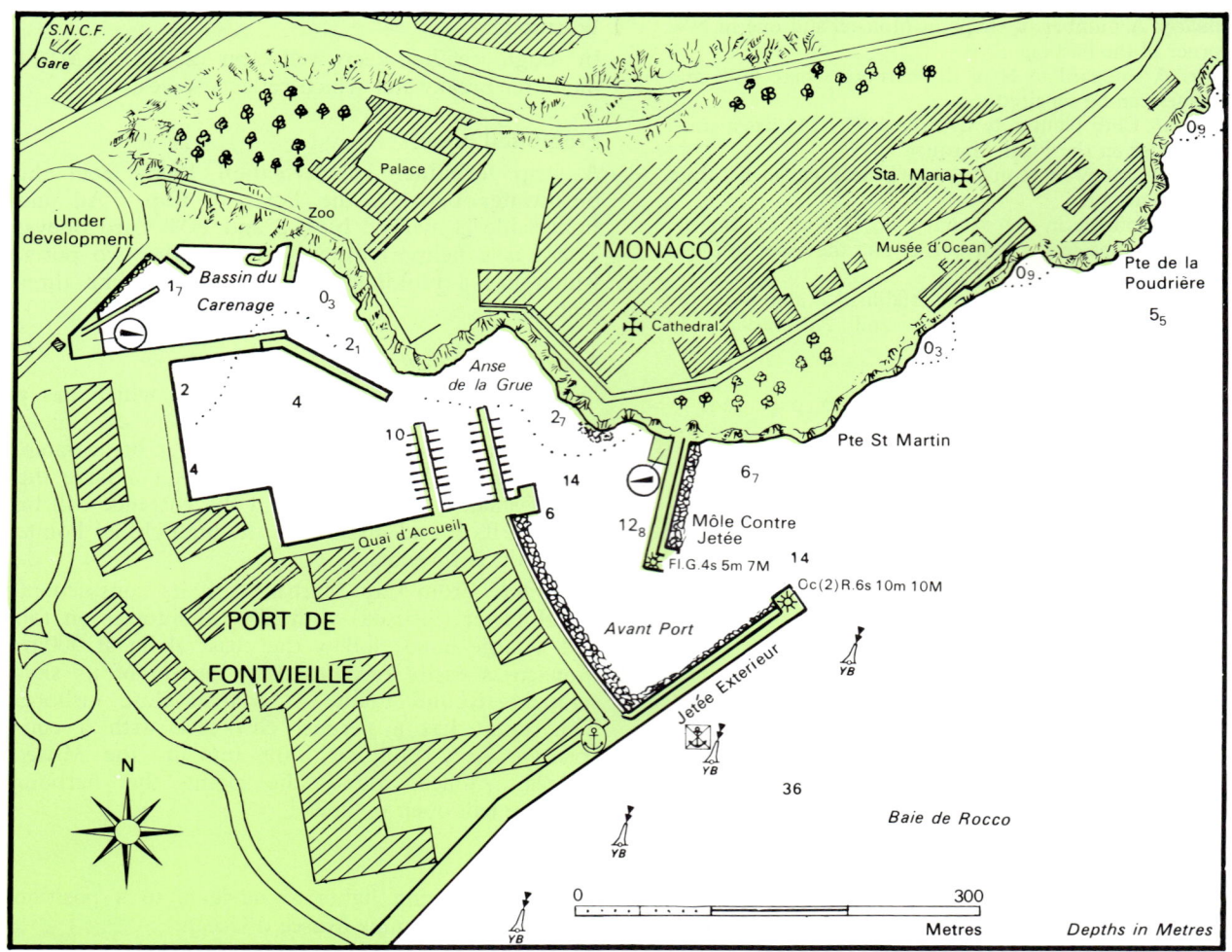

Port de Fontvieille

Port de Fontvieille, entrance looking W

Port de Fontvieille, approach looking W

Port de Fontvieille

Port de Fontvieille looking W

Port de Fontvieille looking S–SW–W–NW

South France Pilot

Facilities
Slip A slip in the NW corner of the inner harbour and at the root of the *môle*.
Water Water points on all quays and pontoons but not on the *môle*.
Electricity 220v AC and 380v AC supply points provided on quays and pontoons but not on the *môle*.
Provisions Many shops in Monaco ½M away.
Ice Supply locally.
Showers Two blocks with 4 showers and 4 WCs.
Garbage Rubbish containers around the harbour.
Beach A beach to SW of the harbour.
Communications Bus and rail services. Helicopter service alongside the harbour.

For other facilities see Port de Monaco, page 118.

Musée d'Océan
A very conspicuous building partially built into the face of the cliffs of Pointe St Martin.

---

143 PORT DE MONACO (MONTE CARLO)
Principauté de Monaco

Position 43°44'·2N 7°25'·6E
Minimum depth in the entrance 30m (98ft)
　　　　　　　　in the harbour 22 to 4m (72 to 13ft)
Width of the entrance 100m
Maximum length overall 150m (492ft)
Number of berths 450
Population 23,000
Rating 3–2–3

General
An old natural harbour that has been improved by the addition of two jetties and quays. It is open to the E and any swell from this direction makes it very uncomfortable inside the harbour. In bad winds from NE–E–SE the normally easy approach becomes difficult. The harbour is often crowded and berths are difficult to find. The attractiveness of the old town is being rapidly eroded as featureless highrise buildings proliferate all over the area and massive road improvements are put in hand.

Data
Charts Admiralty 2167, 149
　　　　French 6863
　　　　Spanish 121
　　　　ECM 500

Magnetic variation 1°09'W (1990) decreasing by about 8' each year.

Port radio VHF Ch 16, 6 and 12. *Bureau de Port* through Monaco (3AH) Ch 16, 12 (French and English).

Coast radio station Monaco (3AF) VHF Ch 16, 20, 22, 86 (French and English).

Weather forecast Published once a day at the *Bureau de Port*. Automatic prerecorded forecasts (*Navimet*) or ☎ 93 83 17 24.

Speed limit 5 knots.

Storm signals Staff from the *Bureau de Port* warn yachts in the harbour.

Pilots The pilot station is in the light tower at the head of Jetée Nord and pilots control the movement and berthing of yachts. They have a small white launch with a black 'P' on it. ☎ 93 30 19 21 ext 8577. Monaco (3AG) and (3AH) VHF Ch 16, 12.

Lights
Jetée Sud Head Oc.R.4s16m11M. White eight-sided tower, red top.
Jetée Nord Head Oc.G.4s16m11M. White eight-sided tower, green top.

Buoys There are several unlit mooring and warping buoys in the harbour. Wave recording R and Y conical buoy (Fl(5)Y.20s) halfway between Port de Fontvieille and Cap Martin.

Warning
It is forbidden to enter the area marked by buoys near l'Anse de Larvotte which is a bathing area located ¾M to the E of the harbour. Anchorage is prohibited within an underwater nature reserve area off Monte Carlo which is marked by Y buoys and also inside a 400m circle described around a Y conical buoy 600m E of Pte de la Veille. The harbour is very deep near the mouth.

Approach by day
From SW Cross the wide Baie de Beaulieu and round the very high Cap d'Ail which has a conspicuous rock outcrop on its summit, le Tête de Chien. Pass the new long high breakwater off Port de Fontvieille and round the vertical cliffs of Pointe St Martin with the conspicuous grey Musée d'Océan building on its face. Follow the coast round to the entrance of the harbour which has two conspicuous light towers.

From NE Round Cap Martin, a low promontory, tree-covered with a rocky point which has a large hotel on its point and a disused signal station on its summit (with TV/radio tower on top). The mass of buildings of Monaco will be seen from afar with the rocky outcrop, Le Tête de Chien, showing well behind. In the closer approach the entrance will be seen with two light towers either side of it.

By night
Using the lights listed below navigate to a position where the entrance is 300m to W:
Menton VQ(4)R.3s10M
Cap Ferrat Fl.W.3s25M
Beaulieu Q.R.10M
Fontvieille Oc(2)R.6s10M

Anchorage in the approach
The only anchorage is 200m to W of Pointe de la Veille in 6m (20ft) sand and mud which is located 1M to NE of the harbour, open to E–SE–S–SW. At night it is permitted to anchor in the W centre of the harbour. Anchor lights to be shown.

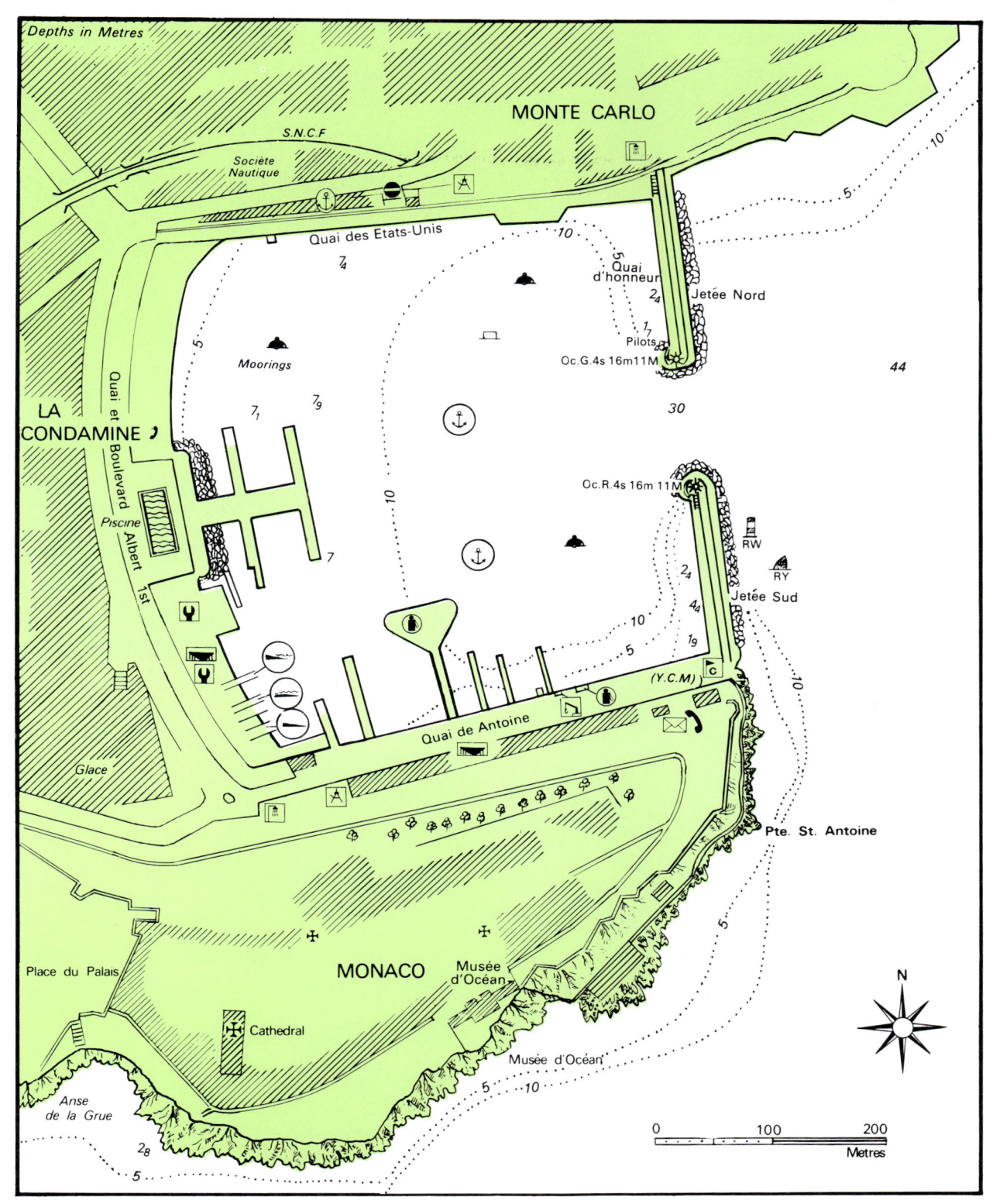

Port de Monaco (Monte Carlo)

Port de Monaco (Monte Carlo)

South France Pilot

Port de Monaco looking NW

Musée d'Océan   Entrance   Tête de Chien

Musée d'Océan   Pointe St Antoine   Entrance

Port de Monaco (Monte Carlo), approach looking W

Port de Monaco (Monte Carlo), approach looking N

Port de Monaco (Monte Carlo)

Lighthouse   Jetée Sud   Entrance

Port de Monaco (Monte Carlo), entrance looking W

Entrance

By day Enter on a W course between the two lighthouses. It is forbidden to cut the corner.

By night From a position 200m to E enter on a W course leaving Oc.G.4s to starboard and Oc.R.4s to port.

Berths

Berth stern to quay or pontoon as instructed by the pilot from the head of the Jetée Nord, bow to anchor laid well ahead with a trip line. Some berths have mooring chains. If no instruction is received, secure to Quai d'Honneur near the head of Jetée Nord. Berths on the N side of the harbour are subject to the worst effects of the swell.

Anchorage

Temporary anchorage at night in the centre of the harbour in 13m mud. Anchor lights must be shown.

Formalities

It is essential to contact the pilot on duty at the head of the Jetée Nord (☎ 93 30 42 46 ext 3268) on entering the harbour, open 0800 to 2300 in summer, 0800 to 2000 in winter. He will allocate a berth and hand over a form to be completed which will be collected by the *gendarmes* who then produce yet another form to be completed. If required, customs (☎ 93 30 26 00) have an office near the *Bureau de Port*. The *Bureau de Port* is located on the N side of the harbour (☎ 93 30 19 21 ext 8578, telex 489 035), open summer 0800–2300, winter 0800–2000.

Charges

There are harbour charges, but not excessive. A two-hour wait is free.

Courtesy flags

As the Monagesque have their own flag it is advisable to purchase one at a previous harbour and to exchange it for the French *tricolore* courtesy flag while in these waters.

Facilities

Slip A slip in the SW corner of the harbour.
Slipway Two slipways to the SW of the harbour, one of 100 tonnes and the other of 20 tonnes capacity.
Cranes There are two cranes of 10 and 20 tonnes to S of the harbour and mobile 12 and 50-tonne cranes are available.
Travel-lift An elevator of 15 tonnes.
Fuel Diesel (*gasoil*) and petrol are available from pumps on the head of a pontoon on the S side of the harbour, 0800–2000 hours in summer, 0800–1400 hours in winter. Petrol is also available from pumps on the quays on the S side of the harbour.

Port de Monaco (Monte Carlo) looking N–NE

South France Pilot

Water Many water points around the harbour.
Electricity 220v AC and 380v AC supply points are available around the harbour.
Provisions A supermarket to the W of the harbour and a market to SW.
Ice From fuel station, the factory is to SW of the harbour.
Duty-free goods There are shops to the N and S of the harbour who will provide duty-free goods.
Garbage A limited number of rubbish containers around the harbour.
Chandlery Ships' chandlers to the N and S of the harbour.
Repairs Major repairs to hull and engine are possible by the shipyards to the SW of the harbour. Electronic equipment can be repaired, also sails.
Laundrette A laundrette in the town.
Post office The PTT is located in the SE corner of the harbour.
Hotels Six **** deluxe, one ****, six ***, two **, four * and several unclassified hotels.
Restaurants Over one hundred and twenty restaurants of all types and quality. There are also many café/bars.
Yacht club The Yacht Club de Monaco (YCM) (☎ 93 50 58 39) has a very palatial clubhouse with all facilities located in the SE corner of the harbour, but unlike almost every yacht club in the world visiting yachtsmen are not welcome here unless they are guests of a member.
Showers 4 blocks with 20 showers and 20 WCs near the NE and SW corners of the harbour.
Information office The office of the Service du Tourisme is located to the NE of the harbour on the higher road at 2A Blvd des Moulins, Monte Carlo 9830 (☎ 93 30 87 01 and 93 50 60 88).
Visits There are many places to visit including the old Monaco-Ville, the Palace, Palace Museum, the Musée d'Océan, the Zoo, Museum of Prehistoric Anthropology and the Casino.
Beaches Some beaches to the NE of the harbour.
Communications Bus and rail services.

Future development
Facilities are to be improved.

History
Legend has it that Monaco was founded by Hercules. It was certainly occupied as a small fishing harbour in the 10th century BC by the Phoenicians. In the 4th century BC in succession to the Menockos a Ligurian tribe took over followed by the Romans who left some remains which are still existing despite the Barbarians and Saracens who ravaged the area. The Counts of Provence acquired it in 972 AD. It was held by the church from 1075 for one hundred years until the Genoese took over and built its first fortress. In 1297 the Grimaldis seized it and have held it ever since despite numerous wars in which they only lost Menton and Roquebrune (1842). The establishment of the Casino and the rail services for tourists encouraged the development of the area during the last hundred years.

⚓ **W of Pointe de la Veille**
A semi-open anchorage off a sandy and rock beach, anchor in 4–5m sand. Road, houses and large hotels ashore, open to E–SE–S–SW.

⚓ **Baie de Roquebrune**
Anchorage is available in sand and weed N of a line joining Pointe de la Veille and Cap Martin. The coast is rocky with close inshore rocks and shingle sandy beaches. Sound carefully and anchor in 5m depth. Railway, roads and large houses with pine trees ashore, open SE–S–SW.

Cap Martin
A prominent and conspicuous headland with a slightly sloping ridge covered with trees and houses (74–105m). A water tower and disused signal station (now a TV/radio relay) on the top with an hotel on the point which is steep-to.

⚓ **E of Cap Martin**
A semi-open anchorage off Carnolès sandy beach. Anchor in 2 to 5m sand and weed. Coast road, many houses, shops etc. ashore. Open to NE–E–SE with swell from S.

Port de Monaco   La Tête de Chien

Baie de Roquebrune looking SW–W–NW

Anchorage to W of Pointe de la Veille looking NW

Baie de Roquebrune looking NW

South France Pilot

Cap Martin looking NE with anchorage beyond.

Port de Menton-Ville looking NW

Port de Menton-Ville (Vieux Port)

Port de Monaco   La Tête de Chien   Pointe de la Veille

W of Pointe de la Veille looking SW–W–NW

Hotel   Old signal station

Hotel

Cap Martin looking SW

Cap Martin looking E

To W of Cap Martin looking NW–N

144 PORT DE MENTON-VILLE (VIEUX PORT)
06500 Alpes-Maritimes

Position 43°46'·2N 7°30'·8E
Minimum depth in the entrance 7m (23ft)
   in the harbour 5 to 1·5m (16 to 4·9ft)
Width of the entrance 35m
Maximum length overall 25m (82ft)
Number of berths 440
Population 30,000
Rating 1–3–3

General
An old fishing and yachting harbour that has been much improved by the addition of jetties and pontoons. Approach and entrance are easy but can be difficult in strong E–SE winds which tend to make the harbour uncomfortable. Facilities are limited but the old town is unique and the surroundings are very attractive. The shops are good. In the season the area is crowed with tourists and holidaymakers especially from England.

South France Pilot

Data

Charts Admiralty 2167
French 6863
Spanish 121
ECM 500

Magnetic variation 1°09′W (1990) decreasing by about 8′ each year.

Weather forecast There is an automatic prerecorded coastal forecast at the *Bureau de Port (Navimet)* or ☎ 93 72 31 32.

Speed limit 5 knots.

Port radio VHF Ch 9 (French).

Lights

Jetée Sud Head VQ(4)R.3s16m10M. White tower, red top. Obscured when more than 036° by Cap Martin.

Warning

In very heavy weather from E–SE the approach and entrance can become dangerous.

Approach by day

From SW Round Cap Martin which is low, tree-covered and has a large hotel on its point and a squat TV/radio tower on its summit which was a signal station. The concentration of houses and a church spire (illuminated at night) mark Menton

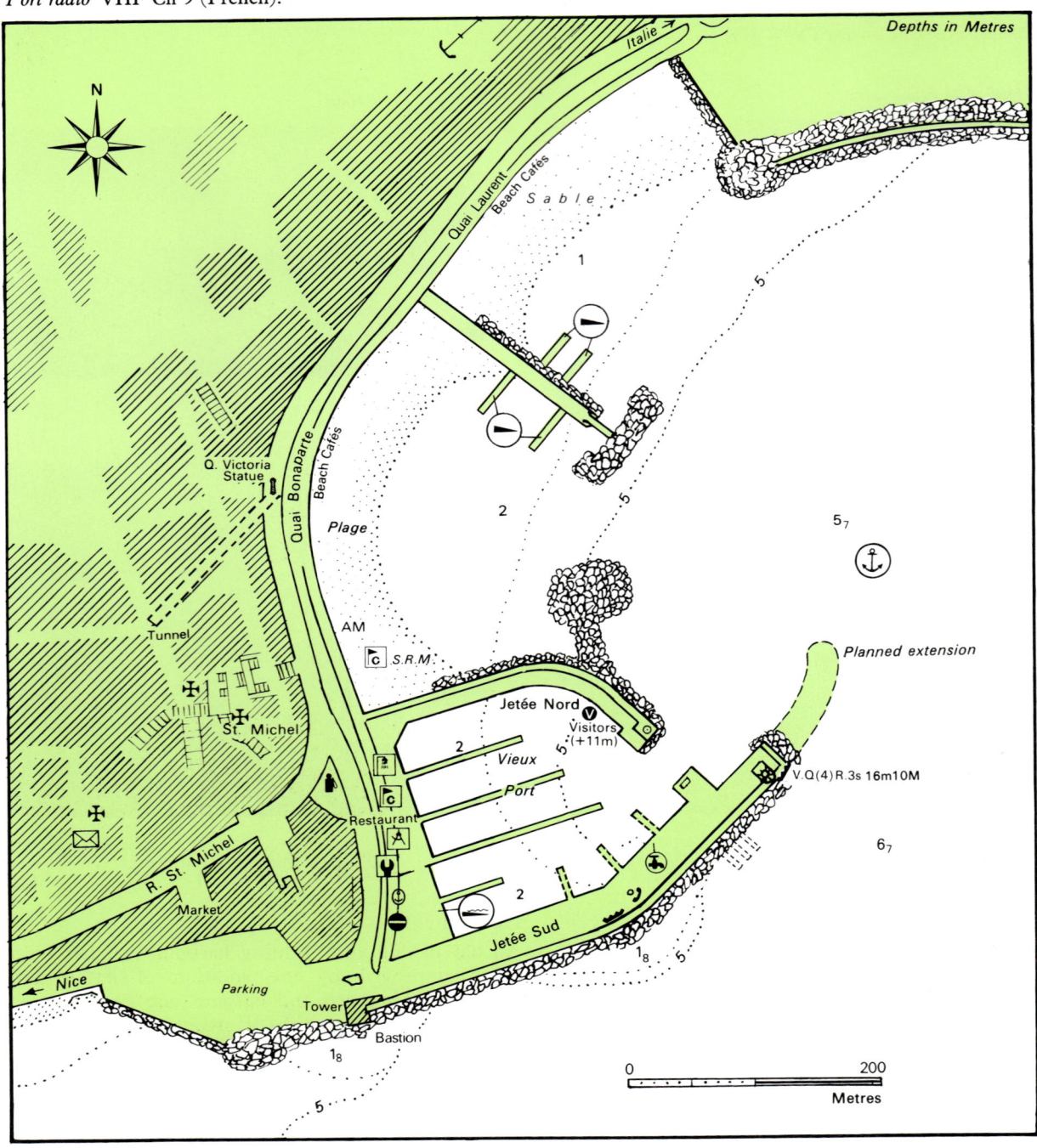

Port de Menton-Ville

122

Port de Menton-Ville (Vieux Port)

Lighthouses Head of Jetée Sud   Church spire

Port de Menton-Ville looking W

tration of houses at Menton will be seen from afar especially the church spire which is conspicuous and illuminated at night. Closer in, the Jetée Est, its Bastion tower and light tower will be seen.

By night
Using the lights listed below navigate to a position where the entrance to the harbour is 200m to W:

Cap Ferrat Fl.W.3s25M
Monaco Oc.R.4s11M
Menton-Garavan Fl(2)R.6s10M
Cap d'Armes Fl(2)W.10s29M

Anchorage in the approach
Anchor 200m to NE of the entrance in 6m (20ft) sand, shingle and weed. Open to E–SE–S.

Port de Menton-Ville looking SW–W–NW

Port de Menton-Garavan Cap Mortola   *Port de Menton-Ville*

Port de Menton-Ville looking NE–E–SE

and are easy to recognise. In the closer approach the Bastion tower (a fort-like building) on the Jetée Sud and a light tower on its E head will be recognised.
From NE Round the high sloping Punta della Martola which has outlying small rocky islets extending some 400m off the point. Two rail viaducts cross the valleys above the coast. From this direction the yacht harbour of Menton-Garavan and the concen-

Entrance
By day Approach the head of Jetée Sud on a W course and round it at 20m leaving it to port and enter on a SW course.
By night Approach VQ(4)R.3s on a W course, leave it 20m to port and round it to enter on a SW course.

123

South France Pilot

Berths
Stern to quay or pontoon in a vacant berth with bow to anchor or mooring chain, but anchors need trip lines. The heads of the three pontoons are usually the best place for visiting yachts to secure to. Report to the *Bureau de Port* for allocation of a berth.

Formalities
Report to the *Bureau de Port* (☎ 93 35 80 56), open 0800–1800 winter and 0730–2000 summer on arrival and if necessary to the customs (☎ 93 35 93 18) in the same office building.

Charges
There are harbour charges.

Facilities
Slip A large slip to the SW of the harbour but there is only 1·5m of water. Four dinghy slips to N of the harbour.
Crane A mobile 5-tonne crane.
Fuel Diesel (*gasoil*) and petrol are available from pumps at Menton-Garavan just inside the entrance on the Quai Est or by can from a garage to W of the harbour.
Water Water points are available on the quays.
Electricity 220v AC supplies are available on the quays.
Provisions A number of shops near to the harbour and a good covered market is just to the W of the harbour.
Ice Ice available from the chandlers to W of the harbour.
Duty-free goods Duty-free goods can be supplied by contacting the ships' chandler.
Chandlery A ships' chandler just to the W of the harbour.
Repairs Local yards can carry out simple repairs to the hull and engine. Electrician and sailmaker.
Laundrette There are several in the town.
Post office The PTT is located in the centre of the new town to W of the harbour.
Hotels Three ****, two ***, twenty-six **, twenty * and twelve unclassified hotels.
Restaurants Over fifty restaurants and many café/bars.
Yacht club The Société des Régates de Menton (SRM) (☎ 93 35 77 37) has a small office and a shower to the NE of the harbour. The Club de Voile (CNVP) close to the *Bureau de Port*.
Showers Showers at W side of harbour, obtain pass from *Bureau de Port*, 8 showers, 8 WCs. 78 06).
Information office The Syndicat d'Initiative has an office next to the casino at Palais de l'Europe, Av Boyer (☎ 93 57 57 00).
Lifeboats A *vedette* lifeboat, 1st class, kept here (☎ 93 35 78 06)
Visits The old town should be visited as it is unique being the only 'Kasbah' type of town in Europe. There is also a Musée Municipale of paintings and archaeology and in the Bastion tower is the Musée J.Cocteau.
Beach There is a sand and pebble beach to the NE of the harbour.
Communications Bus and rail services.

Future development
More pontoons to be provided and Jetée Sud to be extended.

History
Menton lies on the old Roman road to Gaul but the first records of the town only date from 1251. The ancients called it the Bay of Peace. In 1318 it was besieged by Doria who obtained a ransom of 16,000 gold florins from the Grimaldis of Monaco. In 1641 the town came under the protection of France but it changed hands a number of times and was the scene of frequent skirmishes. In 1848 it was proclaimed a free city. In 1890 the Jetée Sud was constructed and the harbour established. It grew into a popular winter resort for the English at the end of the last century. An Anglican clergyman was one of the first foreigners to live here and the area was soon colonised by other English expatriates. Queen Victoria visited the settlement in 1882.

⚓ **N of Port Menton-Ville**
Anchorage off sandy beach and breakwater in 4–6m sand. Coast road and town ashore, beach cafés, landing slips. Open E–SE–S.

145 PORT DE MENTON-GARAVAN
96502 Alpes-Maritimes

Position 43°47'·1N 7°31'·5E
Minimum depth in the entrance 6m (20ft)
    in the harbour 5·5 to 1·6m (18 to 5·2ft)
Width of the entrance 50m
Maximum length overall 40m (131ft)
Number of berths 800
Population 30,000
Rating 3–3–2

General
A large modern artificial yacht harbour which has good facilities for yachtsmen. It is easy to approach and enter but in strong winds from E–SE–S it could become difficult. The attractive old town of Menton is 1M away but everyday requirements can be bought locally.

Data
Charts Admiralty 2167
    French 6863
    Spanish 121
    ECM 500

Magnetic variation 1°09'W (1990) decreasing by about 8' each year.

Port radio VHF Ch 9, 16 (French, little English).

Weather forecasts A forecast is posted once a day at the *Bureau de Port* and there is also an automatic pre-recorded coastal forecast (*Navimet*) or ☎ 93 72 31 32.

Speed limit 3 knots.

Storm signals Assistant sent round the harbour with a loud hailer.

Port de Menton-Garavan

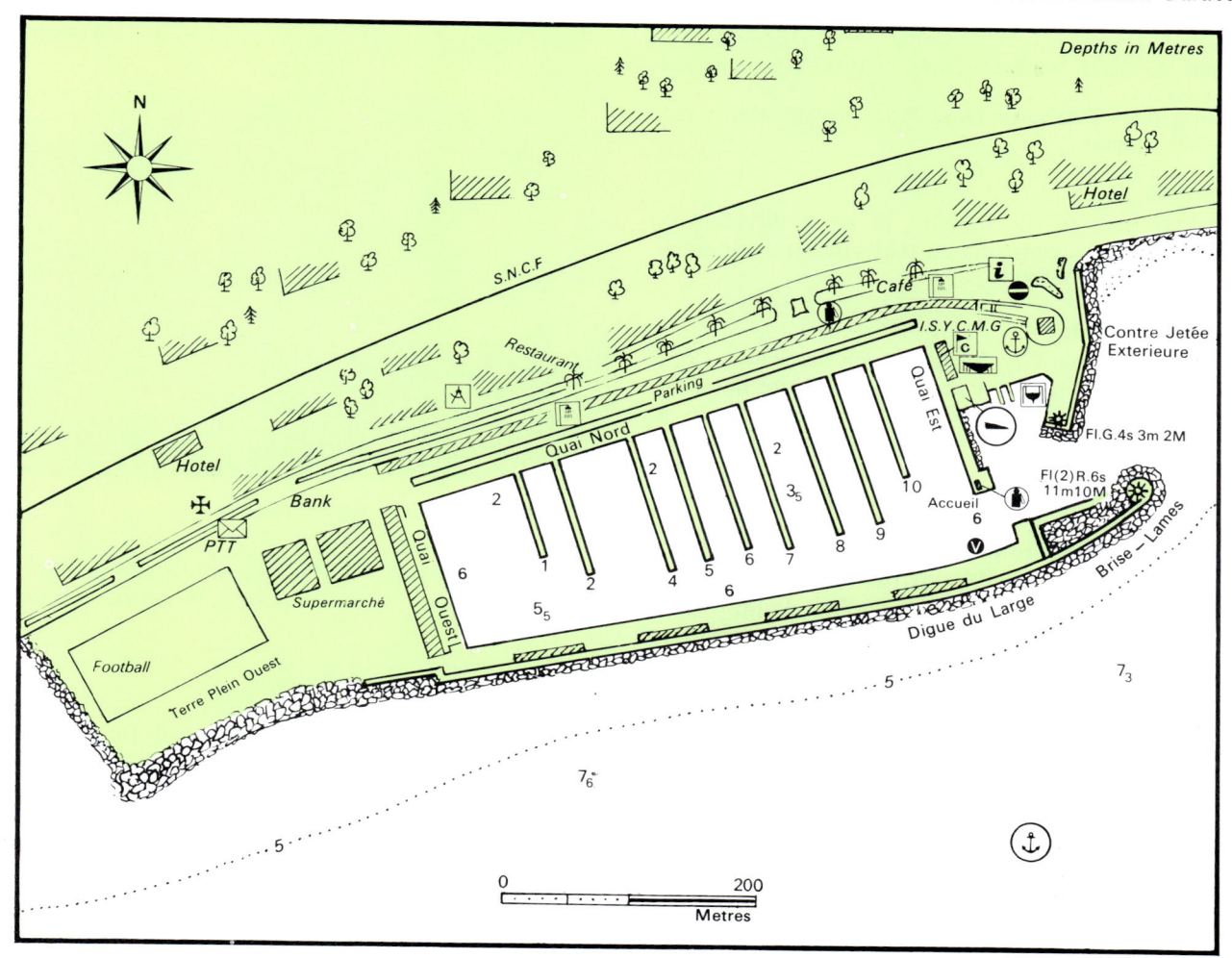

Port de Menton-Garavan

Port de Menton-Garavan looking N

125

South France Pilot

Lights
Digue du Large Head Fl(2)R.6s11m10M. White and red tower.
Contre Jetée Extérieure Head Fl.G.4s3m2M. Green and white support.

Warning
An extension of the harbour in an E direction is planned and its construction may affect the entrance to the original harbour.

Approach by day
From SW Round Cap Martin which has a low, sloping wooded promontory with a large white hotel on its point and a squat TV/radio tower which was a signal station on its summit. Pass the mass of houses topped by a conspicuous church spire at Menton-Ville and the jetty of its harbour. The long Digue du Large will now be seen with its light tower and the square white tower building of the *Bureau de Port* which has a blue balcony round its top.

From NE Round the high sloping Punta della Martola which has offlying rocky islets extending some 400m offshore. Punta Garavano is lower and has a cluster of houses at its foot beside the frontier with Italy. The harbour entrance is open from this direction and is located to the N of the head of the Digue du Large which is conspicuous in the close approach.

By night
Using the following lights navigate to a position where the entrance to the harbour lies NW at 300m:
Cap Ferrat Fl.W.3s25M
Monaco Oc.R.4s11M
Menton VQ(4)R.3s10M
Cap d'Armes Fl(2)W.10s29M

Anchorage in the approach
Anchor 300m to SE of the entrance in 6m (20ft) sand and shingle. Open to E–SE–S–SW.

Entrance
By day Approach the head of the Digue du Large on a NW course leaving it 20m to port rounding it and entering on a W course.

Bureau de Port

Port de Menton-Garavan, entrance looking W

Entrance

Port de Menton-Garavan, approach looking N

By night Approach Fl(2)R.6s on a NE course, leave 20m to port and round it onto a W course leaving Fl.G to starboard.

Berths
Secure alongside the head of Quai Est just inside the harbour on port hand marked 'Accueil' by the fuel pumps and report to the *Bureau de Port* for the allocation of a berth. Secure in allocated berths stern-to, bow to mooring chain. Visiting yachts are usually berthed inside the Digue du Large near its head.

Formalities
Report to the *Bureau de Port* (☎ 93 28 78 00 and 93 35 70 19), open day and night, on arrival and if necessary to the customs (☎ 93 35 93 18) whose office is just to N of the *Bureau de Port*.

Charges
There are harbour charges.

Facilities
Slip A slip just inside the entrance to starboard.
Cranes Two 40-tonne cranes just inside the harbour on the N side, and also a 5-tonne mobile crane is available.
Fuel Diesel (*gasoil*) and petrol are available from pumps at the head of Quai Est, 0700–2000 hours in summer, 0900–2000 in winter (☎ 93 28 78 00) also a fuel station on the main road.
Water Water points on all quays and pontoons.
Electricity 220v AC and 380v AC supply points are on quays and pontoons.
Provisions Some shops near the harbour mouth and a large supermarket at the W end. There are many shops and a market at Menton-Ville about 1M away.
Ice Ice can be bought from a shop at the N side of the harbour also from fuel station.
Duty-free goods Duty-free goods can be obtained from a shop on the N side of the harbour.
Garbage Rubbish containers round the harbour.
Chandlery Two ships' chandlers to the N of the harbour.
Repairs A shipyard at the E end of the harbour and there are mechanics who can repair engines.
Laundrette There are laundrettes in the town and one on the N side of the harbour.

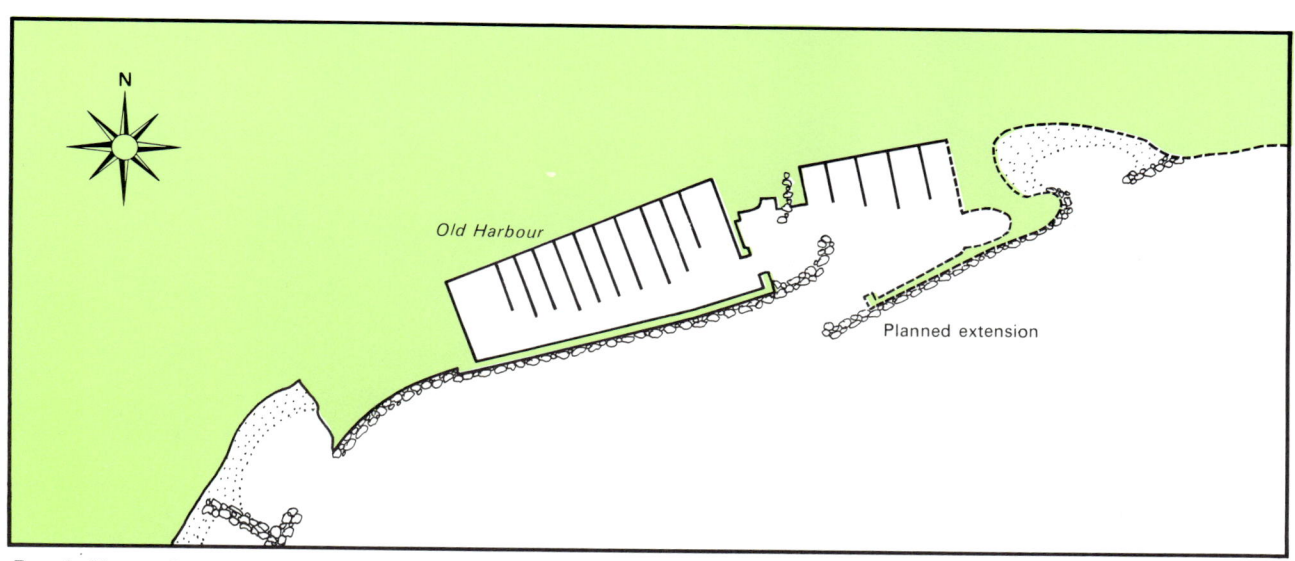

Port de Menton-Garavan showing planned extension

Post office There is a branch of PTT to the NW of the harbour.
Hotels Three ****, two ***, twenty-six **, twenty * and twelve unclassified hotels.
Restaurants Very many restaurants in the area and a number of café/bars.
Yacht club The International Sporting Club de Menton-Garavan (ISCMG) (☎ 93 35 70 19) has a new clubhouse to the NE of the harbour with a bar, lounge, restaurant and showers.
Showers There are four sanitary blocks with 18 showers and 19 WCs.
Information office The Syndicat d'Initiative has an office next to the customs office.
Lifeboats Small lifeboats stationed here.
Beaches Pebble beaches either side of the harbour.
Communications Bus and rail services.

See also Port de Menton-Ville page 124 for additional data.

Future development

Extension of harbour towards E providing four more pontoons and a sail-boarding area.

Index

Aiguille, Pointe de l', 6-7, 18
Ail, Port de Cap d', 107-111
air radiobeacons, 2
Anges, Baie des (Port de Marina), 73-75
Anse de l'Argent Faux, 63, 65
Anse de l'Espalmador, 91, 93
Anse de la Garoupe, 63, 65
Anse de Grasseut, 91, 93
Anse de Passable, 92
Anse de la Salis, 67
Anse de la Scalletta, 92, 94
Anthéor, Calanque d', 6-8
Antibes, Cap d', 66, 65
Antibes, Port Vauban, 68-72
Argent Faux, Anse de l', 63, 65
Aurelle, Calanque d', 10-11

Bacon, Pointe, 2, 66
Baie des Anges (Port de Marina), 73-75
Baie de Roquebrune, 118
Baie de St Laurent, 106
Baumette, Pointe de la, 6-7
Béal, Port du, 35-37
Beaulieu-sur-Mer, Port de, 99-103
Bijou, Port, 44-45
buoys, 2

Calanque d'Anthéor, 6-8
Calanque d'Aurelle, 10-11
Calanque des Deux Frères, 15-16
Calanque de Maubois, 10
Cannes, Vieux Port de, 37-41
Cannes-Marina, Port de, 30-32
Cap d'Ail, Port de, 107-111
Cap d'Antibes, 64, 65
Cap de l'Esquillon, 14
Cap Ferrat, 87, 92
Cap Gros, 65
Cap Martin, 118-121
Cap de Nice, 85
Cap Roux, 105
Cap Roux, Pointe de, 6-10
charts, 2
Colombier, Pointe du, 92
Croisette, Pointe de la, 45, 48
Croisette, Les Ports de la, 44-45
Cros-de-Cagnes, Port de, 75-78
Crouton, Port du, 61-65
currents, 2

dangers, 2
Deux Frères, Calanque des, 15-16

Espalmador, Anse de l', 91, 93
Esquillon, Cap de l', 14
Eze-sur-Mer, Port d' (Port de Silva-Maris), 103-106

Ferrat, Cap, 87, 92
festivals, 3
Figueirette, Port de la (Port Miramar-le-Trayas), 12, 15
Fontvieille, Port de, 111-114
Fort Carré, 72
Fosses, Les, 92, 94
Fossettes, Les, 92-94
Fourmis, Port des, 98-99

Galère, Port de la, 16-18
Gallice, Port (Juan-les-Pins), 58-62
Garoupe, Anse de la, 63, 65
Golfe Juan, head of, 58
Golfe-Juan, Port de (Vallauris), 55-58
Grasseut, Anse de, 91, 93
Gros, Cap, 65

history, 2

Ile St Honorat, 48-49
Ile Ste Marguerite, 47-49
Iles de Lérins, Les, 1, 3, 46-53
Ilette, Pointe de l', 65

Juan, Golfe, 55-58
Juan-les-Pins, 58

Lérins, Les Iles de, 1, 3, 46-53
lights, 2
Lilong, Pointe de, 92, 93

Mallet, Port 65
Mandelieu-la Napoule, Port de, 25-28
Marco-Polo Marina, Port de, 33-34
marine radiobeacons, 2
Martin, Cap, 118-121
Maubois, Calanque de, 10
Menton-Garavan, Port de, 124-127
Menton-Ville, Port de (Vieux Port), 121-124
meteorological offices, 2
Miramar-le-Trayas, Port (Port de la Figueirette), 12-14
mistral, 1
Moines, Port aux (Ile de St Honorat), 49-51
Monaco, Port de (Monte Carlo), 114-118

Monte Carlo (Port de Monaco), 114-118
Mouillage du Piton, 65
Mouré-Rouge, Port du, 53-55

Napoule, Port de Mandelieu-la, 25-28
Nice, Cap de, 85
Nice, Port de, 82-85
Nice-Côte d'Azur, Aéroport, 81

Olivette, Port de l', 65
Ours, Pic de l', 10-11

Palm Beach, Port de, 44-45
Passable, Anse de, 92, 93
Passable, Pointe de, 91-92, 93
Paume, Pointe de la, 14
Pic de l'Ours, 10-11
Pierre-Canto, Port, 41-44
Piton, Mouillage du, 65
Pointe de l'Aiguille, 6-7, 18
Pointe Bacon, 2, 66
Pointe de la Baumette, 6-7
Pointe de Cap Roux, 6-10
Pointe du Colombier, 92
Pointe de la Croisette, 45, 48
Pointe de l'Ilette, 65
Pointe de Lilong, 92, 93
Pointe de Passable, 91-92, 93
Pointe de la Paume, 14
Pointe Rompa-Talon, 98
Pointe du Rube, 91, 93
Pointe de St Hospice, 92
Pointe de Trayas, 10-11
Pointe de la Veille, 118
Port de Béal, 35-37
Port de Beaulieu-sur-Mer, 99-103
Port Bijou, 44-45
Port de Cannes, Vieux, 37-41
Port de Cannes-Marina, 30-32
Port de Cap d'Ail, 107-111
Ports de la Croisette, Les, 44-45
Port de Cros-de-Cagnes, 75-78
Port du Crouton, 61-65
Port d'Eze-sur-Mer (Port de Silva-Maris), 103-106
Port de la Figueirette (Port Miramar-le-Trayas), 12, 15
Port de Fontvieille, 111-114
Port de Fourmis, 98-99
Port de la Galère, 16-18
Port Gallice, Juan-les-Pins, 58-62
Port de Golfe-Juan (Vallauris), 55-58
Port Mallet, 65

Port de Mandelieu-la-Napoule, 25-28
Port de Marco-Polo Marina, 33-34
Port de Marina, Baie des Anges, 73-75
Port de Menton-Garavan, 124-127
Port de Menton-Ville (Vieux Port), 121-124
Port de Miramar-le-Trayas (Port de la Figueirette), 12-14
Port aux Moines (Ile de St Honorat), 49-51
Port de Monaco (Monte Carlo), 114-118
Port du Mouré-Rouge, 53-55
Port de Nice, 82-85
Port de l'Olivette, 65
Port de Palm Beach, 44-45
Port Pierre-Canto, 41-44
Port de la Rague, 22-25
Port du Riou de l'Argentière, 28-30
Port de St Honorat, 49-51
Port de St Jean-Cap Ferrat, 95-98
Port de St Laurent-du-Var, 78-81
Port de Ste Marguerite, 51-53
Port de la Salis (Rous-Chaffey), 66-67
Port Sec (Port de la Siagne), 35
Port de la Siagne (Port Sec), 35
Port de Silva-Maris (Port d'Eze-sur-Mer), 103-106
Port de Théoule-sur-Mer, 19-22
Port Vauban-Antibes, 68-72
Port de Villefranche-sur-Mer, 88-91

Rade de Villefranche, 85-91
radiobeacons, 2
Rague, Port de la, 22-25
restricted areas, 2
Riou de l'Argentière, Port du, 28-30
Rompa-Talon, Pointe, 98
Roquebrune, Baie de, 118
Rous-Chaffey (Port de la Salis), 66-67
Roux, Cap, 105
Roux, Pointe de Cap, 6-10
Rube, Pointe du, 91, 93

St Honorat, Ile de, 48-49

129

South France Pilot

St Honorat, Port de, 49-51
St Hospice, Pointe de, 92
St Jean, Port de (Cap Ferrat), 95-98
St Laurent, Baie de, 106
St Laurent-du-Var, 78-81
Ste Marguerite, Ile, 47-49
Ste Marguerite, Port de, 51-53
Salis, Anse de la, 67
Salis, Port de la (Rous-Chaffey), 66-67
Scalletta, Anse de la, 92, 94
sea levels, 2
Sec, Port (Port de la Siagne), 35
Siagne, Port de la (Port Sec), 35
Silva-Maris, Port de (Port d'Eze-sur-Mer), 103-106
sports, 3
submarines, 2

Théoule-sur-Mer, Port, 19-22
tides, 2
Trayas, Pointe de, 10-11

Vallauris (Port de Golfe-Juan), 55-58
Vaquette, La, 13, 14-15, 17
Var River delta, 1, 2, 81
Vauban-Antibes, Port, 68-72
Veille, Pointe de la, 118
Vieux Port de Cannes, 37-41

Villefrance, Rade de, 85-91
Villefranche-sur-Mer, Port de, 88-91

weather forecasts, 2
winds and seas, 1